Cosmetics in Shakespearean and Renaissance Drama

Revised Edition

Farah Karim-Cooper

EDINBURGH
University Press

Edinburgh University Press is one of the leading university presses in
the UK. We publish academic books and journals in our selected subject
areas across the humanities and social sciences, combining cutting-edge
scholarship with high editorial and production values to produce academic
works of lasting importance. For more information visit our website:
edinburghuniversitypress.com

First published in hardback by Edinburgh University Press, 2006, and in
paperback in 2012.

Edinburgh University Press Ltd
The Tun – Holyrood Road, 12(2f) Jackson's Entry, Edinburgh EH8 8PJ

Typeset in Sabon and Futura by
Servis Filmsetting Ltd, Stockport, Cheshire
and printed and bound in Great Britain.

A CIP record for this book is available from the British Library

ISBN 978 1 4744 5271 7 (hardback)
ISBN 978 1 4744 5273 1 (webready PDF)
ISBN 978 1 4744 5272 4 (paperback)
ISBN 978 1 4744 5274 8 (epub)

Contents

List of Illustrations

Acknowledgements

Thank you to the British Academy for their financial support, and to the library at the University of Leiden, Dulwich Picture Gallery, the V&A picture library, the British Library, Glasgow University Library and Shakespeare's Globe for the illustrations that are crucial to this book. Thanks are due to Michelle Houston for her support for this new edition.

For Angus Lamming

Chapter 1

Defining Beauty in Renaissance Culture

'Womens *supplimentall Art, does but rather bewray Natures Defects Perfuming, Painting, Starching, Decking . . .*'[1]

For centuries cosmetics have offered the promise of perfection. Paints and powders, brushes and pencils are the artistic tools with which woman can re-create the self. Yet historically, cosmetics have been perceived as mere ornament, secondary, trivial, even deceptive. The subject of beautification, however, was an important discourse within the dramatic, social and literary worlds of early modern England. Domestically, kitchens were actively engineering the cosmetics that would be on display in the public sphere as well as on the stage. This book will draw attention to the cultural preoccupation with cosmetics by exploring a wide range of early modern texts and the theatrical appropriation of cosmetic metaphors and materials. It also places overdue importance upon the subject of early modern beauty practices by arguing that the contemporary culture of cosmetics extended beyond practice and vanity and into the domains of theatre, art and poetry. Given the prominence of the phenomenon of cosmetics in Shakespearean and Renaissance drama, surprisingly little attention has been paid to it as a whole in the Renaissance period. Certainly, there have been excellent studies, such as Annette Drew-Bear's brief survey of face painting conventions on the Renaissance stage, and Frances Dolan's article, 'Taking the Pencil out of God's Hand: Art, Nature and the Face-Painting Debate in Early Modern England', which charts the analogous relationship between the art/nature debate and moral discourse on cosmetics. Equally important is Dympna Callaghan's work on cosmetics, theatre and negritude in her book *Shakespeare Without Women*, and Tanya Pollard's recent work on 'cosmetic theater' in her book, *Drugs in Early Modern Theater*, in which she examines the poisonous properties of cosmetics and their metaphorical relationship to theatricality. Yet, no one has conducted a comprehensive enough analysis of what can be termed the early modern culture of cosmetics and how it impacted upon the contemporary world of drama.

Since this book was first published in 2006, a number of studies have emerged that demonstrate the growing interest in and importance of the history of female beauty and cosmetic practice. All of these studies, I might add, are by women. I eagerly await the day when male scholars and critics see this subject as a crucial factor in the development of early modern literary, dramatic, material, social, political and cultural history. Published at virtually the same moment as this book in 2006, Patricia Phillippy's *Painting Women: Cosmetics, Canvases, and Early Modern English Culture* examines the intersections of cosmetic and visual art, focusing on women's self-representations. By 2011, the intellectual debates surrounding beauty and cosmetic practice were still gaining traction. In a collection of essays edited by Edith Snook, *Women, Beauty and Power in Early Modern England: A Feminist Literary History*, the contributors consider female attitudes towards 'beauty culture' and the ways in which skin, clothing and hair were used to portray racial, class and gender identities; the essays do not really take into account, though, how these various identities are constructed across various artistic media. In the same year, art historian Aileen Ribeiro published *Facing Beauty: Painted Women and Cosmetic Art*, which takes as its subject the shifting perceptions of beauty from 1540 to 1940. The intersection of race and beauty was an important and seminal consideration for Kim F. Hall's *Things of Darkness: Economies of Race and Gender in Early Modern England* (1995), but since then the relationship between race and cosmetic beauty has largely been overlooked.[2] However, Kimberley Poitevin's article 'Inventing Whiteness: Cosmetics, Race, and Women in Early Modern England', in the *Journal for Early Modern Cultural Studies* (2011), begins to redress this imbalance in the critical attention to the construction of beauty in early modern culture.

Focusing on early English theatre practice, *Inventions of the Skin: The Painted Body in Early English Drama, 1400–1642* by Andrea Ria Stevens (2013) takes into account the use of paint as an essential and transformative technology of the theatres. Romana Sammern's 2015 article 'Red, white and black: colors of beauty, tints of health and cosmetic materials in early modern English art writing', in *Early Science and Medicine*, examines cosmetic practice as a science. This piece, like Stevens' *Inventions*, takes a somewhat forensic look at the semiotics of paint and colour as it relates to the aesthetic, medical and cosmetic practices and theories of the early modern period, beginning with the 'ideal colors of beauty': white and red.

The arguments of this book are, in part, a response to the questions raised by the authors of *Subject and Object in Renaissance Culture*: 'should or shouldn't seemingly vain objects be deemed worthy of serious attention?'[3] While most critical attention to cosmetics in Renaissance literature has focused on the moral denigration of feminine rituals of beautification, this book observes that early modern dramatists attempt to *revalue* the cosmetic, first by transporting it out of the feminine domestic interior and into a theatrical and poetic context, and secondly, by reasserting its materiality rather than merely endorsing its hypothetical usage in contemporary debates. Fundamentally, this repositioning of cosmetics suggests that they resist a univocal reading on the stage and within dramatic play texts. Painted faces on the stage do more than evoke poison, moral corruption and feminine deception. They signify power, art, poetics, and are crucial to theatrical performance.

In Act III, scene ii of John Marston's *Antonio and Mellida* (1601), Balurdo and Rossaline enter the stage, peering into their looking glasses ready to have their faces painted. With stage directions like the following, one has little trouble seeing the humour in staged representations of Renaissance cosmetic culture:

> *Enter* Balurdo, *backward*, Dildo *following him with a looking glass in one hand and a candle in the other hand*, Flavia *following him backward with a looking glass in one hand and a candle in the other*, Rossaline *following her*. Balurdo *and* Rossaline *stand setting of faces; and so the scene begins*.

The gallant, Feliche, calls them 'fools', informing the audience that they are about to witness 'a rare scene of folly' (III, ii, 117, 119). The 'face-setting' scene continues with Balurdo, a gentleman of the court in Venice, whose view of the world is conveyed in highly superficial terms, as is evidenced when he commands his servant Dildo: 'By the sugar-candy sky, hold up the glass higher, that I may see to swear the fashion' (III, ii, 120–1); simultaneously, Flavia, the gentlewoman, is hard at work on Rossaline's face. 'Here wants a little white, Flavia' (III, ii, 138) instructs Rossaline; Flavia tells Rossaline that she looks like the Princess. Insecurely, Rossaline compares herself to the Princess and recognises that 'her lip is – lip is a little – redder, a very little redder. But by the help of Art or Nature, ere I change my periwig mine shall be as red' (III, ii, 146–7). On the surface, this scene appears merely to confirm the conventional view that beautification registers idleness and vanity; and the entrance of characters *backwards*, gazing narcissistically at their reflections, is meant to signify the immorality and monstrousness of people with 'set' faces. But Marston, like many Renaissance play-wrights, also captures the visual appeal of cosmetics through this type of spectacle. Moreover, this scene, which uncovers the intimate link between cosmetic and dramatic practice, is typical of many face-painting scenes in early modern drama in that it functions as a meta-theatrical device, a staged representation of a cultural practice that is implicitly performative.

Most commonly, satire is the primary generic mode through which dramatists highlighted the culture of cosmetics. For instance, in *Cynthia's Revels* (1600), Ben Jonson exposes the Elizabethan court as a type of effeminate cosmetic pageant through Crites' bitter denunciation of contemporary practice:

> Some mincing marmoset
> Made all of clothes and face; his limbs so set . . .
> His breath between his teeth, and dares not smile
> Beyond a point, for fear to unstarch his look . . .
> There stands a neophyte glazing of his face,
> Pruning his clothes, perfuming of his hair . . .
>   (III, iv, 22–7, 55–6)

The satiric representation of cosmetics occurs overtly in compelling scenes of face painting, subtly in the language and imagery of the texts, and in malcontented diatribes against vanity, such as the one cited above. It is sometimes explicit; for example, in John Webster's *A Cure for A Cuckold* (c. 1624), Lessingham refers to women in a misogynistic fulmination as 'witches' and argues that

> All that they have is feigned: their teeth, their hair,
> Their blushes, nay their conscience too is feigned.
> Let 'em paint, load themselves with cloth of tissue,
> They cannot yet hide woman; that will appear
> And disgrace all.
>   (IV, ii, 78–82)

At times, cosmetics are referred to implicitly, most notably through subtle allusions to stock subjects as disguising, deception, appearance and reality. Whether it is explicit or implicit, however, it is a dramatic trope that has not yet been examined in depth, and that deserves closer scrutiny because it sheds fresh light on an important preoccupation of Renaissance culture. Annette Drew-Bear in her 1994 study identifies face painting as a dramatic convention. I argue in this book that it is not just face painting, but the notion of a culture of cosmetics that is at the heart of these dramatic representations. Significantly, dramatic representations of cosmeticised bodies are not merely exercises in moralistic didacticism. Scenes such as the cosmetic spectacle in Marston's *Antonio and Mellida* do more than satirise a contemporary custom; they, in fact, comment on the paradoxical attraction to painted beauty and indicate the underlying contradictions inherent in the contemporary discourse on cosmetics.

There is a wide range of early modern texts preoccupied with the subject of cosmetics, such as sermons, homilies, courtesy books, conduct manuals, polemical tracts (including treatises on women, pride, folly, witchcraft, history, cosmography, zoology and travel), anti-Catholic diatribes, anti-cosmetic treatises, literary and artistic criticism, recipe manuals and miscellanies, and of course dramatic texts; it is here that we can observe a distinct culture of cosmetics. While the anti-cosmetic tracts vilify cosmetics and those who use them, recipe manuals promote the engineering of cosmetics within the domestic space and suggest their economical viability. The stage energises and animates the subject of cosmetics, reflecting and embodying the contradictory discourses through 'lively action' and the materiality of visual representation. Cosmetics operate in Shakespearean and Renaissance drama in several ways. First and foremost, we see them in their material form; face paints allow for a variety of significations: femininity, identicality, supernaturalism, for example. Intrinsic to representation on the stage, cosmetics are a poignant reminder of the performativity of gender and race. Identifiable by secondary, prosthetic accoutrements, gender, race and monarchy are enactments of identity regardless of the bodies behind them, and cosmetics signify and help to construct these enactments. Secondly, makeup decorates, enhances and re-materialises the body. Jonathan Sawday identifies a 'culture of dissection' that was striving to bring forth the internal realities of the body. Cosmetics complicate this cultural compulsion by obscuring and concealing the body further; simultaneously, the 'laying on' of cosmetic paints paradoxically laid the body open to contamination, therefore judgement and vilification. Plays such as *The Revenger's Tragedy* and *The Second Maiden's Tragedy* satisfy the desire for such exploitations of the body, in particular, the female body, while reasserting the materiality of cosmetics by pointing to the impermanence of flesh and the posterity of art.

Dramatists also use cosmetics metaphorically. The word 'cosmetic' does not appear in English until 1605 in Francis Bacon's *Advancement of Learning*, and it is not used commonly until well after the 1650s. Early modern writers refer to cosmetic adornment when they speak of beautifying, decking, tricking and adorning, and cosmetics are themselves commonly denoted as 'ceruse', 'fucus' (both face paints/foundations), 'paintings', 'paint'. However, for the purposes of my argument, I use the terms 'cosmetics' and 'cosmetic' to describe the early modern materials, methods and discourses associated with makeup. Linguistic allusions to beautification reveal an intertextual dialogue between drama and the social discourse on cosmetics. While dramatists seem to appropriate language from the debate, the anti-cosmetic argument adopts imagery from a wide range of topics. A marvellous example of this is in Richard Brathwait's *Time's Curtaine Drawne* (1621) where he compares cosmetics to religious idolatry as he thunders against the use of makeup by women:

> Lascivious Idoll, that with painted cheeke,
> Sinne-drawing eye, thy sacred vow doest breake
> With thy *Creator*.[4]

A few years earlier, Barnabe Rich compared painted women and painted harlots to ships that need 'rigging', 'but not like a marchantes ship, but in truth like a *Pyrat* a *Rover*', he argues, '*like* such a ship as lieth still in waite for rapine and spoyle'.[5] A link is also made between cosmetics and traps, with many references to women as painted 'snares', 'mouse-traps' and 'birdlime'. Whether it is an unconscious or conscious response to this discursive field, Shakespearean and Renaissance drama nevertheless engages in such acts of linguistic colonisation.

Allusions to the notion of the cosmetic are likewise found in texts unrelated to material makeup, and this relationship is made clear through words such as 'beautify', 'deck', 'trick', 'adorn', 'bedawb', 'trim' and 'trappings'. In *A Treatise Against Witchcraft*, Henry Holland writes that witches hide their identities because 'they must be carefullie bent, to beautifie and adorne their profession with a goodly, sober, and innocent life'.[6] In this passage, Holland makes the link between witchcraft, femininity and the cosmetic, a connection that Webster also unlocks in *The Duchess of Malfi*. Another metaphorical resonance of cosmetics is detectable in their relationship to art. In Richard Haydocke's translation of Paulo Lomazzo's *A Tracte Containing the Artes of curious Paintinge Carvinge & buildinge* (1598), painting is defined as '*an arte which with proportionable lines, and colours answerable to the life, by observing with Perspective light, doeth so imitate the nature of corporall thinges, that it not onely representeth the thicknesse and roundnesse thereof upon a flat, but also their actions, gestures, expressing moreover divers affections and passions in the minde*'.[7] Painting, therefore, is seen as an organic as well as a mimetic exercise, imitating and uncovering not only the appearance of the figures painted, but also the very details on their faces inspired by their imagined psychological and emotional conditions.

Face painting is seen, by Lomazzo and other contemporary commentators upon art, as a similar, though less noble, process. Rather than illuminate the internal condition of a subject as canvas painting would, face painting conceals, obscures and disfigures.

Significantly, cosmetic discourse is ideological, since it involves questions about gender, art, theatre, race and politics. This book will take its reader through the compelling debate about cosmetics and the recipe manuals that provide the methods and materials for transforming, colouring, painting, perfuming, dyeing, waxing and the wide range of technologies available to early modern women for beautifying the body. It will then turn to the stage to glimpse how the dominant media of the age expressed a subversive and cynical discontentment with varnished faces, authoritative and domestic, public and private, while, paradoxically, revaluing cosmetics and indulging itself in a self-reflexive cosmetic spectacle. This study locates itself within a critical discourse centred upon the materials and material practices of early modern English culture. Studies such as Ann Rosalind Jones's and Peter Stallybrass's *Renaissance Clothing and the Materials of Memory*, Wendy Wall's *Staging Domesticity*, and, among others, Jonathan Gil Harris's and Natasha Korda's collection of essays *Staged Properties in Early Modern English Drama*, do more than simply examine textiles, objects or ingredients and their origins, but they show how these materials help in the formation of cultural identity within a burgeoning global economy, while recognising the early modern stage to be the space upon which the circulation of objects and their signifying practices work to establish and memorialise early modern identities.

The anti-cosmetic argument, which is textually prolific, levels the charge that primping and painting are 'whorish', dangerous and potentially life threatening; so what made early modern woman paint? I suggest that it is the same demand imposed upon women today: beauty means acceptance and the pressure is always on. The desire to be beautiful is a social and cultural construct. In this opening chapter I argue that early modern woman's drive to refashion herself cosmetically was a response to a particular standard inherited from classical and continental models of female beauty. Sixteenth and seventeenth-century love poetry, definitions of beauty, visual art and emblem books reveal the inculcation of a standard of beauty that is not only politically embodied in the central icon of the court and country, Queen Elizabeth I, but that promises the procurement of courtship and marriage. Furthermore, male authors of printed recipe manuals (English and translated continental books) dating well into the seventeenth century draw heavily upon this archetype of beauty repeatedly imaged in literature and art as they include in their cosmetic recipes ingredients such as flowers, stones, minerals and jewels that correspond to the common conceits found in many sixteenth and seventeenth-century love lyrics. Did early modern woman have a conscious desire to transform herself into the poetic embodiment of beauty? I would say yes. The poetic representation of female beauty is a portrait of an ideal, one impossible to achieve, and therefore, fictitious, but women nevertheless attempted to duplicate physically this idealised version of femininity through the reactionary practice of beautification.

'Beauty's red and virtue's white': Treatises on Beauty

> The contours of the flesh, being highly variable, can be manipulated in any number of ways; so too can posture and movements. Enter an array of helpful devices: laces, fabrics, color, infinite modification of the hair and speech . . . the goal of all this reconstruction is 'beauty'.[8]

Klaus Theweleit suggests that the surface of the body has an elasticity, that flesh is easily manipulable, but the search for physical perfection is a procedure requiring various 'devices' of cosmetic contrivance. The quotation implies that physical beauty is achievable by means of prosthesis. What is considered beautiful, however, complicates and undermines the pursuit of beauty, since beauty, as they say, is in the eye of the beholder. Yet there is a collective notion of female beauty operating in the early modern consciousness that helps to reinforce the idea that the white race is superior to all others, which is based on a classical definition that is still fundamental to our cultural perception of beauty today: symmetry and the perfect balance of colours on the face. The humanistic revival of classical expectations of aesthetic pleasure extended itself into the ideology of human beauty. Personifying beauty, Plato saw it as 'the goddess who presides at childbirth', deigning it a privilege given only to some, but he also refers to two types of beauty: beauty 'absolute' and 'divine beauty', both of which are associated with purity, cleanliness and virtue.[9] Plato remarks that such beauty is 'not polluted by human flesh or colors or any other great nonsense of mortality'.[10]

Aristotle's definition of beauty, which was generally adopted by Renaissance artists, consists of 'order and symmetry'.[11] Plotinus adds to this by suggesting that 'a certain charm of colour constitutes the beauty recognized by the eye, that in visible things, as indeed in all else, universally, the beautiful thing is essentially symmetrical, patterned'.[12]

The emphasis on symmetricality is what unifies Western notions of physical beauty. In the seventeenth century, according to Thomas Browne's *Pseudodoxia Epidemica*, beauty is defined in Aristotelian terms, in which the essence of beauty is placed 'in the proportion of parts, conceiving it to consist in a comely commensurability of the whole unto the parts, and the parts between themselves'. Logically, Browne says, measuring beauty in this way means that 'the Moors are not excluded from beauty: there being in this description no consideration of colours, but an apt . . . frame of parts and the whole'.[13] Such allowances gesture toward the paradox of black beauty often referenced in early modern drama as well as reflected in the recipe manuals of the period, which offer suggestions for dying the hair, brows, and even skin black.

On the whole, the classical paradigm of beauty requires proportion, symmetry, and the visible synthesis of colour. Italian Renaissance thinkers developed further these classical ideals of beauty and had, perhaps, the most impact upon the English literary imagination of the sixteenth and seventeenth centuries. Fusing the classical paradigm with Christian spiritualism, Marsilio Ficino was the first of the neo-Platonists to argue that 'Beauty is a kind of force or light, shining from Him through everything, first through the Angelic Mind, second through the World-Soul and the rest of the souls, third through Nature, and fourth through corporeal Matter'.[14] For neo-Platonists, beauty is still a measure of virtue, but it stems from the light and purity of the soul, which ultimately should reflect God's unadulterated image.

The translation of Thomas Buoni's *Problemes of Beavtie* into English in 1606 reveals that enquiries into the nature of beauty were still prominent in seventeenth-century English discourse. This treatise offers several definitions of beauty, and sets up an anonymous dialogue to pose questions or 'problemes' about its uses, while providing a set of answers. What we are given is Buoni's neo-Platonic philosophy of beauty. Like many writers before him, Buoni celebrates the colours of nature, which are 'the white in the snow, red in the rose, gratious in the violet, delightfull in the flowers, rich among the plantes, wonderfull among the beastes of the field & glorious amongst men'.[15] He goes a step further and praises the celestial beauty of the cosmos and the glimmering beauty of the earth's treasures: 'who beholds & rests not astonished at the cleare light of the Moone, the bright beams of the sun, the whiteness of siluer, the splendor of gold, the purity of marble . . .'[16] Correspondingly, the idea of woman's beauty is drawn out in very similar terms privileging whiteness as the superior aesthetic: she is bright, white, even figured as silver, gold and shining marble. Buoni asks later why beauty shines, especially in women. The only answers he can offer are that women, knowing they are beautiful, 'seeke to attaine that of the minde'; because men have intelligence, so women must have the physical lustre of beauty; or because she has been given beauty she should 'learne of her mother nature, to hide it . . . and not to lay it open as a thing common'.[17] Whatever the reason for woman's beauty, it is manifestly clear that its survival depends upon her careful behaviour and modest practice.

As I have suggested, beauty for Renaissance writers relied upon symmetry and the very careful balance of colours. Problem 14 of the tract raises the question 'Why doth the Beauty of Women consist sometimes in one colour, sometimes in the variety of colours?' A very curious proposition is offered when Buoni writes 'because corporall *Beauty* is not onely placed in the due proportion, or site, or quantitie, or quality of the members, but much more in the appetite', and therefore, desire and preference may vary; for example,

> to the eye of the *Moore*, the blacke, or tawny countenance of the *Moorish* damosell pleaseth best, to the eye of another, a colour as white as the Lily, or the driuen snow, to another the colour neither simply white, nor black, but that well medled *Beauty* betwixt them both, like the red rose in pure milke, or the purple violet amongst the white Lillyes.[18]

Here, Buoni suggests that the consideration of beauty depends upon social, cultural and ideological factors. Geography plays a large part in determining the colours on a woman's face that make her aesthetically acceptable, which reinforces anxieties about racial intermingling. In essence, a woman is generally attractive to the men in her own racial group. Yet, startlingly, Buoni's claim that neither colour, but their 'well medled Beauty' is preferable to some, complicates questions about race and gestures toward the practice of racial intermingling, even while accommodating within the standard of beauty varied complexions.

The paradox of neo-Platonic standards of beauty is that, although physical loveliness is meant to be a sign of virtue, purity and simplicity, there is always a suggestion that it hides sinfulness. This is the point at which cosmetics come under fire, because they are perceived as a material barrier, concealing what is inscribed beneath. Although Buoni, in response to the question 'Why is the Beauty of a light woman lesse esteemed?', suggests that 'Vntrue & deceitful thinges neuer pleased, and therefore the *Beauty* of the bodie being an outward signe of the inward *Beauty* of the minde, but in such a woman made a cloke for sinne, she belieth her bodily *Beauty*', he does not offer a way to distinguish between such women.[19]

In *Haec Homo, Wherein the Excellency of the Creation of Woman is Described* (1639), William Austin argues that there are three types of beauty: 'Corporall, Vocall, or Spirituall', in addition to arguing that a woman's face is 'an *epitome* of *Heaven*'.[20] However, when defining the beauty of the body, the author insists on '*a good and proportionable agreeing coherence, and compacture of all the several parts of the body in one fairenesse; as it doth especially in woman*'.[21] Again, what is being stressed is the importance of 'coherence' and proportion; one gets the impression that without these attributes a woman might look monstrous or deformed. This particular standard for beauty is also the basis for the opposition to prosthetic accoutrements: cosmetics, jewels, bodices, corsets, gowns, sleeves, farthingales and the like. These prosthetic attachments suggest an underlying fragmentation to contemporary critics. Ben Jonson, as I will show, satirises this very fragmentation and prosthetic compensation and stages the monstrous opposite to the conventional beauty standard.

Annibale Romei's *The Courtier's Academie*, translated into English in 1598, is one discourse on beauty that suggests alternative means of obtaining what he calls 'a most pretious qualitie, which shineth in the universall frame, growing from proportions of colours'. He recommends developing an 'intelligible' beauty, one that can be secured by 'bedecking our soules with prudence, fortitude, temperance & iustice'; this would make a woman 'most beautiful'.[22] This recipe for beauty echoes the admonitions of the early Church Fathers, such as St Jerome, St Augustine, Tertullian, and St Chrysostom, who (often quoted by Renaissance anti-cosmetic authors) admonished women to adorn their souls in order to improve their faces.

Widely discussed by Renaissance historians, Agnolo Firenzuola's fifteenth-century treatise on beauty was influential in the formation of English Renaissance perceptions of beauty. The treatise takes the form of two dialogues, one set in a natural landscape, the other during a lavish dinner party, indicating each dialogue's devotion to nature and art respectively. The discoursers are four women and one man, Celso, whose initial claim is that the face is the 'seat' of beauty, a notion that would remain popular throughout the sixteenth and seventeenth centuries in Europe and in England. The face, according to John Downame's much later dialogue on 'auxillary beauty' published in 1656, 'is the chief *Theater*, Throne, and *center of Beauty*, to which all outward array is subservient'.[23] Significantly, Firenzuola's tract makes clear that perfect beauty requires not only the typical physical prescriptions, but also abstractions, such as 'elegance', 'charm', 'grace', 'loveliness', 'air', and 'majesty', but since no woman, he claims dismissively, has all of these qualities, he must paint the 'perfect' beauty in words. To create his verbal portrait of a truly beautiful woman, Celso invokes the method of the ancient artist 'Zeuxis, who chose the five most elegant girls of Croton and, taking from each her most exquisite feature, painted such a beautiful picture of Helen of Troy'.[24] Leon Battista Alberti's guide for artists also tells the story of Zeuxis, who

> thought that he would not be able to find so much beauty as he was looking for in a single body, since it was not given to a single one by nature. He chose, therefore, the five most beautiful young girls from the youth of that land in order to draw from them whatever beauty is praised in a woman.[25]

The problem is that the beauty this creates is fragmented and fictitious, seemingly perfect only in its artistic state, leaving woman no choice but to attempt to create a similar portrait upon herself.

Complementing his description of the perfect beauty whose attributes are taken from disparate women, Firenzuola later defines beauty, saying that it is

> nothing else but ordered concord, akin to a harmony that arises mysteriously from the composition, union, and conjunction of several diverse and different parts that are, according to their own needs and qualities, differently well proportioned and in some way beautiful, and which, before they unite themselves into a whole, are different and discordant among themselves.[26]

The emphasis on the separate 'parts' uniting in perfection, creating a composite whole, reintroduces classical ideologies of beauty. This notion of perfection deriving from a union of fragments is significant when one considers the literary affirmation of such definitions. The poetic blazon can be seen as a reaction to this ideal. Significantly, Firenzuola's *definition* of what is beautiful leads into a point-by-point blazoning *description* of the ideal woman, when he insists that 'the cheeks must be fair (*candido*). Fair is a colour that besides being white, also has a certain lustre, as ivory does; while white is that which does not glow such as snow'.[27] Here, Firenzuola makes an important distinction between white and fair. Because the word 'fair' is frequently used in poems and pamphlets on beauty, it is crucial to analyse carefully this curious distinction. It would seem that the terms 'fair' and 'white' are not always to be taken as interchangeable. Stephen Greenblatt also observes this distinction when he suggests that for Shakespeare there are two senses of what is beautiful: radiance and unblemished smoothness. Greenblatt comments that the word 'fair' provides a 'distinct sense of shining'.[28] Paleness or whiteness is one thing as complexions go; however, fairness is quite another. It conveys a lustre that is comparable to silver; perhaps then, if a woman is unfortunate enough not to have a natural lustre, she must obtain it with an egg glaze or oil of poppy or, if she is wealthy, crushed pearl. William Warde's translation of *The Secrets of Alexis of Piemont* hearkens back to the distinction made between white and fair when he offers a 'water of white Mellons, that maketh a faire skinne'.[29] The same recipe manual instructs women how 'To make a water that maketh the face white and shining'. One must take 'the Milke of an asse, and egge shelles, and make thereof distilled water, and wash your face with it, and it will be white, faire and glistering'.[30] Although white is the complexion that is being offered in this recipe, the marketing tenor of the piece lies in its promise of skin that will be 'faire' and 'glistering'. Buoni's views coincide with Firenzuola's differentiation between colour and lustre when he insists that '*Beauty* consisteth not so much in coulour as in the illumination or illustration of those coulours, which giueth grace, and lustre to euery countenance, and without which all *Beauties* are languishing'.[31] Problematically, the question arises as to how a 'virtuous' woman is able to achieve this lustre realistically without crushed pearl, silver and gold foile, or a simple egg glaze. Neo-Platonists would argue that her virtue and spiritual luminescence would make themselves visible upon her cheeks. This common fantasy of feminine virtue constructs the ideal woman through spiritual abstractions; thus the introduction of material compounds would undoubtedly destabilise, but ultimately help to reconfigure the ideology of beauty.

Firenzuola goes on to describe the necessity of colours in composing a beautiful appearance. He says there should be a 'different color in different parts', for example, 'somewhere white, as in the hands, somewhere fair and vermilion, as in the cheeks, somewhere black, as in the eyelashes, somewhere red, as in the lips, somewhere blonde, as in the hair'.[32] Again Firenzuola distinguishes between the 'white' of the hands and the 'fair' of the cheeks, revealing that it was not enough just to be pallid. The arousing glister of the fair face is also detectable in sixteenth-century art that sought to capture visually the ideal woman. Brian Steele notes that in sixteenth-century paintings of Venetian beauties, 'the erotic imagery parallels themes in Petrarchan lyrics; visual details constitute analogues to poetic metaphors; and both arts catalog identical standards of beauty'.[33] What we also have to consider are the material ties that the lyrics and the paintings have to cosmetic practice. Some of the period's poetic metaphors consist of roses, lilies, ivory, gold, silver and vermilion hues, which are also properties used to make cosmetics. And the lead-based paints used to create the Venetian beauties Steele writes about are the same paints that create the lustre on women's faces. These two facts suggest that Renaissance cosmetic practice was a reaction to the period's artistic expressions of beauty.

Firenzuola's disquisition on feminine beauty forms the basis for such standards in the Renaissance. He argues that the lips should 'seem to be of finest coral, like the edges of a most beautiful fountain', and that the colours needed to depict the perfect woman are 'blonde, tawny, black, red, fair, white, vermilion, and flesh-pink'. He also describes how one can obtain such colours; for example, the colour red 'is that bright color we find in cochineal, in corals, in rubies' and that 'flesh-pink' is 'a white shaded with red, or a red shaded with white, such as the roses we call incarnate'.[34] At this point, ironically, Firenzuola's text becomes an instructional guide to artists and a recipe manual for women hoping to paint the perfect beauty upon the canvas of their own skins, constructing note only a feminine ideal but also a racial one. Lomazzo's tract on painting instructs artists on the 'Matter of colours': '*Reddes* are made of the two *cynnabars called Vermilions* Natural and Artificial, and of the red earth called *Maiolica*, otherwise browne of *Spaine*'; he then goes on to suggest that '*Vermilion* and *lake* make the colour of ripe *strawberries, roses, red lippes, rubies, bloud* and *scarlet*; the same mixtures with *white*, make the colour of red cheeks, of faire carnation and damaske roses'.[35] However, Lomazzo's digression on the dangers of face painting is a sharp reminder that his text is strictly for artists and not meant to assist in female beautification, which implicitly conveys Lomazzo's awareness of the frequent intersection of both arts. Nevertheless, it does not change the fact that artists were involved in shaping the standard of beauty that required fair faces, red lips and 'flesh-pink' cheeks. The portraits 'seem to epitomize contemporary notions of beauty . . . The type idolises the same features – golden hair, white flesh tinged with rose, shell-like ears and symmetrical features, firm breasts, and so on',[36] and women also responded artistically, inscribing beauty on to their own skins.

Highlighting a familiar paradox, although Firenzuola insists upon stringent prescriptions for beauty, he does not hesitate to suggest that such beauty should be natural: 'I said fair because it should not be a washed-out white, without any lustre, but shiny like a mirror; not shiny because of lotions or polishes or powders'.[37] Firenzuola has Celso fantasise about the delicate balance of colours that should be visible on the female face and body; first of all her eyes should be as stars, so bright that they would 'seem to be like the two great luminaries in the sky', while the eyebrows should be 'the color of ebony, thin, with short, soft hairs, as if they were of fine silk'. The hollow around the eyes should be the same colour as the cheeks; but if women hope to achieve this look cosmetically, they must do so with care, for 'when they use cosmetics (those that have a darker complexion, I mean), because very often that part is badly suited to receiving color – or, to speak more clearly, eyeshadow – in its hollowness, or to keep it, because the motion of the eyelashes creates lines that look very bad'.[38] Ideally, beauty should be natural, but for those with a 'darker complexion', Celso argues, concessions may be made. However, one of the 'naturally' beautiful ladies present in the dialogue, Mona Lampiada, shows a disdain for women who use cosmetics:

> Waters and powders were invented in order to remove scales, or freckles and other such marks, and today they are used to paint and to whiten the face, not unlike plaster or gypsum on the surface of walles. And perhaps these little simpletons believe that the men they seek to please are not aware of such concoctions which, besides ruining their time, also ruin their teeth and make them look like carnival clowns all year round.[39]

The mocking tone of condemnation of cosmetic embellishment places women in a paradoxical trap in which strict codes are set down, but the artificial pursuit of such codes is unacceptable. In an anonymous dialogue entitled *The Problemes of Aristotle*, the author poses the question: 'Why do women desire rather to go trim, and decke themselves than men?' The answer he provides further complicates the female predicament, when he suggests that perhaps it is because 'the nature of women is unperfect' and that 'they endeuor to supplie the want of nature with the benefit of art . . . or is it bicause that wanting the beautie of the minde, they are forced to studie how to trim and deck their bodies?'[40] The author suggests here that there is no such thing as a woman's natural lustre. Similarly, in Castiglione's *The Book of the Courtier*, the Count discloses an awareness that women are 'extremely anxious to be beautiful' and that, at times, 'Nature has fallen short', so women may be forced to become beautiful by cosmetic means; however, although the Count allows for physical adornment, he insists:

> surely you realize how much more graceful a woman is who, if indeed she wishes to do so, paints herself so sparingly and so little that whoever looks at her is unsure whether she is made-up or not, in comparison with one whose face is so encrusted that she seems to be wearing a mask and who dare not laugh for fear of causing it to crack.[41]

Further on, the Count declares:

> how much more attractive than all others is a pretty woman who is quite clearly wearing no make-up on her face, which is neither too pallid

nor too red, and whose own colouring is natural and somewhat pale (but occasionally blushes openly from embarrassment or for some other reason), who lets her unadorned hair fall casually and unarranged, and whose gestures are simple and natural, betraying no effort or anxiety to be beautiful.[42]

Here the Count suggests that it is a woman's shame and embarrassment that would give her a natural blush and glow, and indicates that metaphorical cosmetics, such as modesty, would do the trick. Castiglione, however, offers no alternative for women who do not measure up to the ideal beauty, which leaves them 'anxious' about their appearance, aware that beauty is what leads to visibility, acceptance, love and marriage.

Although it can be argued that beautifying was, for a woman, a way of securing loving relationships or marriage, it is also likely that it allowed Renaissance woman to enact her fantasies about textual production, theatrical participation and visual painting, activities from which she was traditionally excluded. At the very source, 'cosmetic artifice', as Katherine Stern argues, 'expresses even more fundamentally a mode of relation to one's own body, a mode of cultivating transience instead of stasis, multiplicity instead of singularity, elaboration instead of simplicity, and extension instead of limitation of one's self-image', thus giving woman a sense of ownership when it came to her body and providing her with a mode of artistic, even intellectual expression.[43] Paradoxically, cosmetic ritual, in early modern England, was artistically, socially and sexually empowering, even though woman was striving ultimately to escape invisibility.

In her study of Italian Renaissance woman, Ruth Kelso writes that 'if painting within reason was permissible to the girl not yet furnished with a husband and therefore anxious to present as attractive an appearance as possible, the argument was no longer applicable to the married woman, who had no acceptable incentive to attract the eyes of men'.[44] It would appear from the dialogues that cosmetics were somewhat 'permissible', but upon a closer reading it becomes clear that natural beauty achieved by means of a virtuous soul and a gentle temperament, grace and elegance, is preferred, and that cosmetically enhanced women are not the exemplar of the ideal. Kelso is right when she claims that 'physical beauty . . . was argued to be necessary to perfection not only as an external sign of goodness, the perfect body furnishing fewer impediments to the working of the soul'.[45] But, realistically such perfection could not be found in one woman, and therefore cosmetic attachments became a necessity; for many of the Renaissance courts, they were an expectation, no matter how many writers spoke out against them: 'being dissatisfied with the attractions bestowed upon you by Nature, you go to extraordinary lengths in trying to improve them'.[46] What, however, created such an intense, and gut-level dissatisfaction in women? The answer is quite simply the media: the vehicle for the delineation of the male sexual fantasy about ideal womanhood, which undermines the physical uniqueness of women by imagining, through hyperbole, fictitious female bodies.

The Poetry of Love, Beauty and Courtship

The description of the Temple of Venus by Scudamor in Spenser's *Faerie Queene* points out the Temple's function as an allegory of female beauty. Spenser describes the beautiful women around 'Womanhood' and 'Shamefastness':

> Euen in the lap of *Womanhood* there sate,
> The which was all in lilly white arayd,
> With siluer streames amongst the linen stray'd:
> Like to the Morne, when first her shyning face
> Hath to the gloomy world it selfe bewray'd
> That same was fayrest *Amoret* in place,
> Shyning with beauties light, and heauenly vertues grace.
> (*FQ*, III, x, 52)

In this excerpt, Spenser posits the neo-Platonic assumption that 'heavenly grace' should be bodied forth as radiant beauty in a woman. The passage seems to prove Sara Matthews Grieco's argument that, thanks to a neo-Platonic influence, 'beauty was no longer considered a dangerous asset, but rather a necessary attribute of moral character and social position'.[47] However, the poetry and drama of the period show that beauty was still considered 'a dangerous asset'. In Book I, Canto ii of Spenser's epic, the narrator provides a picture of both a virtuous beauty and a duplicitous one. The distinction can be detected in the physical description of Duessa, who is not only a symbol of outlandish sumptuousness and popery, but also a signifier of false or cosmetic beauty, and therefore extremely dangerous:

> He had a faire companion of his way,
> A goodly Lady clad in scarlot red,
> Purfled with gold and pearle of rich assay,
> And like a *Persian* mitre on her hed
> She wore, with crownes and owches garnished,
> The which her lauish lovers to her gaue;
> Her wanton palfrey all was ouerspred

With tinsell trappings, wouen like a waue,
Whose bridle rung with golden bels and bosses braue.
(I, ii, 13)

The allusion to Catholic idolatry, the Whore of Babylon and the references to 'scarlot', 'pearle', gold and 'trappings' testify to the author's notion of what comprises dangerous beauty and immoderate representation; these are also references to cosmetic materials: gold foil, liquid pearl and the 'scarlot' effect of cochineal. On the contrary, the description of Una as a 'louely Ladie', who was 'whiter' than the ass upon which she rode and accompanied by the 'milke white lamb', points to her purity, naturalness, and 'divine beauty' (I, i, 4). Further evidence that, despite neo-Platonic models, beauty was still seen as something dangerous can be found in various tracts. When John Hynd argues that 'beauty hath detained many from embracing honesty', and, he continues, 'Beauty hath made many adulterous, but few or none at all chaste',[48] he is suggesting the power beauty has over behaviour, specifically sinful behaviour. Peter Boaystuau writes that the face can be so beautiful 'that sometimes we desire of our good willes, and gladly sacrifice oure selves for the beautie of some persones, and we are so stirred even to become out of our wits, by the prickings and provocations of this faire and beautiful face'.[49] According to many contemporary theorists, whether cosmetic or natural, a woman's beauty is hazardous, a notion that is satirised in poisonous kiss sequences on the stage and encapsulated in the cliché that painted women are traps.

The great question remains: how can neo-Platonic theory claiming that beauty is a reflection of inner virtue, and the misogynistic supposition that beautiful women are dangerous coexist? The eponymous protagonist of Lyly's *Euphues, or The Anatomy of Wit* (1578) wonders, 'time it is that the disposition of the mind followeth the composition of the body; how then can she be in mind anyway imperfect who in body is perfect every way?'[50] Lyly raises the question that Renaissance love poetry and painting answer by settling upon the artistic representation of women; for, in physical terms, art is the only real source of true beauty. And if this is the case, then it may have driven women to paint themselves, transfiguring their perceived inadequacies into artistic beauty. In the third book of *Ars Amatoria* (a popular text in the Middle Ages and Renaissance), Ovid instructs women how to procure the love and affections of the opposite sex. Primarily, a woman must attend to her beauty: 'let not your locks be lawless: a touch of the hand can give or deny beauty'. Realising that not all women are naturally beautiful, Ovid promotes cosmetics, plugging his own publication of recipes, *Medicamina Faciei* (Face Cosmetics): 'from it seek means to rescue impaired beauty: my art is no sluggard in your behalf. Yet let no lover find the boxes set out upon the table'.[51] Ovid suggests that the answer to this dilemma lies in the cosmetic strategy deployed by the woman. If she paints herself, she must do so discreetly, secretively and pretend that her beauty is natural: he asks for deception. Ovid's text, read widely in the Renaissance, and other recipe books suggest that this subtlety, this type of deception is not only at the heart of cosmetic representation, but that lovers actually want to be deceived.

An anonymous collection of poems entitled *The Phoenix Nest*, published in 1593, also contains lyrics that describe the norms of beauty. The following verses adhere to the extremely popular practice of comparing the red and white beauty of women to the rose and lily:

> Hir eies showed pitie, pietie, and pure,
> Hir face shields Roses, Lillies, and delight,
> Hir hand hath powre, to conquere and allure,
> Hir hart, holds honor, loue, remorce, and right,
>> Hir minde is fraught, with wisdome, faith, and loue,
>> All what is hirs, is borrowed from aboue.

The poet provides an anatomical blazon of the woman's face. He alludes to images of war and fortitude in anticipation of the last two lines, which highlight the lady's chastity by gesturing toward the spiritual mysteries surrounding her inner virtue. The rose and lily are important images as they signify not only the perfect beauty, but they are also very popular ingredients in the cosmetic recipes of the period, providing a link between poetic prescriptions and cosmetic practice. A second poem in the collection emphasises the importance of a woman's complexion to beauty:

> The Lillie in the fielde,
> That glories in his white:
> For purenes now must yeelde,
> And render vp his right:
>> Heau'n pictur'de in hir face,
>> Doth promise ioy and grace.
> Fair Cinthias siluer light,
> That beates on running streames;
> Compares not with hir white,
> Whose haires are all sunbeames;
>> Hir vertues so doe shine,
>> As daie vnto mine eine.

It is not merely paleness that is being worshipped in these lines, but rather a shimmering, shining, or glistening paleness, no doubt the type of lustre that Firenzuola fantasised about. Another poem comes from the Earl of Oxford in 1593; questioning the ability of any artist, he asks 'What Cunning can express' the *true* beauty of a woman:

> This pleasant lily white,
>   This taint of roseate red,
> This Cynthia's silver light,
>   This sweet fair Dea spread
>   These sunbeams in mine eye;
>   These beauties make me die.[52]

Both Oxford and Spenser wrote poems in honour of Queen Elizabeth I. Many have argued that she influenced the standard of beauty, recalling the many poems of this ilk written in her honour. But, as we have established, the standard of beauty (red lips, fair complexion, blushed cheeks) had been around for centuries and had been renewed and recycled by poets and painters from each generation perpetuating the racially superior ideal of 'fair' or white beauty. Thus Elizabeth I herself not only came to symbolise but also may have fallen victim to these structured and well-rooted prescriptions when she came to power, which is likely to have been one reason why she was painted with cosmetics. Her red and white painted beauty held a double significance though: it was a symbol of virtuous beauty, but simultaneously, a signifier of political authority and the stability of that authority.

During the reign of Henry VIII, a poem by John Skelton fuses the imagery of red and white with the theme of monarchical stability:

> The Rose both white and Rede
> In one Rose no dothe grow:
> Thus thorow every stede
> There of the fame dothe blow:
> Grace the sede did sow:
> England now gladdir flowris
> Exclude now al dolowrs.[53]

Skelton celebrates the Tudor monarchy, which, with the ascension of Henry VII in 1485, united the white rose of the house of York and the red rose of the house of Lancaster, thus establishing the Tudors as personifying the union of the two colours. A struggle between the colours continued, however, on a smaller scale, which would provide the imagistic fuel for Elizabethan poets to mythologise Elizabeth I and emblematise the conflict as the two colours embattled upon the cheeks of the queen and the mistresses of the period's poetry of courtship. The queen's habit of painting her face with red and white is significant, because her face was a symbolic register for the body politic. Pictorial representations of the queen were, in essence, pictorial representations of her country and subjects; she is depicted usually as an awe-inspiring monarch embodying the national identity of the English people. Charting the allegorical tenor of Elizabeth's portraits, Roy Strong argues that

The 'Ditchley' portrait is a logical progression from its predecessors in one aspect. In the 'Sieve' portraits England is depicted glowing mysteriously on a globe in the background behind the Queen; in the 'Armada' portrait that globe is brought forward and she holds it; in the 'Ditchley' portrait Queen, crown and island become one. Elizabeth is England, woman and kingdom are interchangeable.[54]

On another level, the paintings of the queen acted as a type of fashion spread, which displayed the queen in her cosmetic glory, thus helping to perpetuate the standard that would be emulated by her followers at court.

'In thee, the whole kingdom dresseth itself, and is ambitious to use thee as her glass', says Jonson in *Cynthia's Revels*, but he goes on in an attempt to teach through his own art, 'It is not powdering, perfuming, and everyday smelling of the tailor that converteth a beautiful object: but a mind shining through any suit, which needs no false light either of riches or honours to help it.' He recommends a neo-Platonic ideal, urging simplicity in a court well known for its sycophancy, cosmetic gloss and ostentatious display. But Jonson must have known that the queen's beauty ritual was not mere vanity, nor an attempt to present herself as some type of icon. Instead, the queen's feminine dissatisfaction with her physicality was fused with her conviction that power resides ultimately in beauty.

The Sonnet is the perfect mode through which to transmit the classical and neo-Platonic ideals of beauty because, as a poetic model, it is a balanced composite, harmonious and symmetrical in its form. In *A Neaste of Wasps Latelie Fovnd* (1615), William Goddard's sonnet sequence combines the exaggerated conceits of the poetry of beauty with a disdain for fading looks and cosmetic anxiety. In Sonnet 2, he praises the ideal:

> My sences amaz'd, my hands doe tremble
> To think to what I should my loue resemble,
> Compare hir to the rose; hir crymson die
> Is farr more pure; hir white excells the Ivorie,
> Vnto hir skynn rug'd is the smoothest Iett
> The softest downe to counterfett
> With in hir faces circute there are plac'd,
> Two heauenlie sonns, by whom the world is grac'd,
> Whose golden beames from-of hir lippes exhales,
> That hunnye dewe which Poets Nectar calls
> Soe faire is shee, soe sweete, smooth, soft, soe cleere
> As on this Earthe naught like hir maie appeare,
> > O what a Matchles, Mistresse haue I caught
> > That iustlie cann compare hir vnto naught

In this excerpt Goddard draws on popular images of rosy cheeks, 'Ivorie' complexion, the eyes as suns or stars, and the hair as 'golden beames'. But in the same sequence, Goddard's later sonnets, unconventionally, do not praise neo-Platonic beauty, but rather contain vituperative attacks on painted ladies:

> Awaie with sicklye wenches (whitelye fac'd)
> And those whose heades with amber lockes are grac'd
> Those puling creatures are vnfit for men
> (Sonnet 75, 1–3)

Curiously, here the poet applies the stringent codes of beauty, while, in the same sequence of sonnets, he demonstrates the common distrust and fear of painted women. The idea of beauty as transient is common to many poetic expressions of praise for the ideal woman. For example, Samuel Daniel writes that 'Beauty, sweet love, is like the morning dew, / Whose short refresh upon the tender green, / Cheers for a time, but still the sun doth shew' (XLVII, 1–3). Ironically, the poems that harp on about the threat of time to the beauty of a mistress, urging her to seize the moment of her *natural* blossom, may have intensified the pressure on women to be aesthetically pleasing. Daniel writes that:

> Old trembling age will come,
>   With wrinkl'd cheeks and stains,
>   With motion troublesome,
>   With skin bloodless weaves,
>   That lively visage reaven,
>   And made deform'd and old,
>   Hates sight of glass it loved so to behold.
>
> Thy gold and scarlet shall
> Pale silver-colour be;
> Thy row of pearls shall fall
> Like wither'd leaves from tree;
> And thou shalt shortly see
> Thy face and hair to grow
> All plough'd with furrows, over-swoln with snow.
> (*A Description of Beauty*, VII, VIII)

That beauty is usurped by age and deformity is a ubiquitous theme in the period's poetry of courtship: 'Then beautie (now the burthen of my song)/Whos glorious blaze the world doth so admire,/Must yeeld up all to tyrant Time's desire'(*To Delia*, 33, 5–7). Michael Drayton uses the same technique to reinforce the myth of physical perfection in Sonnet 8:

> There's nothing grieves me, but that Age should haste,
> That in my dayes I may not see thee old;
> That where those two cleare sparkling Eyes are plac'd,
> Onely two Loope-holes then I might behold.

That lovely, arched, yvorie, pollish'd Brow,
Defac'd with Wrinkles, that I might but see;
Thy daintie Hayre, so curl'd, and crisped now,
Like grizzled Mosse upon some aged Tree;
Thy Cheeke, now flush with Roses, sunke, and leane,
Thy Lips, with age, as any Wafer thinne;
Thy Pearly Teeth out of thy head so cleane,
That when thou feed'st, thy Nose shall touch thy Chinne:
  These Lines that now thou scorn'st, which should delight thee,
  Then would I make thee read but to despight thee.

The ultimate monument to the sonnet mistress is, of course, the sonnet itself; however, in Drayton's poem, the tone is taunting, as it will be a monument to her youthful beauty, one he threatens to use as a retrospective looking glass when she is old and withered purely to torment her. Shakespeare's sonnets to the fair youth exploit further this transience of beauty theme in order to persuade the youth to make a copy of his face by reproducing: 'Then let not winter's ragged hand deface/In thee thy summer ere thou be distilled' (6, 1–2). Reproduction for the purpose of preserving beauty can be viewed as a cosmetic process, a vain beauty ritual stemming from an anxious desire to remain eternally young and alluring.[55]

Two more poems that demonstrate the power of the blazon in helping to promulgate the standard of beauty in England come from Spenser's *Epithalamion* and the lesser-known poet, B. Griffin. Spenser's tenth verse on his marriage not only faithfully exhibits the period's requirements for beauty, but it also lays bare his success as a poet in fusing his secular love for his Elizabeth with his love of God through the neo-Platonic revelation that such beauty is possible in one woman:

Her goodly eyes lyke Sapphyres shining bright,
Her forehead yvory white,
Her cheeks lyke apples which the sun hath rudded
Her lips lyke cherryes charming men to byte.
Her brest like to a bowle of creame uncrudded,
Her paps like lyllies budded,
Her snowie necke lyke to a marble towre,
And all her body like a pallace fayre,
Ascending uppe with many a stately stayre,
To honors seat and chastities sweet bowre,
                              (*Epithalamion*, 10, 5–16)

In this poem Spenser's devotion to the standard of beauty is clear; although he did write his own marriage poem and he did marry a woman named Elizabeth, there is nevertheless a tension between fiction and biography residing in the hyperbolic description of her beauty and her virtue. Towards the end of the poem, Spenser creates a type of goddess, who is the touchstone of virtue as well as the paragon of beauty. The depiction of her body as a marble palace 'ascending' to the heavens illustrates the poet's own belief that this beautiful 'creature' is his stairway to heaven.

Griffin's blazon also engages in a similar technique, which delineates the mistress's beauty through itemisation:

> My ladies haire is threads of beaten gold,
>   Her front the purest Christall eye hath seene;
> Her eyes the brightest starres the heavens hold,
>   Her cheeks red Roses, such as seld have been:
> Her pretie lips of red vermilion dye,
>   Her hand of yvorie the purest white;
> Her blush Aurora or the morning skye,
>   Her breast displaies two silver fountains bright;
> The Spheares her voyce, her grace the Graces three,
>   Her bodie is the Saint that I adore;
> Her smiles and favours sweet as honey bee,
>   Her feete faire Thetis praiseth evermore,
> But ah the wors and last is yet behind,
> For of a Gryphon she doth beare the mind.
>   (Sonnet 39, *Fidessa*)

Of course, the stark difference between this blazon and Spenser's is the poet's disdain for the mistress, which resembles the tone of spite felt in Drayton's poem. It exhibits the resentment of a woman who appears to be physically perfect, but who keeps that perfection to herself. Griffin evokes many cosmetic images as well, fortifying the link between the poetry of beauty or courtship and female cosmetic practice. The perfect woman should have hair of gold, which conveys not only her racial superiority, but also commercial value. Countless recipes from the period's manuals make suggestions for dying the hair gold, blond or 'yellow'; one recommends taking 'the best honey two pints, Gumarabick two ounces, distil them with a gentle fire; the water which comes forth first, doth whiten the face, the second and third makes the hair yellow'.[56] Griffin's mistress, like countless beauties of Renaissance love poetry, has red lips, 'of red vermilion dye'; the term 'dye', meaning the cosmetic act of tincturing or staining the lips with the dye made from a vermilion agent, which was also used in canvas painting as Lomazzo informs us. If a woman hoped to 'make the Lips ruddie', she should 'take the juice of briony, wild cucumber, reeds, rosewater each one *ounce*, clarified hony four *ounces*, boile all together, strain it and keep it in a glas: it is exceeding good to anoint the lips and gives them a ruddie and vermilion hue'.[57] Griffin's poem uses the image of 'Christall' to describe her eyes;

later I will argue that the many references to crystal in the imagery of early modern poetry and drama is an allusion to looking glasses made of crystal, which were tinted slightly so that the reflection would be more flattering to the eyes, thus crystal becomes a material symbol of illusion giving it a cosmetic quality. This image in love poetry like Griffin's gestures to the neo-Platonic idea that when lovers gaze into each other's eyes it is their own reflections they see, and the projection is made more flattering because of the intensity of the lovers' feelings for each other. This aspect of neo-Platonic theory, ironically, insinuates that love itself is a cosmetic process.

Beauty in Pictures: Plays and Emblem Books

It is impossible to deny the powerful impact visual media has on our own definitions of beauty. Through its poetry and stage pictures, Shakespearean and Renaissance drama contributed to contemporary notions of beauty. The painted boy actors, donned in red and white pigments, were also, though quite loosely, visual markers of early modern standards of beauty. The language of the plays also disseminated a picture of beauty that was remarkably similar to the classical paradigm. Stephen Greenblatt contends that Shakespeare's notion of beauty revealed a 'pragmatic distaste' for specificity. In Shakespeare's *The Taming of the Shrew*, however, Lucentio, having fallen in love with Bianca, characterises her winning looks:

> I saw her coral lips to move,
> And with her breath she did perfume the air.
> Sacred and sweet was all I saw in her.
> (I, i, 168–70)

Shakespeare's description here is conventional, so we have to ask ourselves if the playwright is being ironic. We know from Sonnet 130 that the poet enjoys mocking the trite poetic descriptions of beautiful women. Moreover, his dramatic representations of beauty are never straightforward; for example, in *The Two Gentlemen of Verona*, he explores creatively a popular idea in the Renaissance that love can affect a woman's beauty, that, in fact, love is inextricable from beauty. Julia is in disguise and, realising that Proteus loves another, she describes its toll on her appearance, indicating that a woman's prettiness cannot exist without a man to appreciate, write about and praise it:

> She hath been fairer, madam, than she is.
> When she did think my master loved her well

> She, in my judgement, was as fair as you.
> But since she did neglect her looking-glass,
> And threw her sun-expelling mask away,
> The air hath starved the roses in her cheeks
> And pinched the lily tincture of her face,
> That now she is become as black as I.
>
> (IV, iv, 141–8)

Here Shakespeare draws upon the rose and lily motif in beauty poetry and indicates, ironically, that the one very important cosmetic for women – love – has been taken away; therefore, Julia vows to neglect all of her cosmetic duties. Similarly, in *The Comedy of Errors* Adriana characterises her husband's neglect in terms of her beauty: 'Then he is the ground/Of my defeatures. My decayed fair/A sunny look of his would soon repair' (II, i, 96–8). Here the implication is that her husband's love would 'repair' her facial imperfections, suggesting the cosmetic powers of emotionality. In Shakespeare's *Sonnets* the poet personifies beauty but refuses to engage in the popular practice of describing the beloved's beauty, but rather draws upon the speaker's love as a determining marker of the young man's beauty. However, the poems do reflect a departure from the cultural ideal of beauty by suggesting that it is embodied within, as Greenblatt suggests, the individual emerging from the featureless collectivity.[58]

Jonson's *Volpone*, parodically, contributes to early modern definitions of beauty as well, when in Act I, scene v, Corvino's wife, whom Volpone will try to seduce later in the play, is poetically praised; he calls her the 'blazing star of Italy!'

> A beauty ripe as harvest!
> Whose skin is whiter than a swan, all over!
> Than silver, snow, or lilies! A soft lip,
> Would tempt you to eternity of kissing!
> And flesh that melteth in the touch to blood!
> Bright as your gold! And lovely as your gold!
>
> (I, v, 108–14)

This extract relies upon the conventional images associated with beauty – the skin as white and glistening as 'silver', 'snow' and 'lilies' – which simultaneously mocks and perpetuates the standard. Celia's beauty is also seen as financial property, a commodity, suggested by the reference to her flesh as 'gold', an image that reflects the pervasive, textual prescriptions for female beauty. An unfamiliar, yet intriguing example comes from *The Tragi-Comedy of Calisto & Melibaea* (1520). Calisto, who is excessively in love with Melibaea, attempts to justify his emotions by defending his position in a blazon:

I begin at her hair, which is so goodly,
Crisped to her heels, tied with fine lace.
For shining beyond fine gold of Araby:
I trow the sun colour to it may give place;
That who to behold it might have the grace . . .
Her gay glossing eyes so fair and bright;
Her brows, her nose in a mean no fashion fails;
Her mouth proper and feat, her teeth small and white;
Her lips ruddy, her body straight upright . . .
Her skin of whiteness endarketh the snow,
With rose-colour ennewed . . .
Her fingers smal and long, with nails ruddy: most pure
Of proportion, none such in portraiture.[59]

Differing from the moralising prescriptions of the authors of treatises and the hyperbolic representation of white beauty in the poetry, this passage seems to suggest that painted beauty might be not only acceptable, but also alluring: the word 'ennewed' means 'painted', which also creates a fusion of portrait painting and face painting. Thus the conventions of female, physical beauty are closely tied to their painted representations on canvas. If these paintings are acceptable and arousing, then a painted lady may be even more exciting, making fantasies about the period's painted pin-ups a reality.

The expectations for women with regard to beauty are also depicted in emblem books, which were useful for authors as they had the advantage of conveying through picture and poetry the formal codes of feminine beauty. In Henry Peacham's famous collection, *Minerva Britania*, published in 1612, three emblems quite conventionally associate beauty with chastity. *Pulchritudo foeminea* (Figure 1.1) shows a lady on a dragon with a 'christall glass' in one hand. Metaphorically, this material property proved useful to moralists who knew that crystal glasses often reflected a more flattering image. In the other hand the woman in the engraving holds a dart, symbolising love, the (sometimes) dangerous effect of beauty; however, although the virgin holds a mirror, Peacham assures us that 'she needes no art'. The flowers on her head represent the transience of natural beauty and, ultimately, the message is that pride or vanity is useless in a world governed by time and impermanence. This emblem not only participates in the cultural formation of beauty standards, but also speaks out against cosmetics.

Philautia (Figure 1.2) pictures a lady gazing into a glass, and poetic images calling attention to her face as 'light' evoke the neo-Platonic conventions of beauty. However, this emblem speaks vehemently against vanity and 'Selfe-loue', while it demonstrates the paradox of the beauty standard. Peacham expresses the widely felt distaste for cosmetic

A VIRGIN naked, on a Dragon fits,
One hand out-ftretch'd, a chriftall glaffe doth fhow:
The other beares a dart, that deadly hits;
Vpon her head, a garland white as fnow,
Of * print and Lillies. Beautie moft defir'd,
Were I her painter, fhould be thus attir'd.

* Alba liguftra cadunt ----

Her nakednes vs tells, fhe needes no art:
Her glaffe, how we by fight are mooud to loue,
The woundes vnfelt, that's giuen by the Dart
At firft, (though deadly we it after prooue)
The Dragon notes loues poifon: and the flowers,
The frailtie (Ladies) of that pride of yours.

Cumque aliquis dicet, fuit hæc formofa, dolebis;
Et fpeculum mendax, effe querére tuum.

Ovid: 2. de Arte amandi.

Nec femper violæ, nec femper Lilia florent:
Et riget amiffa fpina relicta rofa.

Idem.

K I.

Nil

Figure 1.1 *Pulchritudo foemina*, Henry Peacham, *Minerva Britania* (1612) c. 38.
f. 28, by permission of the British Library.

'5   *Philautia.*

Vide Alciatum.   A *VIRGINS face with Robes of light aray* ,
Embl: 69 .   *Why hath (Selfe-loue) our Poets thee aſsign'd?*
                   Philaut :   Loue ſhould be young, and freſh as merry MAY,
                          Such clothing beſt agreeth with my mind.
                   What meanes that poiſonous Serpent in thy hand?
                   Philaut :   My bane I breed , by this you vnderſtand.

                   I' th other hand ſay why that looking glaſſe ?
                   Since in thee no deformitie I find ,
                   Philaut :   Know how in Pride Selfe-loue doth moſt ſurpaſſe,
                          And ſtill is in her Imperfections blind :
* Quod volumus   And ſaue her owne deviſes * doth condemne ,
ſanctum eſt .
Auguſtin : contra   All others labours , in reſpect of them.
Creſconium
Grammat :

                   Cur Virgo incedis Philautia?   *P HI LA:* Virginis ora
Baſili : Doron.   Malit amor . *Serpens quid ſinuoſa manu?*
lib: 2 . pag: 65 . *Philaut :* Pectore virus alo . *Speculum ſed conſulis .* *P HI:* inde
                          Cætera dedignor , dum mea ſola placent .

                                               Humanæ

Figure 1.2   *Philautia*, Henry Peacham, *Minerva Britania* (1612) c. 38. f. 28, by
              permission of the British Library.

embellishment and vanity, yet upholds a standard of beauty that seems impossible to achieve naturally. In the same vein, *Salomone pulchrius* (Figure 1.3) remarks that there is no substitute for natural physical perfection. All that is pictured in this emblem, in fact, is a lily, signifying woman in an imagined natural state. Woman is not represented in her human form, though, which suggests that the ideal of beauty does not even translate into any physical reality. The artist's imaginings are consistently far more powerful than any cosmetic. Ironically, as many early modern cosmetic recipes show, the lily is an important ingredient in ointments and powders to make the face white or fair, illustrating the material relationship between standards of beauty expressed in literary texts and responsive cosmetic practice. For instance, Gervase Markham ensures that after reading his household guide, a woman 'shall know that the best waters for smoothing of the skinne, and keeping the face delicate and amiable, are those of which are distilled from Beaneflowers, from Strawberies, from Vine leaues, from Goats milke, from Asses milke, from the whites of Eggs, from the Flowers of Lilies . . . any of which will last a yeere or better'.[60]

Thomas Combe's translation of La Perriere's emblems also form part of the network of texts that issue requirements for beauty. Emblem XVIII (Figure 1.4) shows how women can, through behaviour, create for themselves a natural beauty. They must not 'gad' about; they must be silent, and their chief virtue should be their willingness to provide comfort for their husbands, while Emblem XXXVII (Figure 1.5) promotes the neo-Platonic paradigm of virtue as the chief begetter of female beauty. The looking glass provides an apt metaphor for spiritual reflection; women must look within and adorn their souls to achieve the beauty they feel may be lacking externally. Many anti-cosmetic authors use a careful strategy to influence women's behaviour, by appealing to the desire to be beautiful, a desire constructed by the early modern cultural media of texts and images. The use of the veritable buffet of cosmetics was considered indecent, wanton and depraved. Yet painted faces materialised male fantasies and were boldly brandished at court. Appropriated by dramatists and popularised by the stage, the cosmetic materials, language and face painting scenes enraptured audiences, while plunging them into the thick of a cultural phenomenon that would gesture towards monarchy, death, art, poetry, race and gender.

Salomone pulchrius.　116

L ET Courtly Dames, their coftly Iewells boaft,
　And *Rhodopis*, in filkes and fattens fhine;
Behold the *Lillie*, thus devoid of coft,
In flowery feildes, is clothd by power divine,
　In pureft white, fair'ft obiect of the eie,
　Religions weede, and badge of Chaftitie.

Why fhould ye then as flaues to loathed pride,
And frantique fooles, thinke ye are halfe vndone,
When that ye goe not in your cullors pide,
Or want the grace, of neweft fafhion :
　When even the *Lillie*, in glorie doth furpaffe,
　The rich, and roiallft King, that ever was .

Matb: 6. 24.

Albedo obieƈtuui
vifus . *Arift*

　　Splendida fluctivagos quid iactitat Aula lapillos?
　　　Intumet et Rhodopis bombycis arte levis?
　　Regibus anteferor, mediis quod veftit in agris
　　　Vita oculi candor, virgineumque decus.

Soboles

Figure 1.3　*Salmone pulchrus*, Henry Peacham, *Minerva Britania* (1612) c. 38.
　　f. 28, by permission of the British Library.

Figure 1.4   Emblem XVIII, La Perriere, *Theatre of Fine Devices* (1614), Glasgow
University Library, Department of Special Collections.

EMBLEME XXXVII.

Herein the chiefest cause is taught,
For which the glasses first were wrought.

A woman should, and may well without pride,
Looke in a looking-glasse, and if she find
That she is faire, then must she so prouide
To sute that beautie with so faire a mind;
If she be blacke, then that default to hide
With inward beautie of another kind.
    ... women would do so, they were but asses
        should dislike the vse of looking-glasses.

Figure 1.5   Emblem XXXVII, La Perriere, *Theatre of Fine Devices* (1614), Glasgow
University Library, Department of Special Collections.

Notes

1. Gaule, *Distractions*, p. 134.
2. See my article, '"This alters not thy beauty": face-paint, gender, and race in *The English Moor*', in *Early Theatre* (2007).
3. Cited in Harris, 'Shakespeare's hair: staging the object of material culture', p. 484.
4. Brathwait, *Time's Curtaine Drawne*, Sig. A5*v*.
5. Rich, *The Excellency of good women*, p. 78.
6. Holland, *A Treatise Against Witchcraft*, Sig. K3*r*.
7. Lomazzo, *A Tracte Containing the Artes of curious Paintinge*, p. 13.
8. Theweleit, *Male Fantasies*, vol. 1, p. 335.
9. Plato, *Symposium*, p. 489.
10. Ibid. p. 494.
11. Aristotle, 'Beauty' from *Metaphysics*, p. 96.
12. Plotinus, 'Beauty' from *The Enneads*, p. 46.
13. Browne, *Pseudodoxia Epidemica*, p. 355.
14. Ficino, *Commentary on Plato's Symposium*, p. 213.
15. Buoni, *Problemes of Beavtie*, Sig. A2*v*.
16. Ibid. *Sig.* A2*v*.
17. Ibid. *Sig.* A2*v*.
18. Ibid. pp. 26–7.
19. Ibid. pp. 18–19.
20. Austin, *Haec Homo*, pp. 100, 105.
21. Ibid. p. 120.
22. Romei, *The Courtier's Academie*, pp. 6, 11.
23. Downame, *A Discourse of Auxillary Beauty*, p. 23.
24. Firenzuola, *On the Beauty of Women*, p. 43.
25. Alberti, *On Painting*, p. 93.
26. Firenzuola, *On the Beauty of Women*, p. 14.
27. Ibid. p. 15.
28. Greenblatt, 'The Mark of Beauty', paper given at 2005 Shakespeare Association of America meeting.
29. Ruscelli, *The Secrets of Alexis of Piemont*, p. 66.
30. Ibid. p. 121.
31. Buoni, *Problemes of Beavtie*, p. 27.
32. Firenzuola, *On the Beauty of Women*, p. 15.
33. Steele, 'In the Flower of their youth', p. 481.
34. Firenzuola, *On the Beauty of Women*, pp. 28, 45–6.
35. Lomazzo, *A Tracte Containing the Artes of curious Paintinge*, pp. 100, 104.
36. Steele, 'In the Flower of their youth', p. 494.
37. Firenzuola, *On the Beauty of Women*, pp. 51–3.
38. Ibid. p. 51.
39. Ibid. p. 54.
40. Anonymous, *The Problemes of Aristotle*, Sig. G7*v*–G8*r*.
41. Castiglione, *The Book of the Courtier*, p. 86.
42. Ibid. p. 86.
43. Stern, 'What is femme?', p. 186.

44. Kelso, *Doctrine for the Lady of the Renaissance*, p. 107.
45. Ibid. p. 202.
46. Boccacio, *The Decameron*, p. 170.
47. Grieco, 'The body, appearance, and sexuality', p. 58.
48. Hynd, *The Mirrour of Worldly Fame*, pp. 36–8.
49. Boaystuau, *Theatrum Mundi*, p. 248.
50. Lyly, *Euphues*, p. 32.
51. Ovid, *Ars Amatoria*, pp. 127, 133.
52. De Vere, Earl of Oxford, 'What cunning can express', in *The New Oxford Book of Sixteenth Century Verse*, p. 162.
53. Skelton, 'A Lawde and Prayse Made for Our Sovereigne Lord the Kyng', in *The Penguin Book of Renaissance Verse 1509–1659*, p. 79.
54. Strong, *Gloriana*, p. 136.
55. I have deliberately omitted a discussion of Shakespeare's *Sonnets* because I am currently working on a shorter study of the cosmetic trope in the sonnet sequence.
56. Culpeper, *Arts Master-piece*, p. 7.
57. Jeamson, *Artificiall Embellishments*, p. 136.
58. In a paper given at the 2005 meeting of the Shakespeare Association of America, Greenblatt argues that for Shakespeare, beauty is identifiable through the individuation of a subject. He provides as an example the mole on Immogen's breast as a 'brief touch' of ugliness that intensifies, like most 'love-spots', 'the beauty of the ambient flesh'.
59. Anonymous, *The Tragi-Comedy of Calisto & Melibaea*, p. 62.
60. Markham, *Countrey Contentments*, p. 129.

Chapter 2

Early Modern Cosmetic Culture

Women 'goe up and downe whited and sised over with paintings laied one upon another, in such sort: that a man might easily cut off a curd of cheese-cake from either of their cheeks'.[1]

Though satirical and intentionally humorous, this colourful excerpt from Thomas Tuke's anti-cosmetic tract betrays an anxiety about woman's fundamental lack of readability. Tuke reveals an implicit distrust of artifice. To understand the relationship between cosmetic drama and early modern society, it is necessary to get to grips with the cultural reception of beautification found within the non-dramatic writing of the period. I want to suggest that from a wide range of early modern texts, what we see emerging is the formation of a culture of cosmetics that found its visual footing on the stage.

In the oppositional texts there are three primary objections to cosmetics: the belief that alteration of the body is a crime against God; the ethnocentric fear of foreign ingredients and commodities of a cosmetic nature; and the necromantic effect of face paint, which suggested not only the physical unreliability, but also the poisonous and contaminative nature of women and even art. Anti-cosmetic diatribes unearth a deeply rooted fear not just of cosmetic paint and its potential toxicity, but rather of what it signifies: gender, theatricality, race and the performative nature of political power. Stephen Greenblatt's comments on the inherent theatricality of kingship in his essay 'Invisible bullets' forced me to consider the role cosmetic paint must have played in legitimating Queen Elizabeth I: whether she was painted in order to fashion herself into the quasi-divine icon she is now perceived to have been, or her cosmetic practice was simply to preserve her youth motivated by a fear of the effects ageing would have on her ability to command an increasingly superficial court. Greenblatt suggests that 'the charismatic authority of the king, like that of the stage, depend upon falsification'.[2] Given that power, authority and legitimacy are nurtured by public perception, the manipulability of the Queen's body seems not only a practice fuelled by a desire to be attractive, but is also a declaration of unmistakable potency. Thus the theatrical representation of cosmetics speaks to this central anxiety, not just about the 'falsification' of power, but also, specifically, the varnished authority of Queen Elizabeth I.

A by-product of the Queen's open use of facial cosmetics is the social legitimising of cosmetics for other women, at least at the upper levels of society. For if the Queen can paint and be forever conceptualised as a virgin, what about other women at court? This legitimisation undermines the anti-cosmetic argument, which attempts to stamp on to the painted woman the brand of whore, a word, which Dympna Callaghan insists, was 'probably the worst name you can call a woman in Shakespeare's England', owing to 'its capacity to deprive women . . . of all means of social and economic support'.[3] However, paradoxically, women of the upper court circles and social levels were not only openly painting, but were, strikingly, expected to have a working knowledge of the rituals and intimate secrets of the female dressing chamber. Yet, how do we reconcile this expectation and the painted Virgin Queen with the pervasive concept of the painted whore? The answer lies in an analysis of the symbolism of the material face paint. The Queen's use of cosmetics was linked to her power and the aesthetic. Once the paint is applied to the face of a housewife, however, it becomes a sign of her deceptiveness, infidelity and lack of care to her household duties. Thus the social meaning of cosmetics is subject to the status of the woman wearing them. Significantly, the meaning of the actual paints becomes heightened when we realise that they are the material link between the private and the public domain. A woman paints or is painted within the secret walls of her chamber and she shows her face in the public sphere. The paradox of cosmetic paint is that it simultaneously conceals and displays. The cosmetics debate is one discourse in which the social relationship between cosmetics and feminine display is seen taking shape. The early modern discussion of cosmetics is not, as it may seem, simply about face paint and female vanity. Neither is it a simplified collection of moralistic prescriptions. It is rather a register of contemporary attitudes towards women, art and visible power, and it contributed to the formation of individual and cultural identities. This chapter will provide a context for the dramatic appropriation and revaluation of cosmetic signifiers by examining the religious, political and social opposition to cosmetics as well as some of the recipes, which provide a unique history of the materials and technology of beauty.

'The Devil's craft': The Opposition to Cosmetics

Following the Reformation, humanism helped to reshape perceptions of the body. At this time, the notion that the body belonged to God begins to change to a sense that the body is one's own. The Burckhardtian formulation of the emerging individual is right when we consider the relationship people had to their bodies in this period. Although anti-cosmetic arguments grounded in the notion that 'God has given you one face' mark a permeable shift in cultural attitudes toward the body, individual ownership of the body was not as pervasive a concept as it is now. The reconfiguration of ideas about the human body is marked by Francis Bacon, who was the first to use the term 'cosmetic' in English. In Book II of *The Advancement of Learning* (1605), Bacon describes the types of knowledge necessary to maintain the 'good of a man's body', which he divides into four categories: 'Health, Beauty, Strength and Pleasure: so the knowledges are Medicine, or art of Cure; art of Decoration, which is called Cosmetic; art of Activity, which is called Athletic; and art Voluptuary, which Tacitus truly calleth *eruditus luxus*'.[4] He goes on to describe the cosmetic art: 'it hath parts civil, and parts effeminate: for cleanness of body was ever esteemed to proceed from due reverence to God, to society, and to ourselves. As for artificial decoration, it is well worthy of the deficiencies which it hath; being neither fine enough to deceive, nor handsome to use, nor wholesome to please'.[5] From the moment of its first usage, the term 'cosmetic' and the idea of 'artificial decoration' were problematic. Nevertheless, Bacon's description of 'cosmetic' redefines attitudes towards the individual and the presentation of the physical self. He also carves out a place for cosmetic decoration in the study of human development by placing it alongside other subjects of learning.

Bacon's acknowledgement of the cosmetic arts, coupled with the 'increased self consciousness about the fashioning of human identity as a manipulable, artful process,'[6] invited discussions about decorating the self, a discourse that would continue throughout the seventeenth century. Much of this literature was addressed to women in order to assist in their own self-fashioning: a self-fashioning that for some authors focused upon the internal, and for others, upon the external self. Kate Aughterson's study of books for women suggests that women underwent a self-shaping process that differs greatly from that of men: 'women did not experience the same self-fashioning as did men, but . . . the proliferation of discourses, the discoveries, the economic, political and religious changes in which Renaissance man was involved, also embedded and constructed woman, albeit in differing and different ways'.[7] The texts for women are distinctive in that they appeal to what was, and still is, perceived as a feminine desire for physical beauty. These texts consist of household guides, theological instructional guides, misogynous diatribes, culinary manuals, medicinal tracts and blatantly anti-cosmetic treatises.

In the anti-cosmetic arguments the simile seems to be the device most authors rely upon, evoking a wide range of comparisons: painted women are like ships that need rigging and repairing, bird-lime, or other types of traps and objects of deception. Additionally, moralists liken painted ladies to animals, witches, foreigners, prostitutes and even criminals. Those who use cosmetics are deemed fundamentally idle, unnatural, sinful, hideous and monstrous. Yet, as I pointed out in the opening chapter, there is a simultaneous expectation that women model themselves upon the female ideal found in art and poetry: eyes like stars or the sun; a mouth like coral, rubies, vermilion; cheeks or a complexion like the moon, alabaster, lily mixed with rose, silver, glistering gold, cream or milk; blue veins in the breast like azure rivers; and teeth like pearls or ivory. This ideal portrayal of women coupled with the polemical and misogynistic representation of women who paint conspire to polarise them, demonstrating the perpetual paradox that locked women into the myth that natural physical perfection should be attainable.

One principle admonition to women (and men)[8] in the prescriptive texts of the anti-cosmetic argument is to beautify internally, rather than adorn the external body. This is a reflection of many fears, one that people were replacing their religion with vanity. Railing against the seventeenth-century male fashion of lovelocks, one Puritan worries that 'the Barber is *their* Chaplaine: *his* Shop, *their* Chappell: *the* Looking glasse, *their* Bible; and *their* Haire, and Lockes, *their* God'.[9] Another author addresses the ungodly women he has in mind directly:

> you that take more care to trick your bodies to the pleasure of men, then to deck your soules to the will of God, you that had rather spend two houres at ye glasse, then a minute at the bible, taking more delight to dew your faces, then to behold your consciences.[10]

This passage urges self-reflection, arguing that faith no longer occupies the minds and hearts of the vain. Many moralists regarded the Bible as a symbolic looking glass, meant for internal refashioning, while actual mirrors conversely were symbols of vanity and excess. Actual looking glasses (Figure 2.1), crucial to the cosmetic process, were signifiers of vanity; however, the concept of the looking glass was also 'intended to provoke women to concentrate upon their moral advancement, rather than embellish their physical adornment'.[11] Herbert Grabes finds that

Figure 2.1   Venetian looking glass, V & A Images/Victoria and Albert Museum.

the pervasiveness of 'mirror-metaphors' is contextualised within the medieval and Renaissance perception of the cosmos; Grabes observes that 'the world and the universe were, of course, considered to be a hierarchical structure or great chain of being, in which one level reflected the order of the others'; he goes on to say that 'a predilection for mirror-metaphors could be expected in such a context of thought, particularly in view of the Neo-platonic model underlying this world-picture'.[12]

The materials out of which looking glasses were made were of significance when it came to spiritual versus physical reflection. Many early modern texts of a didactic nature refer to 'flatt'ring glasses', or false glasses as well as 'true glasses', which calls to mind the fact that mirrors were constructed out of different materials, such as crystal or metal. Philippa Kelley's study of looking glasses in Shakespeare is useful here: 'the term "mirror" referred to metal mirrors as well as to "water mirrors," crystal mirrors and mirrors of glass, while "looking glass" (or, less commonly, "seeing glass") designated mirrors made of glass compound'.[13] Kelley also finds that crystal glasses 'provided a novel way of distorting the face', while mirrors with a metal backing 'gave a very good reflection'.[14] Such material differences afforded authors the opportunity to construct symbolic differences; in other words, flattering glasses embody vanity, and lies, while the true or 'steel' glass is much like the instructional text, which allows readers to see the absolute truth as they reflect upon their souls. George Gascoigne's satire entitled *The Steel Glas* is an example of such a text, with its description of steel glasses as 'trusty' and 'true'; however, 'our curious yeares can finde / The christal glas, which glimseth brave & bright, / And shewes the thing, much better than it is'.[15] At times, the looking glass appears on stage as a stock property in scenes of face painting; although dressing table mirrors were not widely used until the end of the seventeenth century, hand mirrors, long mirrors, and snuff boxes that contained a tiny mirror on the inside of the lid were used, especially among court circles, hence the association with vanity and affectation.[16] Grabes reveals that metal mirrors or 'mirrors of steel, silver or gold were in use well into the seventeenth century', and that the glass mirrors initially made in Venice 'gradually spread to England, becoming very popular, particularly in the form of the more mass-produced article developed by the Venetians in the sixteenth and then copied by the English at the beginning of the seventeenth century'.[17]

Many anti-cosmetic authors appealed to what was believed to be women's inherent desire for physical beauty by urging them to deck themselves with qualities compliant with patriarchal expectations, such as modesty, chastity, grace and moderation. William Prynne demonstrates this view when he suggests 'let us paint our Faces with the candor of Simplicitie, and Vermilion-blush of Chastite: and our Eyes, with Modestie: let Silence, or Holy conference, bee the ornament of our Lips'.[18] Similarly, Richard Brathwait accuses women of religious negligence: 'you neglect the incomparable beauty of your Soules. For with what ornaments doe ye adorne them? With what sweet odors of Spiritual graces doe ye perfume them?'[19] Painting the soul would result in a naturally beautiful appearance, so women should not need material compounds; instead the desired cosmetics are abstract notions, such as 'simplicitie', 'chastitie', 'modestie', 'silence' and 'holy conference'. The language that Prynne and Brathwait use emphasises its metaphorical suggestion that internal decking is still in the category of physical beautification; the imagery attempts to appeal to female sensibilities of the time. Additionally, the passage from Prynne is a type of anatomical blazon, which reduces the body into a face, and then divides it into eyes and lips. Such imagery occurs frequently in the discourses criticising adornment, to reinforce to the reader that physical mutability is subject only to God's discretion, that individuals do not own their bodies. Thus to alter one's self by external means is offensive to God's image and a violation of his property.

Polemicists argued that face paints, lip colours, wigs, perfumes and other accessories that serve to alter or enhance the external body destroyed divine workmanship. Hamlet reminds Ophelia that women's paintings are an affront to God: 'I have heard of your paintings, too, well enough. God hath given you one face, and you make yourselves another' (III, i, 142–3). Hamlet is not necessarily suggesting that the character of Ophelia is painted, but in addition to undermining Ophelia's physicality he is repeating a frequently cited argument against artificial beauty that often accompanies a misogynistic diatribe. Philip Stubbes's tract *The Anatomie of Abuses* (1583) famously rebukes English women for indulging in cosmetic practices: 'Doo they think thus to adulterate the Lord his woorkmanship, and to be without offence?'[20] Stubbes deliberately poses questions designed to diminish a woman's artistic compulsion to paint herself: 'Thinkest thou that thou canst make thy self fairer then God, who made us all?'[21] And later in the seventeenth century, another tract argues that women who paint 'pretend by such *Fucus* to make themselves seem more fair and comely then ever God made them'.[22] This is the crux of the religious opposition to cosmetics.[23] Such arguments reveal three main concerns: an anxiety of transformation, an anxiety that God's workmanship is being altered, and an anxiety about recognisability. These tracts provide some insight into why the devil is consistently associated with adornment: 'the devil's craft hath dyed and stained' because cosmetics undermine God's creation and distract one from spiritual meditation and reflection.[24] In the cosmetics debate the material is always pitted against the spiritual.

Comparing a painting woman to an amateur artist who boldly repairs the work of a master painter is another convention of the anti-cosmetic polemics.[25] Juan Luis Vives's *A very Fruteful and pleasant booke called the Instruction of a Christian Woman* also draws on this popular analogy, and he indicates that a professional artist would be offended if an amateur presumed to 'amend' the artist's creation.[26] Thomas Tuke objects to cosmetics on the same grounds: 'sure there is wrong done to God, whose workmanship they would seame to mend, being discontented with it'.[27] No doubt this particular strain of the anti-cosmetic argument highlights the aesthetic undercurrent of cosmetic practice and aligns cosmetics with canvas paints on a very tangible and material level. However, the comparison between God and a professional artist suggests that it is not art that the writers are protesting about; rather, the audacious woman, who appropriates the 'pencil' of the artist and paints upon herself, is the targeted subject of the religious polemics.

Another common yet forceful argument against the use of cosmetics is that God will not recognise a woman who has spent her life painting her face and adorning her body. Many polemicists insist on this, yet in doing so they are paradoxically placing more power in a woman's ability to create than in God's. Stubbes insists that 'those which paint or collour them selves in this world otherwise than GOD hath made them, let them feare, least when the day of judgement commeth, the Lorde will not knowe them for his Creatures.'[28] The sixteenth-century preacher Roger Edgeworth warns women that their maker will not recognise them: 'thee that paintest thyself, art thou not afraid, lest when thou shalt appear afore the Judge . . . he will not know thee'.[29] Vives expresses the same anxiety: 'How dare she lifte up towarde heaven that face, that hir maker will not knowe'.[30] The religious opposition to cosmetics became intrinsic to Puritan exhortations making it less convincing and a target for satire on the stage. Hence the social influence of such prescriptions appears to be virtually negligible. Early modern England was devoted to ornament, decoration and artifice, and cosmetics became a material signifier of this devotion, fuelling anxieties and attacks which ultimately had little effect.

In addition to the theological opposition to cosmetics, there is also an argument based on a sense of national identity. The fear of a diminishing Englishness in an ingredient culture that thrived upon foreign commerce is quite central to the anti-cosmetic case. Many oppositional authors suggest that English women had a responsibility to help preserve the national identity because of the centrality of their role in the household. Lisa Jardine attributes the 'national isolation' of the English to the Papal Bull of 1570, which excommunicated Elizabeth I and her followers, subsequently opening trade routes to the East. The exchange of goods with the 'infidels' allowed English merchants to monopolise trade and commerce in Europe for a time, though many (including the Venetians) ignored such prohibitions.[31] The booming trade economy in England, however, antagonised ethnocentric sensibilities and moralists raised concerns about foreign 'thinges' and the increasing consumerist drive for material possessions. During the reign of Edward VI, the Bishop of Winchester, Hugh Latimer, was already voicing his concerns about women's love of foreign decorative commodities. He calls the dressing process 'pricking-up' and complains that 'we must have our power from Turkey, of velvet, and gay it must be; far-fetched, dear-bought'.[32] John Hoskins calls upon 'daughters of England' to avoid building 'turrets or castles on your heads'.[33] William Averell tells the story of a wife of Constantinople, whose husband was a captain governing a band of Venetians. This wife would have her servants assist her as she delighted in 'artificial pleasures', and 'her bed chamber was garnished' with commodities that are implicitly exotic and cosmetic: 'sweete hearbes, such varietie of fragrant flowers, such chaunge of odiferous smelles, so perfumed with sweete odours, so stored with sweete waters, so beautified with tapestrie, and decked so artificially'.[34] The story might make us think about the term 'cosmetic' and what it means as I apply it to early modern discourse. If something is 'cosmetic', it is material and symbolic; it is that which beautifies. It refers not only to makeup, but also to perfumes, herbs, and even aesthetic commodities such as tapestries, which 'beautify' a room. Eventually, in the story, God punishes the wife for her pride; Averell therefore warns English women: 'your washing in sweet waters, your anoynting with sweete odours, your muske, your civitte, your baulme, and a number of devises, to make the body sweete . . . do make your soules to stincke'.[35] Averell, in addition to making an argument against foreign perfumes and cosmetic waters, is stressing the need for internal painting. He is suggesting that no matter how much perfume a woman puts on her body, if her soul is neglected, she cannot conceal the stench.[36]

Barnabe Rich distinguishes between the qualities of merchants and suggests that a good merchant of England is one who brings back items necessary or beneficial to society: 'such commodities as may best serve necessitie'; a merchant less worthy is one who 'bringeth in toyes and trifles, and such other fantasies as are both vain and needles'.[37] Kim F. Hall observes that many male writers 'worry that female vanity will feed the market for foreign ornaments'.[38] She also argues that in addition to a fear of foreign cosmetic goods, the fear of colour difference is also inherent in the discourses that express a disdainful apprehension of foreign exchange. The fear of the Other is projected on to women who paint, because if they are painted, they must be hiding a metaphorical blackness that qualifies their souls as strange and deformed. Although it is not solely preoccupied with skin colour, John Bulwer's *Anthropometamorphosis* shows a concern for the increasing mutability of the English people, which was still a concern in the mid-seventeenth century. He describes the cosmetic practices of many different cultures, including Europeans, Native Americans, and 'Japonians'. His concern is that the English retain a unique identity in the shrinking world, since they simply imitate the fashions and customs of 'barbarians' as well as Europeans:

> the Spanish women when they are married, they have a privilege to weare high shooes, and to paint, which is generally practiced there; and the Queen useth it her selfe; which brings on great decay in the naturall Face: For it is observed, that women in *England* look as youthfull at fifty as some there at twenty-five. This . . . is to be reproved in your Spanish women, that they now and then deforme their face with washes of Vermilion & Ceruse, because they have lesse native colour than your French women; and indeed other nations learnt from them the use of Spanish paper . . .[39]

It is clear from this extract that the fear of foreign infiltration is tied closely to anxieties about bodily infiltration, especially when it comes to cosmetics. The foreign custom of using poisonous, foreign ingredients will contaminate the English body as well as the English state. He argues:

> our English Ladies, who seeme to have borrowed some of their Cosmeticall conceits from Barbarous Nations, are seldome known to be contented with a Face of Gods making; for they are either adding, detracting, or altering continually, having many Fucusses in readinesse for the same purpose . . .[40]

Cosmetics worn by women were undoubtedly a reminder of the permeability of the flesh and the permeability of England's borders. Stowe's *Annales* show that in 1563 many Dutch and French people emigrated to England, and London's foreign population increased with each year, as did 'the greate freedome, of Traffiqus, and commerce into France, Spayne, Italy, and Turky'.[41] He goes on to say that England was 'plenteously abounding in Free Trade and Commerce with all nations, richly stored with gold, silver, pearle; spice, peper & many other strange commodities . . . Oyles from Candy, Cyprus, and other places under the Turkes dominion'.[42] Many writers, including Barnabe Rich, did not see this economic expansion as advantageous, but rather as threatening to the more vulnerable components of England, such as the unique cultural identity of its people, an Englishness that was fast dissolving into an indiscernible multi-cultural hodgepodge. Rich calls the age one of 'fearfull times', and cosmetics were foreign sins 'ingrossed and transported into England'.[43]

'All the favoure of the face waxeth olde, and the breath stynketh; and the tethe rusten, and an evyll ayre all the bodie over, bothe by reason of the ceruse, and quicke silver'.[44] The stringent objection to cosmetics not only stemmed from a pathological desire for religious or national preservation, but was deeply embedded in the preservation of the natural body, giving the anti-cosmetic argument a cosmetic element itself, paradoxically. The neurotic fears about poison were not entirely unfounded in early modern England, since poisons were quite ubiquitous in medicines, ointments and cosmetics. But the fear of the contamination of cosmetic poisons was a fear of sexual contamination, which had literal implications when it came to painted prostitutes who hid their syphilis scars underneath thick layers of cosmetics. This reason often provides a thematic framework for the cosmetic sequences in many of the plays discussed in this book. The passage quoted above is a typical example of the awareness of the dangerous ingredients in many cosmetic bases, and it uncovers a link between the poison in cosmetics and metaphorical poison. Nowhere is the dangerous materiality of cosmetics made more explicit than in Lomazzo's *Tracte Containing the Artes of curious Paintinge Carvinge & buildinge*, translated into English in 1598. This text provides sufficient evidence that face paints and canvas paints customarily contained the same materials. Richard Corson is not far from the truth when he argues that sixteenth-century women treated their faces as 'living canvases'.[45] In his tract, Lomazzo exhaustively instructs artists about the symbolism of colour, the blending and manipulation of paints to create certain pigments, and the physical motions of the human body. However, Lomazzo feels compelled to digress upon women's cosmetics and warn them about the dangers residing in the various colours, ingredients, and methods of beautification. The author hopes to reveal what women are using on their faces 'because it often falleth out, that in steede of beautifying, they doe most vilely disfigure themselves'.[46] The deeply rooted belief that a woman's face is often made worse after she treats it is captured most compellingly in John Webster's *The Duchess of Malfi* (1614), when Bosola describes a woman who flayed her face in order to achieve a smoother complexion, but ended up no more attractive than 'an abortive hedgehog' (II, i, 27).

Lomazzo's text goes on to describe in detail cosmetic technology. Much of his discussion provides the modern reader with insight into the various techniques used by Renaissance women in Italy and in England. He warns against Mercury Sublimate 'and the bad effects thereof'; it is 'offensive to mans flesh, and that not only to the face; but unto all the other parts of the body besides, where it is applied'.[47] He indicates that cosmetic paints were not only applied to the face, but other parts of the body, most likely the hands, neck and breasts.[48] Lomazzo's text suggests that people were aware of the dangers involved in painting the face and body, but indulged in it anyway. He describes the ravaging effects of the sublimate in detail: 'wherefore such women use it about their face, have always black teeth, standing far out of their gums like a Spanish mule; an offensive breath, with a face halfe scorched, and an uncleane complexion'.[49] The picture he paints is a beastly, burned, dirty face. And there is the latent suggestion that women do not know what they are doing as they clumsily burn themselves and destroy their teeth as well as the natural cleanliness of their faces. Such descriptions of the grotesque effects of beauty rituals make it even more impossible for women who were caught between the cultural ideal and the potentially monstrous ramifications of proactively attempting to create their own beauty. What is more, that an artist would describe it and Richard Haydocke translate the text for English eyes in the late sixteenth century is especially curious. We are made to recall the religious argument of women usurping the role of *the* master painter. In a secular context, Lomazzo, and by extension, Haydocke, is suggesting the same thing: women are amateurs and should not paint, end of story.

The text then details the effects of 'ceruse', a blend of white lead and vinegar, which dries up the moisture on women's faces and makes their complexions become 'withered and gray-headed'.[50] This is something of a stock theme in the anti-cosmetic argument, that while women are attempting to stave off the ageing process, the use of ceruse or other mineral cosmetics, ironically, brings it on more rapidly. A 'Sermon Against Excesse of Apparel' in a book of homilies (1547–63) points out this ironic dimension of face painting: 'smells and savours . . . do rather deform and misshape thee, than beautify thee'.[51] As Montaigne clearly indicates about the women of his country, skin flaying was another common activity among English women of the upper classes as well as the country wives, 'who hath not heard of her at Paris, which only to get a fresher hew of a new skin, endured to have her face flead all over?'[52] Haydocke's translation reveals how it was done by scaling or 'Plume-Alume': 'with this some use to rubbe the skinne off their face, to make it seem red, by reason of the inflammation it procureth'.[53] The digression closes with a warning:

> all Paintings and colourings made of minerals or halfe minerals, as iron, brasse, lead, tinne, sublimate, cerusse, camphire, iuyce of lymons, plume-alume, salt-peeter, vitrioll, and all manner of saltes, and sortes of alimes . . . are very offensive to the complexion of the face.[54]

Following this scare tactic, he offers a familiar method of beautifying the face as he instructs women to be 'cheerful' and content in order to achieve an attractive complexion, advice which falls into the same category as the religious arguments encouraging women to choose silence, contentment, and chastity as their preferred cosmetics. Lomazzo's final moralistic admonition is curious given its secular context.

The devastating effects of poisonous cosmetics were more than likely gradual, which is why many women persisted in painting throughout their adult lives, including Queen Elizabeth herself. Although some effects of the poisons were fatal, apothecaries and physicians continued to supply women with the ingredients. Strikingly, John Manningham's diary (1602–8) gives an account of 'one Trystam Lyde, a surgeon, admitted to practise by the archbishop letters, was arraigned for killing divers women by annoynting them with quicksilver'.[55] Similarly, Montaigne warns against mineral cosmetics: 'their very skin, and quicke flesh is eaten in and consumed to the bones; whereby they sometimes worke their owne death'.[56] Examples such as these make it clear that early modern society was aware of the physical dangers that cosmetic materials posed, and that the use of poisonous ingredients could lead to death in some instances, but nevertheless, painting the face was an activity similar to painting a portrait and practitioners of both arts employed the same mineral ingredients.

In Richard Brathwait's treatise against cosmetics he tells the story of a woman, who understanding one to be much inamoured of her, called him aside and told him:

> Sir, I honour you so much, as I have chosen rather to suffer, than by my beauty to make you a prisoner: wherewith discovering her face, in complexion much altered, by some colours which she had caused to be laid upon it: he vowed to relinquish his suit, imagining that shee had poisoned her face, to waine him from his affection.[57]

Here we see cosmetics acting as a deterrent to love and courtship. The intended message to women is that if you paint your face you will not be loveable or marriageable in this society. The extract also demonstrates another stock theme of the anti-cosmetic argument, that cosmetics are 'birdlime,' a sexual trap to make men captive to female sexuality, an idea interred in the word 'prisoner'.

Sexual entrapment is one of the chief accusations polemicists level at painted women. John Donne's Sermon 8 proclaims that 'our women are not so carefull, but they expose their nakedness professedly, and paint it, to cast birdlime for the passenger's eye'.[58] However, this notion that cosmetics are birdlime complicates issues of beauty in the period. The paradox lies in the cliché that a painted face symbolised an evil heart, and a beautiful woman was a sexual trap; yet the standard of beauty laid heavy upon the shoulders of women in a society in which marriage was the ultimate goal for them. The anti-cosmetic argument sometimes had a caveat: if we do not know you are painted, it would be better – this is how women were expected to get around the central paradox of beauty. John Donne speaks to this in Paradox 2, 'That Women Ought to Paint Themselves', which is repeated by John Manningham, who writes: 'fowleness is loathsome; can it be soe that helpes it? What thou lovest most in her face is colour, and this painting gives it that; but thou hatest it, not because it is, but because thou knowest it is. Foole whom ignorance only maketh happie'.[59] This paradox criticises the male *desire* to be fooled by outward show and the hypocrisy at pretending to condemn it, an idea that is perfectly embodied in Bassanio's 'deceived by ornament' speech in *The Merchant of Venice*. The Paradox deduces that if a painted portrait of a woman is loved by man (as we see in Bassanio's admiration of Portia's min-iature), why should she not be lovely if the portrait is living: 'if her face be painted on a board or a wall, thou wilt love it, and the board and the wall. Canst thou loathe it then, when it smiles, speekes, and kisses, because it is painted?'[60] This point raises questions about the psychology behind oppositions to painted faces. Even today there are those who dislike women who wear too much makeup, a natural (or seemingly natural) beauty is once again preferable, the irony being that in the opposition to deception there lies a preference for it. But funda-mentally, Donne is asking what is the difference between a painted face and a painted wall or canvas. Again, the meaning of the paint changes depending upon its signifying function and on the person applying it to its designated medium. Michael Price argues that Donne's preoccu-pation with face painting stems from his religious theory. For Donne, Price proposes, Catholic dissimulations and cosmetics were linked: 'he devises the analogy that likens women who paint to sinners who conceal their offences'.[61] Although Price recognises the contemporary links made between Catholic idolatry and female cosmetic practice, he simplifies Donne's interest in cosmetics here as a 'stock metaphor'. Paradox 2 is not only an attempt to hide 'subversive subtexts', but it also raises questions about art and highlights the contemporary distinction between acceptable and unacceptable deception.[62]

Joseph Swetnam's notoriously misogynistic treatise demonstrates the beauty paradox in its claim that 'a fair face . . . is ever matched with a cruel heart'.[63] Both beauty and plainness count against women, and trying to enhance or rectify either cosmetically is treated with suspicion. It is assumed by many moralists that women under painted faces are duplicitous traps for unsuspecting men: 'how many vices are hidden under these painted faces, what deformities covered with vailes & masks, what crooked minds under straightened bodyes?'[64] In *The Second Maiden's Tragedy* (1611) the painted face of the dead Lady does indeed function as a trap for the Tyrant, who is physically contaminated by the paint when he kisses the Lady's corpse. This dramatic event encapsulates the anti-cosmetic cliché that painted ladies are traps but, as I will show in the next chapter, the painted Lady in this play is virtuous and her cosmetic tincture restores health to the political body by cleansing the court of its perverse usurper. The dramatisation of the poisoned kiss framed by the notion that cosmetics are the contaminants is paralleled by theories about cosmetics that are explored in related discourses. Tanya Pollard's study of the poisonous properties of cosmetics investigates the social and political implications of the contagiousness of cosmetic material, a dimension of cosmetics which no doubt deepened anxieties about painted women. Pollard argues that 'socially and politically . . . the idea of cosmetic infiltration came to be aligned with concerns about the contamination of national and class identity'.[65] Pollard observes that this anxiousness about national identity is bound up with the contemporary attitude towards poison, both being key to the anti-cosmetic argument, as I have shown. The notion of a painted lady as a snare is tied closely to this neurotic fear of poison in early modern England, and is at the root of the anti-cosmetic sentiment: 'a woman is a stinking rose, a pleasing evill, the mouse-trap of a mans soule . . . a sweete poison'.[66]

Women of all social backgrounds wore cosmetics in the early modern period. Prostitutes were particularly notorious for their painted faces. It was assumed they painted to hide the external scarring of venereal diseases, which materialised contemporary fears of sexual entrapment and poisoned kisses. Moralists argue that prostitutes paint their faces to capture men: '*the Harlot* is like a ship too, but not like a marchantes ship, but in truth like a *Pyrat* a *Rover* . . . like such a ship as lieth still in waite for rapine and for spoyle'.[67] Thomas Gainsford echoes this belief, and suggests that, when confronted with a painted harlot, a man's entire being is at stake, his spiritual, emotional self as well as the sensual, bodily self: 'Beauty of a curtisan is a meete trap to deceive one, and a worse danger: for the one peradventure catcheth but our goods, or bodies; but the other ravisheth both our senses and our harts'.[68] Barnabe Rich argues that whores have '*Lippes*, to inchant, *kisses* to inflame, a *body* to performe, and all these to poison'.[69] This strain of the anti-cosmetic argument is incongruent with contemporary practice, since prostitutes were not the only women who painted their faces. The implication, then, is that any woman who paints is a 'whore' or 'harlot'. Since women from the Queen to her court attendants painted their faces, the anti-cosmetic tracts were not only moralistic prescriptions, but also politically subversive, expressing anxieties about painted authority and excessive pageantry.

The time and money spent on the cosmetic ritual are wasteful, according to many anti-cosmetic rhetoricians. A popular analogy was the comparison of an overly dressed lady to a 'rigged-up' ship:

> There is now one other qualitie that a good woman must in no wise borrow from a ship and that is too much ridginge, and it is a great deale of charge and to very little purpose that is bestowed on some ships in superfluities in the paintinge of *Caage workes* like the painting of womens faces . . .[70]

This trope is appropriate when one considers some early modern perceptions of mercantilism and the importation of foreign goods, including cosmetics. In the quotation from Rich's tract, we learn that the 'rigging up' obviously takes great pains, and the time spent on the cosmetic ritual is often railed against in other anti-cosmetic polemics. Prynne expresses a similar frustration: 'much is the time, that many spend between the Combe and the Glasse'.[71] Robert Burton's *The Anatomy of Melancholy* (1632) expresses frustration at the time, energy, and cost of the cosmetic process: 'why doe they use and covet such novelty of inventions; such new fangled tyres, and spend such inestimable summes on them?' He continues his interrogation of women's dressing practices when he asks: 'but why is all this labour, all this cost; preparation, riding, running, farre fetched, and dear bought stuffe?'[72] Burton asks, 'why doe they make such glorious shewes with their scarfes, feathers, fannes, maskes, furres, laces, tiffanies, ruffes, falls, calls, cuffes, damasks, velvets, tinsels, cloth of gold?'[73] The protestations located in the anti-cosmetic discourse suggest that it was dangerous, rebellious and shameful to wear cosmetics in public; however, there is a counter-discourse, which actively promotes cosmetic production and consumption in the middle and upper classes of early modern England. Quite simply, women wore them at court, in the city and even in the country. This acceptance is evident in recipe manuals, household guides, and pro-cosmetic arguments, all of which point to the economic viability of cosmetics and the beginnings of a cosmetics industry, and promote the creative agency of women, at least within the domestic sphere.

'She Shal Appeare to be the Age of Fifteene Yeares'

In his vituperative outburst against cosmetics, Philip Stubbes attempts to create a grotesque picture of the materials used in early modern cosmetic practice by women: 'they are made of many mixtures, and sundry compounded simples, bothe farre fetched and deer bought, cunningly couched together, and tempered with many goodly condiments and holsome confections, I warrant you'.[74] The household texts that contain cosmetic recipes appear 'to be directed primarily to a middle-class audience, to women who perhaps had servants but who were not removed from the mechanics of household affairs'.[75] The recipes reveal that the use of cosmetics, including perfumes and waters, was widespread and that the composition of them took an enormous amount of time, patience and scientific knowledge on the part of the woman. The recipes also indicate that many of the ingredients were foreign, yet easily obtained. One of the most popular practical guidebooks in the period is *The Secrets of Alexis of Piemont*, translated into English by William Warde; this text contains varied recipes, such as 'Against the Stinking of the Breath', 'To Know whether a Woman shall ever Conceive', and 'To make the Skin Stretch, and Return again into his place'. This bizarre collection of recipes is also accompanied by suggestions for personal adornment. William Eamon's study of Italian books of secrets argues that this text 'is considered by modern bibliographers to be a complete fabrication, the creation of the Venetian humanist, Girolamo Ruscelli'.[76] Eamon explains that the text contains approximately 350 recipes, 108 of them being medicinal in nature. However, he does not count the cosmetics recipes in all four parts of the text. While he does acknowledge that there is a chapter devoted to 'recipes for making perfumes, scented soaps, skin lotions, body powders, and suffumigations to scent rooms and clothing', as well as a separate section on 'cosmetics, hair tonics and dyes, depilatories, skin treatments, and cleansers for the teeth', Eamon does not show that approximately 200 recipes are cosmetic in nature, and include recipes for perfumes, face paints and waters, soaps, hair dyes and tonics, and hair removal and hair growth remedies.[77]

In the first part of the manual there are twenty-one recipes for sweet waters and perfumes, thirteen for powders, thirteen for soaps, four for hair pomades and ointments, and thirty-three for face paints, waters and ointments; the second part contains twenty-seven for face paints and waters, one recipe to make the hands white, one for chap stick, nine for toothpastes, six for hair growth, and three hair-dying recipes. Importantly, among the alchemical recipes and experiments in this text, there are instructions that are a vital first step in the preparation of cosmetics; for example, 'To sublime quick-siluer, that is to say, to make common sublime, that Goldsmithes, Alchimistes, & Gentlewomen do vse, and that men vse in many things concerning physick';[78] 'To fine and renew Borax' (a common ingredient in recipes for perfume);[79] 'To sublime Mercurie'; and 'For to make a white colour of Lead' (which would be used by artists and women alike).[80]

It is conceivable that Alexis Piemont was a pseudonym for Ruscelli who, as Eamon notes, published his own book of secrets, *Secret nuovi*, which contained over 1,000 recipes and in which he claims to be the true author of *The Secrets of Alexis of Piemont*. Significantly, Ruscelli founded a research academy to test his recipes before advertising them in his books. The society, called *Accademia Segreta*, hired 'two apothecaries, two goldsmiths, two perfumers, and four herbalists and gardeners'.[81] Eamon does not question how these tests were carried out, but it gives one pause to imagine a research academy of men testing cosmetics such as face paints, lip colours and rouge. An implicitly theatrical quality might well be ascribed to a society that prided itself on making ' "the most diligent inquiries and, as it were, a true anatomy of things and operations of Nature itself . . . In addition to our own pleasure and utility' ".[82] Many of the ingredients in Ruscelli's text evoke the distant places from where large quantities of them were imported; this is especially true of the recipes for perfumes (Figure 2.2, a 'brazen morter'); for example, to make 'Powder of Civet verie Exquisite', one must 'take Sugar candie what quantities you list, and put it in a brazen morter: and after you have well beaten it, adde to it as much Civet as you will, and make thereof powder, the which you must keep always close'.[83] Civet is a name for a 'cat-like animal' (OED) that comes from central Africa; the ingredient is a secretion extracted from the anal glands of these animals.[84] John Taylor mocks the use of such ingredients in his tract against pride: 'Their Civet [that affords such dainty sents]/Is but a poore Cats sweating excrements'.[85]

Figure 2.2   Brazen mortar, sixteenth century, V & A Images/Victoria and Albert Museum.

One English recipe manual offers suggestions for making perfumes, including one entitled 'K. Henry the eighth his perfume': 'take six spoonfuls of compound water, as much of Rose-water, a quarter of an ounce fine Sugar, two graines of Muske, two grains of Amber-greece, two of Civet: boile it softly together: all the house will smell of Cloves'.[86] Hugh Platt's perfume recipes contain some of the most commonly used imports, such as musk, civet, and ambergris. In his tract, Platt teaches women how to make a pomander (perfume-ball) using 'two ounces of Labdanum; of Beniamin and Storax, one ounce: musk, six graines: of civet, six graines: Amber-grease, six graines'.[87] The full title of Platt's text, *Delights for Ladies to Adorne their Persons, Tables, Closets, and Distillatories; with Beauties, Banquets, Perfumes, and Waters*, suggests the knowledge and capability of early modern women. Lynette Hunter argues that Renaissance gentlewomen 'had a developed technical knowledge in order to perform their social and economic functions';[88] and much of this knowledge consisted of aspects of 'physical and organic chemistry'.[89] This type of knowledge, often overlooked, is evident in the fact that many recipes contain precise weights and measurements, and curiously those that do not suggest much of the knowledge to be a part of women's inherited folklore, recipes passed from one generation to the next by word of mouth.

Eamon's study of the Italian books and his comments on Platt are useful in allowing us to gain an understanding of the complexities of these writers; however, Eamon's emphasis lies in what these texts contributed to the field of science, without making much of the recipes for cosmetics found in these texts; nor does he recognise the cosmetic to be a significant field of knowledge, a branch of science itself. In *Delights for Ladies*, Platt dedicates his book 'To all true louers of Art and Knowledge', which places him next to Bacon in acknowledging cosmetics to be a branch of learning in some respects.[90] According to Eamon, Platt was devoted to testing and improving upon the secrets he discovered in books of secrets written before his; additionally, he 'queried artisans, housewives, and other virtuosi'.[91] The cosmetics recipes were doubtless tested and queried too.

No matter how many writers were suspicious of the use of cosmetics in Renaissance England, it cannot be denied that those who used makeup actually played a role in the economy at large. The knowledge of cosmetic technology, the consumption of cosmetic commodities, and the purchase of books with recipes in them all play a role within the early modern economic structure. William London's *A Catalogue of the most vendible Books in England*, published in 1658, indicates that *The Secrets of Alexis, The Ladies Cabinet* Opened, *A Closet for Ladies and Gentlewomen*,

Culpeper's *The Practice of Physick*, *The English Physician, His Last Legacy*, John French's *The Art of Distillation*, the anonymous, *The Queen's Closet Opened*, Thomas Lupton's *A Thousand Notable things, of sundrie sorts*, and Christopher Wirtzung's *The General Practice of Physick* are all among 'the best and most Books printed in England'.[92] And all of these texts contain recipes for cosmetics. Richard Surflet's translation of Steven's and Liebault's *Maison Rustique* talks about the 'fashion for distilling water for Fukes' [Fucus]: 'a good Farmer's wife must not be too busie with Fukes and such things as are for the decking and painting of the bodie . . . I would not have the manner of distilling of waters for Fukes . . . but that shee may make some profit and benefit by the sale thereof'.[93] While it may be inappropriate for a countrywoman to *use* makeup, there is no reason why she should not benefit from the sale of homemade cosmetics. Male authors of household guides and recipe manuals capitalised on the feminine desire for physical beauty, which seems to have been a contributor to the economic structure of the society. Hence many of the recipes resonate with the idiom of commercial advertising. For example, Hugh Platt's recipe for clearing the skin recommends washing

> Barrows grease oftentimes in May-deaw, that hath been clarified in the Sunne, till it bee exceeding white: then take Marshmallow rootes, scraping off the outsides: then make thin slices of them, and mix them: set them to macerate in a seething Balneo, and scumme it well till it bee thorowly clarified . . . Let the mallow roots be two or three daies dried in the shade before you use them. This I had of a great Professor of Art, and for a rare and dainty Secret, as the best fucus this day in use.[94]

The last sentence of this passage has a distinctly marketing objective. Another example that points to the economic impulse behind these manuals comes from *The Secrets of Alexis* for a 'water', in this instance water to make the face as white as that of the ideal Renaissance beauty:

> take the white of eight new laid Egges, and beat them until they be converted into a cleare water, then straine them . . . the Ladie or Gentlewoman that wil use oftentimes to wash her face with this water, yea were shee of threescore yeares, she shal appeare to be the age of fifteene yeares.[95]

This recipe promises the appearance of youth if a woman 'washes' with this concoction frequently. The last line of the recipe claims that the 'water' is the secret of keeping the skin looking youthful, and suggests that this appeal to women was effective. What can also be learned from this recipe is that some poisonous concoctions were not meant to be worn as makeup, but rather applied for short periods of time in order to renew the complexion underneath, the equivalent of a Beverly Hills chemical peel. An example of this type of recipe calls for eggs, vinegar, turpentine, sugar-candy, camphor, rock alum, quicksilver, juice of lemons, 'tartarum', and white onion:

> And at night when you goe to bedde lay the said composition upon your face, neck, and breast, letting it to drie of it selfe . . . you may not take it too soone from your face, for then you shall marre the skinne: but you must let it lie on the space of eight daies. And although you would thinke the said composition burned or flaied off the skinne of your face, you may not for all that take it off, but let it worke his operation, and at the end of eight daies take it off in the manner following: Take Wheat Branne . . . crummes of Bread, and a good quantitie of raw Honey, and boile all these things together, until it be soft, then poure it into some pot, and let it coole until such time as you may endure the smoake thereof, holding your face over the pot . . . and when you perceive your selfe to sweate, take a little of the said water, and put crummes of bread into it, and rubbe with them al about where the composition is laid . . . but beware that in eight daies after you goe not abroad in the open aire, or too nigh the fire, lest the new fine, tender and delicate skin should be burned, or take any hurt. This is a good secret.[96]

A woman who wished for a smooth and white complexion would have to keep this 'composition' on for over a week; women painted quite thickly with this type of paste, pointing to the likelihood that many such pastes were temporary applications. The physical pain would undoubtedly be a result of the use of quicksilver, lemon juice and turpentine. What is worse is the insistence that the woman endure such pain for the purposes of vanity. Giovanni Battista Della Porta, recalling the neo-Platonic standard of beauty, promises in his recipe manual that 'there was nothing better than quick-silver for womens paints, and to cleanse their faces, and make them shine'.[97]

Ben Jonson unquestionably read *The Secrets of Alexis*; in *Catiline* Galla reports that Sempronia 'does sleek/With crumbs of bread and milk, and lies o nights/In as neat gloves' (II, 65–9). Jonson's use of Ruscelli's text is even more extensive in *The Devil is an Ass*, as we will see. The recipe from Ruscelli also provides some evidence as to why women wore masks when they went out. It is agreed that they did so to protect their skin from the sun and wind, but from the recipe we learn that women also wore masks to protect their painted complexions and their *newly* smoothed faces, which they had spent the last 'eight daies' perfecting. Unsettling in the recipes for cosmetics of the period, though, is the irreconcilable dilemma for women who used them. While the manuals provide women with a sense of energetic creativity and suggest the extent of their scientific knowledge, the confinement to their home for sixteen days and the insistence upon the maintenance of a cultural ideal at the great expense of time, money and physical pain point to the double bind inherent in beauty therapy in this period.

Cosmetic compounds contain many ingredients, the most common of which are: alum, musk, civet, ambergris, mercury, white lead, quicksilver, egg whites and shells, crumbs of bread, almonds, milk, rosewater, storax, lemon juice, lilies, roses and other flowers, turpentine, cinnamon, cloves, aloe, labdanum, poppyseed oil, ground jawbones of a hog or lamb, benzoin (resin from an aromatic tree), rosemary, honey, mustard seed, vinegar, rhubarb, myrrh, frankincense, camphor, sulphur, pearl, gold and silver. Such extensive lists of cosmetic ingredients are echoed in Ben Jonson's play *The Devil is an Ass*, in which Wittipol, as the Spanish Lady, satirically catalogues the ingredients for a new Spanish fucus:

> Water of gourds, of radish, the white beans,
> Flowers of glass, of thistles, rosemarine,
> Raw honey, mustard-seed, and bread dough-baked,
> The crumbs o' bread, goat's milk, and whites of eggs,
> Camphor, and lily roots, the fat of swans,
> Marrrow of veal, white pigeons, and pine-kernels
> (IV, iv, 19–24)

Jonson mocks the idea that many cosmetic recipes are not only bound up with culinary recipes, but also require culinary ingredients. One such example is a recipe for a water that will make a 'white and pale person wel-coloured':

> Take white Pigeons, and fat them with Pine Apple kernels the space of fifteene days and then kill them: and having cast away the head, the feet, and the guts with al the garbage, distil them in a Limbeck with halfe a loaf of Sucharine Alome, three hundred leaves of fine silver foile, five hundred of gold foile, and the crum of foure white loaves, steeped or wet in Almond milke, a pound of the marrow of a Calfe.[98]

The use of edible ingredients, such as meat, bread and milk, is one reason why many moralists claim that a vain woman who concocts her own lotions and potions is a neglectful housewife: 'no sooner are they varnished, but they forsake their home'.[99]

The recipe manuals of the sixteenth and seventeenth centuries not only help us to determine what cosmetics were being engineered, they also allow us to reconstruct the fledgling industry of beauty in early modern England. Hugh Platt provides mineral recipes for fucus, which require a woman to 'incorporate with a wooden pestle, and in a wooden mortar with great labour, four ounces of sublimate, and one ounce of crude Mercurie, at the least 6 or 8 houres'.[100] Mercury, an Arabic export, sublimate and other mineral ingredients, contemporary sources tell us, could easily be bought from apothecaries, who 'were concentrated around the central commercial thoroughfares of the city ... about Fenchurch'.[101] Apothecaries could also be located in the 'upper part' of the Royal Exchange.[102] John Manningham reveals that in 1601 'there is a certain kinde of compound called *Laudanum*, which may be had at Dr Turner's apothecary, in Bishopgate Streate; the vertue of it is very Soveraigne to mitigate anie payne'.[103] In addition to its medical properties, 'laudanum' is also frequently cited in cosmetics recipes of the period, specifically in perfumes.

Coryat confirms that apothecaries in Italy did indeed openly sell cosmetics, while simultaneously warning readers about the ill effects of certain cosmetic ingredients: 'if thou hast an exact judgement, thou maist easily discerne the effects of those famous apothecary drugs heretofore used amongst the Noble Ladies of Rome, even ... cerussa'.[104] There is a recipe in *The Ladies Cabinet opened* (1639) for removing wrinkles: 'take a little of the wood of white Vine, that is such as bears white Grapesm or a little Brionym and beat it well in a Morter with a good big Fig or two, such as you may buy at the Grocers'. [105] From this we learn that 'Grocers' commonly supplied women with cosmetic ingredients as well as food. We also discover from Tudor and Stuart accounts of the revels at court that that eggs were purchased to 'trym the vizarde'.[106] Equally, anti-cosmetic texts may tell us about the industry of cosmetics: for example, informing us that in the latter part of the seventeenth century the Exchange was still the place to purchase cosmetic ingredients, Hannah Woolley complains that 'the Exchanges (for now we have three great *Arsenals* of choice Vanities) are furnished with a daily supply and variety of Beauty-spots (with many other things, whose names are only known to the Inventer and Buyer)'.[107] Simion Grahame rails against 'the *charleton* or as the Dutch-man cals him, the *Quick-silver*', and warns that 'he will beginne and tell of many invented miracles, how his Oyles and Waters hath done such rare wonders in restoring health to the diseased persons'.[108] This quotation no doubt refers to the doctors of physic who doubled as cosmeticians. Conflating physicians, artists and beauticians, Grahame writes:

> When the Painter is asked why he left his trade of painting to become a Doctor of Physick. O said he, when I was a Painter, all the world saw my errors, but now being a Doctor of Physick, I make the earth to burie my wrongs, they seeke forth the life and ritches of mankinde.[109]

Physic involves not only medicinal practice, but it also refers to the art of beautification. There are several references in Renaissance drama to physicians who supply and apply cosmetics, from Eudemus in

Sejanus, to the disguised physician in *The Duke of Milan*. John Earle's character of 'A Meer Dull Physician' tells us that 'his learning consists much in reckoning up the hand names of diseases, and the superscriptions of gally-pots in his apothecary's shop'; he continues: 'his two main opposites are a mountebank and a good woman, and he never shows his learning so much as in an invective against them and their boxes'.[110] The interdisciplinary nature of cosmetics and medicine stems from the early modern obsession with disfigurement: 'medical practitioners and the laity alike placed great stress on disfigured conditions, especially those affecting the face'.[111] As a result, the demand for cosmetic reparation increased, which explains why many physicians also practiced cosmetology. The two arts come together as one in cosmetic surgery, often considered a modern invention. There is evidence to suggest that 'early facial surgery . . . was frequently employed to repair the ravages of syphilis'.[112] John Earle's character of 'A Surgeon' confirms this assumption, calling him a 'plaisterer' and pointing out that 'he is a reasonably cleanly man, considering the scabs he has to deal with, and your finest ladies are now and then beholden to him for their best dressing'.[113] An Italian tract by Tagliacozzi entitled *De Chiurgia Curtrum* (1597), arguably the earliest tract on cosmetic surgery, contains engravings of various surgical techniques. Although much of the surgery was for purposes of reparation, it is very likely that beauty was at the heart of most reconstructive desires.

Towards the middle and end of the seventeenth century, we start to see an insurgence of pro-cosmetic literature, suggesting that cosmetic practice was becoming more widely acceptable and also pointing to the fact that men had also started to paint their faces. Such literature argues that facial reconstruction is acceptable when correcting defects and deformities; thus, face repairing instead of face painting allows for the application of cosmetic methods and materials. According to a debate in John Downame's *Discourse of Auxillary Beauty* (1656), the same is true: 'to remove or remedy any pain, sicknesse, maime, misfortune or inconvenience, which happens to us in our health, strength, motion, or estates; and why not in our *looks or beauties* and complexions'.[114] The arguments of texts that seem to tolerate cosmetics are, by their nature, conditional. Downame's text, as we have just seen, has one speaker arguing for cosmetic *reparations*, only if it is to correct a deformity or disfigurement. John Bulwer's conditions are similar: 'yet we cannot say, that it is absolutely unlawfull to use any Fucus, especially when any foule blemish doth disgrace the forme of modest Virgins or Matrons, and we know Physitions are sometimes constrained to satisfie the desires of honourable Ladies'.[115] Bulwer (who was a physician) recognises this demand in society for cosmetic application, but insists that women should not paint themselves:

> and indeed somewhat is to be allowed to women who are studious of their beauty . . . to repaire the injuries of aire . . . or what is wanting to the emendation of the Elegancy of the Epidermis, or skim the Visage is no tresspasse against Piety, but may be honestly endeavoured by a Physitian, since this induceth no Fucus.[116]

Bulwer's argument is that only a physician can 'honestly' apply the cosmetics because of the medicinal need for cosmetic reparation. Frances Dolan writes about Bulwer's acceptance of cosmetics under certain conditions in her study of the role of cosmetics in the art and nature debate in early modern England. She argues that women were seen to be recreating themselves, taking liberties and asserting themselves through the use of cosmetics; this is what is ultimately being opposed in the anti-cosmetic treatises, and it is also being challenged in Bulwer's tolerance of cosmetics. Dolan comes to the conclusion that 'even in the limited defense of corrective cosmetics, it is in taking the pencil into their own hands, in what Bulwer calls their "cosmetique usurpations", that women are shown to err'.[117] In *Artificiall Embellishments*, Thomas Jeamson offers a defence of physical adornment in addition to recipes that will 'teach you creatures of mortality to retrace the steps of youth, and transforme the wrinkled hide of *Hecuba* into the tender skin of a tempting *Helena*'.[118] The author argues that the soul should have an attractive house in which to live, which would make the soul desire to stay longer: 'whose structure and superficial Ornaments might make its Pilgramage pleasent, and invite its stay'.[119] In other words, wearing cosmetics will sustain life, an extraordinary advertising ploy in a society of men and women who use cosmetics that kill! Inspiring competition and objectifying women as the materials they might use to compose the recipes he offers, Jeamson tells his consumers that 'other Ladies in your company shall look like brown-bread sippets in a dish of snowie ceam, or if you will, like blubbered jugs in a cupboard of Venice glasses, or earthen Chamber pots in a Goldsmith's shop'.[120] He appeals to the insecurities of women and what he perceives as an inherent competitiveness amongst them. But why should it take so long for pro-cosmetic literature to appear on the scene? The answer may lie in the anxiety produced by the cosmetic icon of the early modern period.

Painting the Queen

Anti-cosmetic authors continually remind women that they resemble whores when they paint their faces, an argument that stems from the ancient church fathers' opposition to cosmetics. Of course, the Queen is famous for her use of cosmetics and it is understood that she had her face painted to distance herself from her subjects by carving herself out as a featureless icon hidden behind a cosmetic mask, the representation we see in the portraits of her. One author contends that Elizabeth I 'had fully mastered the art of manipulating her image as the 'virgin Queen', so that she appeared perpetually youthful, even perpetually desirable'.[121] Germaine Greer argues that 'with her painted face, her wigs, her false fronts, she looked from a distance as if she were that nonpareil of beauty and virtue that is the centrepiece of her iconography'.[122] The portraits whose artists extolled her as a type of goddess and a timeless virgin also reminded her subjects of her inaccessibility. The cosmetics, incontrovertibly, played an exceedingly important role in this process; in fact, it was the use of paints, cosmetic and aesthetic, that helped to create her fiction and that acted as a barrier between the untouchable queen and her subjects. Roy Strong tells us that 'the demand for the royal likeness had by the nineties far outstripped the number that could be produced by competent artists and in line with government thinking, with the consequent manufacture of debased images of the Queen by hack artists'.[123] This sounds hauntingly like the analogy used by anti-cosmetic authors who compared painting women to 'hack' artists. For as long as she was alive, the Queen had a *certain* amount of control over her visual representations, however; as she aged 'from the mid 1580s onwards her face ceased to be painted from life'; instead, artists relied on earlier face patterns.[124] Strong tells us that it was made law: 'sometime about 1594 a government decision was taken that the official image of the Queen in her final years was to be of legendary beauty, ageless and unfading'.[125] There are some images, though they are few, that depict the Queen's aged face (Figure 2.3). Thus through government legislature, portrait paint would achieve the success that cosmetic paint could not. Elizabeth's control of her image ceased when she died, her death mask revealing that she had aged quite extensively: 'the face is old, the cheeks are sunken and the neck muscles are sagging with age'.[126] However, what is often ignored is the Queen's inherent desire to hide her wrinkles, to maintain her youthful image because even she was subject to the tyrannous threat of receding beauty, therefore receding domination over a culture that deemed beauty and its aesthetic representations extraordinarily powerful ideological influences. John Clapham reports that, 'not long before her death, she had a great apprehension of her own age and declination by seeing her face, then lean and full of wrinkles, truly represented to her in a glass'.[127]

Figure 2.3   Engraving of Queen Elizabeth I, Crispijn de Passé (1592), V & A
Images/Victoria and Albert Museum.

However, Elizabeth's court was perceived to be the epitome of vanity, a notion parodied in Jonson's *Cynthia's Revels* (1600). In his dedication to the court, Jonson moralises:

> Oh vanity,
> How are thy painted beauties doted on
> By light and empty idiots! How pursued
> With open and extended appetite
> (I, v, 21–4)

But it would be useful to consider the word 'vanity' and what it actually means. The Oxford English Dictionary states that 'vanity' comes from the Latin *vanitas*, which means futility. The term 'vanity' is 'the quality of being personally vain; self-conceit and desire for admiration'. But its root meaning is 'worthlessness', or 'futility'. The term was used in the Renaissance with profoundly moral connotations. It is vanity to want to be admired; it is vanity to be consumed with one's personal appearance. This meaning still exists today, but the impact is less severe; now we use vanity tables and vanity mirrors in everyday conversation and in everyday personal cosmetic practice without a thought given to our souls and the moral implications of using such instruments. Vanity in the Renaissance, though seen as sinful and immoral, was inevitable with the emergence of the self or individual. Bacon establishes the term 'cosmetic' in this same context as a necessary evil in these times. Furthermore, the ageing Queen's vanity is tied to her political authority. 'Vanity', we find, is just another term used to demonise the female sex because it was traditionally used in a misogynistic context. Queen Elizabeth I was perhaps the most gazed-upon Tudor monarch. How, then, could her personal appearance and 'self-conceit' not be at the forefront of her political self-fashioning?

The Queen's 'vanity', a subject for Jonson, was not necessarily a safe topic among anti-cosmetic writers. Their admonitions were more often than not directed at the middling classes and gentlewomen. Queen Elizabeth's example was 'the exception that would prove the rule'; in fact, 'the rules were clearly different for commoners'.[128] Although Bishop Aylmer preached about excessive ornamentation in 1593, he soon learned not to preach to the Queen; Janet Arnold cites John Harrington, who reports: 'one Sunday (April last) my lorde of London, preachede to the Queens Majestie, and seemede to touche on the vanitie of deckinge the bodie to finely – Her Majestie tolde the Ladies, that if the Bishope helde more discourse on suche matters she wolde fitte him for Heaven'.[129]

Conclusion

Elizabeth I did not begin to paint her face until she was established on the throne. There is evidence that as a young princess, Elizabeth preferred simplicity. In the 1540s, while she was at Hatfield, Elizabeth's teacher Roger Ascham claimed that Elizabeth chose to dress herself plainly; David Starkey's biography of Elizabeth cites Ascham's observations of the youthful princess: ' "with respect to personal decoration," he writes, "she greatly prefers simple elegance to show and splendour, so despising the outward adorning of plaiting the hair and wearing gold" '. Starkey also cites John Aylmer's testimony to Elizabeth's plain style: ' "I know it to be true," he writes, that Elizabeth, for the whole of Edward's reign, never wore the rich jewels and clothes left her by her father. Instead she offered a "more virtuous example" [. . .] her "maidenly apparel" making the ladies of the court "ashamed to be dressed and painted like peacocks" '.[130] These passages reveal that face painting was fashionable at court before Elizabeth became queen, and that later in her reign she would beautify herself. A letter written on 3 March 1602 by a Jesuit, Father Rivers, points to the older Queen's open cosmetic practice:

> The ache of the Queen's arm is fallen into her side, but she is still, thanks to God, frolicky and merry, only her face showeth some decay, which to conceal when she cometh in public, she putteth many fine cloths into her mouth to bear out her cheeks, and sometimes as she is walking she will put off her petticoat, as seeming too hot, when others shake with cold.[131]

Clearly, it was her youthful appearance that she tried so desperately to maintain, curiously, in this instance, using fabric to puff out her cheeks. Thomas Platter, in his travels in England, gives the impression that the old Queen did indeed have some success in appearing younger than she was: 'she was most gorgeously apparelled, and although she was already seventy four, was very youthfull still in appearance, seeming no more than twenty years of age'.[132] However, contrary to this, the French Ambassador André Hurault, Sieur de Maisse, claims that the Queen's face 'appears to be very aged. It is long and thin, and her teeth are very yellow and unequal . . . many of them are missing so that one cannot understand her easily when she speaks quickly'.[133] It is difficult to determine just how effective the face paint was in preserving the Queen's youth and beauty. Nevertheless, the anti-cosmetics discourses and the satirical passages about cosmetics in the drama both indicate that the long-term effects of the lead paints were unsightly and unhealthy for women, and this must have been the case (as de Maisse suggests) for the Queen. The perception of Elizabeth I as a self-created icon is a valid one; it was not just the woman in her trying to recover the beauty of her youth, it was also the monarch in her who wanted to construct a visually impressive mask of power, varnishing authority in a theatrical proclamation of royal prerogative. The Queen's painted face haunts many dramatic representations of face painting and painted ladies. In *The Revenger's Tragedy* (1607), Vindice wields the painted skull of his dead lover, pointedly dubbed 'Gloriana'. In *The Second Maiden's Tragedy* (1611), the painted dead Lady's iconic status is obvious as her appearance, dressed and painted with the iconographic trappings of a saint, takes on the ghostly significance of the dead, painted Queen of England.

Notes

1. Tuke, *A Treatise Against Paint[i]ng*, Sig. B3*v*.
2. Greenblatt, 'Invisible bullets', p. 63.
3. Callaghan, 'Introduction', in *A Feminist Companion to Shakespeare*, p. xiii.
4. Bacon, *The Advancement of Learning*, p. 208.
5. Ibid. p. 214.
6. Greenblatt, *Renaissance Self-Fashioning*, p. 2.
7. Aughterson (ed.), *Renaissance Woman*, p. 7.
8. This book aims to focus on female cosmetic practice, but there have been questions as to when men started donning face paint. In *Much Ado About Nothing* Benedick is teased for shaving and painting, symbolically to represent love's effeminising effect.
9. Prynne, *The Unlovelinesse of Love-lockes*, Sig. A3*v*.
10. Averell, *A Myrrour for vertuous Maydes*, p. 31.
11. S. P. Cerasano and Marion Wynne-Davies (eds), *Gloriana's Face*, p. 11.
12. Grabes, *The Mutable Glass*, p. 76.
13. Kelley, 'Surpassing glass', p. 2.
14. Ibid. p. 3.
15. Gascoigne, *The Steel Glas*, pp. 147–8.
16. Woodforde, *The History of Vanity*, p. 52.
17. Grabes, *The Mutable Glass*, pp. 72–3.
18. Prynne, *The Unlovelienesse of Love-lockes*, Sig. B3*r*.
19. Brathwait, *The English Gentlewoman*, p. 17.
20. Stubbes, *The Anatomie of Abuses*, p. 64.
21. Ibid. p. 64.
22. Miso-Spilus, *A Wonder of wonders*, p. 1.
23. As early as the reign of Henry VIII, religious anxiety was central to sermons preached against cosmetics: 'some there be that cannot be content with their hair as God made it, but do paint it and set in it another hue . . . and so must their brows and their eyelids be painted proportionably' (Roger Edgeworth in P. Welsby (ed.), *Sermons and Society*, p. 49).
24. Ibid. p. 51.

25. 'Some practise everyday the Painter's trade,/And strive to mend the worke that God hath made. / But these deceivers are deceived farre, / With falsly striving to amend, they marre: / With devlish dawbing, plast'ring they do spread,/Deforming so themselves with white and red' (Taylor, *Superbiae Flagellum*, Sig. C7r).
26. Vives, *A very Fruteful and pleasant booke*, Sig. F5r.
27. Tuke, *A Treatise Against Paint[i]ng*, p. 2.
28. Stubbes, *The Anatomie of Abuses*, p. 66.
29. Welsby (ed.), *Sermons and Society*, p. 50.
30. Vives, *A very Fruteful and pleasant booke*, Sig. F4r.
31. Jardine, *Worldly Goods*, p. 373.
32. Welsby (ed.), *Sermons and Society*, p. 43.
33. Ibid. p. 99.
34. Averell, *A Dyall for Dainty Darlings*, pp. 4–5.
35. Ibid. p. 5.
36. This notion is central to the guilt resulting from Lady Macbeth's neglected and corrupt soul: 'All the perfumes of Arabia will not sweeten this little hand' (V, i, 43).
37. Rich, *The Excellency of good women*, p. 20.
38. Hall, *Things of Darkness*, p. 90.
39. Bulwer, *Anthropometamorphosis*, pp. 259–60.
40. Ibid. p. 260.
41. Stowe, *Annales*, p. 868.
42. Ibid. p. 868.
43. Rich, *My Ladies Looking Glasse*, p. 10.
44. Vives, *A very Fruteful and pleasant booke*, Sig. F3r.
45. Corson, *Stage Makeup*, p. 314.
46. Lomazzo, *A Tracte Containing the Artes of curious Paintinge*, p. 129.
47. Ibid. p. 130.
48. In Philip Massinger's *The Duke of Milan*, the stage directions in the face-painting scene indicate that the disguised physician paints the hands of the body as well as the face (V, ii).
49. Lomazzo, *A Tracte Containing the Artes of curious Paintinge*, p. 130.
50. Ibid. p. 130.
51. Welsby (ed.), *Sermons and Society*, p. 62.
52. Montaigne, *Essays*, p. 285.
53. Lomazzo, *A Tracte Containing the Artes of curious Paintinge*, p. 130.
54. Ibid. p. 133.
55. Manningham, *Diary*, p. 23.
56. Montaigne, *Essays*, p. 285.
57. Brathwait, *Ar't Asleep Husband?*, p. 29.
58. Donne, *Selected Prose*, p. 165.
59. Manningham, *Diary*, p. 134.
60. Donne, 'That Women Ought to Paint', in Donne, *Selected Prose*, p. 38.
61. Price, ' "Offending without witness"', p. 72.
62. Ibid. p. 67.
63. Swetnam, *The Arraignment*, p. 4.
64. Rich, *My Ladies Looking Glasse*, p. 21.
65. Pollard, 'Beauty's poisonous properties', p. 192.

66. Gainsford, *The Rich Cabinet*, p. 162.
67. Rich, *The Excellency of good women*, p. 7.
68. Gainsford, *The Rich Cabinet*, p. 9.
69. Rich, *The Excellency of good women*, p. 13.
70. Ibid. p. 14.
71. Prynne, *The Unlovelinesse of Love-Lockes*, p. 30.
72. Burton, *The Anatomy of Melancholy*, pp. 96–7.
73. Ibid. p. 96.
74. Stubbes, *The Anatomie of Abuses*, p. 65.
75. Hull, *Chaste, Silent, & Obedient*, p. 138.
76. Eamon, *Science and the Secrets of Nature*, p. 140.
77. Ibid. p. 145.
78. Ruscelli, *The Secrets of Alexis of Piemont*, pp. 101–2.
79. Ibid. p. 267.
80. Ibid. p. 235.
81. Eamon, *Science and the Secrets of Nature*, p. 149.
82. Cited in Eamon, ibid. pp. 149–50.
83. Ruscelli, *The Secrets of Alexis of Piemont*, p. 48.
84. Shakespeare parodies the customs of courtiers in *As You Like it* when Corin says hand kissing is not practised in the country because they touch their sheep; Touchstone argues that this is no excuse because courtiers' hands are perfumed with civet, and 'Civet is of a baser birth than tar, the very uncleanly flux of a cat' (III, ii, 59–60).
85. Taylor, *Superbiae Flagellum*, Sig. C4r.
86. Anonymous, *A Closet for Ladies*, Sig. F12v–G1r.
87. Platt, *Delights for Ladies*, Sig. G9v.
88. Hunter and Hutton (eds), *Women, Science and Medicine*, p. 3.
89. Ibid. p. 2.
90. Platt, *Delights for Ladies*, Sig. A3v.
91. Eamon, *Science and the Secrets of Nature*, pp. 312–13.
92. London, *A Catalogue*, Sig. C1r.
93. Stevens and Liebault, *Maison Rustique*, p. 465.
94. Platt, *Delights for Ladies*, Sig. G11v–12r.
95. Ruscelli, *The Secrets of Alexis of Piemont*, p. 65.
96. Ibid. pp. 67–8.
97. Della Porta, *Natural Magick*, p. 242.
98. Ruscelli, *The Secrets of Alexis of Piemont*, p. 64.
99. Welsby (ed.), *Sermons and Society*, p. 100.
100. Platt, *Delights for Ladies*, Sig. G12v.
101. Beier and Finlay (eds), *London 1500–1700*, p. 85.
102. Stowe, *Annales*, p. 869.
103. Manningham, *Diary*, p. 46.
104. Coryat, *Crudities*, p. 42.
105. Anonymous, *The Ladies Cabinet opened*, p. 5.
106. Cunningham (ed.), *Extracts from the Accounts of the Revels*, p. 84.
107. Woolley, *The Gentlewoman's Companion*, p. 59.
108. Grahame, *The Anatomie of Hvmors*, pp. 23–4.
109. Ibid. p. 25.
110. Earle, *Microcosmographie*, pp. 14–17.

111. Beier and Finlay (eds), *London 1500–1700*, p. 89.
112. Davis, *Reshaping the Female Body*, p. 15.
113. Earle, *Microcosmographie*, p. 90.
114. Downame, *A Discourse of Auxillary Beauty*, p. 52.
115. Bulwer, *Anthropometamorphosis*, p. 270.
116. Ibid. p. 270.
117. Dolan, 'Taking the pencil out of God's hand, p. 233.
118. Jeamson, *Artificiall Embellishments*, Sig. A4v.
119. Ibid. *Sig. A5r.*
120. Ibid. *Sig. A5r.*
121. Cerasano and Wynne-Davies, *Gloriana's Face*, p. 11.
122. Greer, 'Uneasy lies the head', A5.
123. Strong, *Gloriana*, p. 14.
124. Cerasano and Wynne-Davies, *Gloriana's Face*, p. 12.
125. Strong, *Gloriana*, p. 20.
126. Ibid. p. 20.
127. Read and Read (eds), *Elizabeth of England*, p. 96.
128. Garber, *Vested Interests*, p. 28.
129. Arnold (ed.), *Queen Elizabeth's Wardrobe*, pp. 4–5.
130. Starkey, *Elizabeth*, p. 83.
131. Rivers, 'The College of St Ignatius', in Foley (ed.), *Records of the English Province*, vol.1, p. 24.
132. Williams (ed.), *Thomas Platters Travels*, p. 192.
133. Arnold (ed.), *Queen Elizabeth's Wardrobe*, p. 8.

Chapter 3

Cosmetic Restoration in Jacobean Tragedy

In his attack on cosmetics Thomas Tuke insists that 'the Ceruse or white Lead, wherewith women use to paint themselves was, without doubt, brought in use by the divell, the capitall enemie of nature'.[1] This clichéd analogy, used time and again by moralists, that painted ladies are like painted devils, draws upon the popular links made between poisonous ingredients, moral corruption and the female body. Curiously, this moral analogy is subverted in two Jacobean revenge tragedies by Thomas Middleton, *The Revenger's Tragedy* (1607) and *The Second Maiden's Tragedy* (1611, now known as *The Lady's Tragedy*). Politically poignant are these two tragedies that dramatise the exhumation of a mourned dead lady (one of them called 'Gloriana', the other simply known as 'the Lady'), whose remains are subsequently painted and used to entrap and kill a sexually perverse tyrant, thereby transforming the notion that cosmetic paint is a corrosive material; instead it becomes a cleansing agent for the political body and a meta-theatrical device used to revalue cosmetic materiality within a theatrical context.

It has long been established that some poisons were key ingredients in mineral cosmetic recipes in the sixteenth and seventeenth centuries and, therefore, a pervasive and realistic threat. Tanya Pollard's analysis of the role of poison in 'cosmetic theater' argues that early modern critics of cosmetics insisted that 'women who adorn themselves with the material poisons of paint not only suffer from spiritual contamination, but translate this taint back into material poisons which they transmit to other victims'.[2] But there is a counter-discourse to this one, which is wholly permissive of poisonous cosmetics, such as the recipe in *A Closet for Ladies and Gentlewomen* (1627), 'To make a Blanch for any Ladies face', which requires two 'drams' of 'white Tartar' and 'white Mercury a peniworth'.[3] Pollard's analysis of *The Second Maiden's Tragedy* does not take into account the fact that the use of cosmetics as political medicine expunges its associations with moral impurity. While it is true that the texts that caution women to 'avoid those things which rather adulterate then adorne the skin, such as *Spanish White* and *Mercury*' – the effects of these ingredients being 'a wrinkle-furrowed visage, stinking breath, loose and rotten teeth'[4] – reflect contemporary fears of contamination and deformity, these fears were not the only register of cultural attitudes towards cosmetics being dramatised on the Renaissance stage. Middleton's revengers use the toxically painted remains of women not just to demonstrate, as Pollard would have, 'the vulnerability of men',[5] but also to demonstrate the power and quixotic seductiveness of cosmetic materiality. The painted women in both plays used to restore political stability are aptly named Gloriana in *The Revenger's Tragedy* and the 'Lady' (who is an iconic virgin) in *The Second Maiden's Tragedy* to recall the painted image of Queen Elizabeth I. Her portraits painted with white lead and mercury helped to establish the late queen as the ideal of womanhood and the defender of the Protestant faith. Elizabethan poets, such as Spenser, endorsed Elizabeth I's beauty as symbolic of the 'true faith'; for example, in Book 1 of the *Faerie Queene* Una is represented as the Protestant ideal of beauty and 'she is strongly associated with whiteness, denoting virginity and purity, which is another link with Elizabeth the Virgin Queen'.[6] By the time the two revenge plays discussed in this chapter were written, Elizabeth was long dead, but her body is exhumed and the two dead ladies in these plays memorialise her political legacy by recalling the late queen's own theatrical display of cosmetic paint to exert her unique brand of political potency. Although the macabre use of female bodies in these plays is irreconcilable to modern sensibilities, contemporary audiences may have needed to reconcile the subversive use of cosmetics as medicine, a harsh cure for the diseased political body. This use of women's bodies as ingredients in a kind of concoction of revenge, art and poison resonates with the contemporary receipt books that combine medicinal with cosmetic ingredients to exorcise the body of ailments in order to beautify it.

Elizabethan and Jacobean tragedies often reflect the anxieties voiced by anti-cosmetic moralists; yet, simultaneously, in the very display of cosmeticised bodies, they celebrate the cosmetic in one form or another. Pollard's view is that 'for audiences, the painted women dramatized and demonised in plays are often closely affiliated with theatricality itself'.[7] While I agree that cosmetics for dramatists and audiences are inextricably linked to theatre, I have to question Pollard's notion that painted women are strictly demonised on stage and that, through the connections between drama and makeup, theatre itself is demonised. Undeniably, what some plays express about cosmetics and death is grounded in material reality. The use of poisonous ingredients in various compounds intrigued most dramatists and attracted them because of the seductive allure cosmetic spectacles had over contemporary audiences. I would argue that dramatists, while reflecting the anxieties about cosmetic materiality, nonetheless celebrate the visual dynamic that is crucial to their theatrical imaginings. Therefore, cosmetics have a double function in the plays discussed in this chapter, since they simultaneously recall the moral discourse that spoke out against painted ladies, referring to them as traps and poisoned harlots; however, the cosmetics in the main plots of both plays take on a reformative value and act as a weapon against sexual sin, or rather a purgative for it. In the case of *The Revenger's Tragedy*, Vindice is contaminated by his excessive involvement in the cosmetic, but he is nevertheless able to use cosmetics to cleanse the political body of corruption. In *The Second Maiden's Tragedy*, while it seems cosmetics are being condemned by some of the moralistic language used to describe them, Govianus deploys face paint paradoxically as a political and spiritual restorative. In this chapter I want to show how the author of both plays appropriates cosmetic materiality by deploying it imaginatively in the language and in the action, through violence and terror. I also want to suggest that both plays reflect the contradictions inherent in the cultural attitudes toward cosmetics, contradictions that permeate the cosmetics discourse beyond the stage.

'The artificial shine': Painted Language

As *The Revenger's Tragedy* opens, Vindice has been preparing for nine years to avenge the old Duke for the poisoned death of Vindice's betrothed, Gloriana, who had resisted the old Duke's sexual advances when she was alive and suffered death as a consequence. In this section, I propose that *The Revenger's Tragedy* and *The Second Maiden's Tragedy* not only dramatise the deceptive, yet restorative, nature of makeup, but point to a cultural cosmetics discourse through the language. In a study of the language of *The Revenger's Tragedy*, Daniel Jonathan Jacobson suggests that 'the image of the mask itself is used to represent the false face of hypocrisy as well as the deceptive painted faces of corrupt ladies'; he goes on to argue that 'the false beauty of cosmetics is another common image of false appearances often associated with the image of "shining" or "gilding" '.[8] Jacobson acknowledges that the play's action revolves fundamentally around the contemporary relationship between hypocrisy and cosmetics. But the idea of the cosmetic is brought to the forefront earlier on through delicate references that construct the cosmetic image patterns in the play. Images of the forehead, clothing and concealment, hot iron and heat imagery, and references to poison form a network of images designed to evoke the cultural fascination with cosmetics and their centrality to the play's outcome.

A spotted face or forehead in the Renaissance carried suggestions of sin and duplicity; allegedly, prostitutes were branded on the forehead as a warning to prospective clients; if this was the case, the physical branding might have taken on a symbolic social meaning, and as a result the forehead could be read as a metaphorical map of the internal moral condition. An example from *Hamlet* shows Shakespeare using this image to insinuate the extent of Gertrude's guilt. Hamlet scolds his mother for not being a faithful widow and says that she has committed

> Such an act
> That blurs the grace and blush of modesty,
> Calls virtue hypocrite, takes off the rose
> From the fair forehead of an innocent love
> And sets a blister there . . .
>   (III, iv, 39–43)

Here Hamlet alludes to the prostitute's 'blister', placing the guilt of all fallen women upon his mother. Barnabe Rich writes that 'a woman that is once tainted in her honour, must be driven to a hard course of recovery she must rubbe of the skinne to wipe out the spot'.[9] Makeup helped to mask syphilis scars, and presumably the branded marks delineating the social status of prostitutes were also covered by face paint; this is why cosmetics came to signify on one level sexual duplicity and entrapment.

In Act I, scene ii of *The Revenger's Tragedy*, Junior, stepson to the Duke, is on trial for the rape of Lord Antonio's wife; the Duke tells the Duchess that he cannot pardon her son's crime because his actions have spotted the body politic, the very reputation of the Duke himself:

> His violent act has e'en drawn blood of honour
> And stain'd our honours,
> Thrown ink upon the forehead of our state . . .
>   (I, ii, 2–4)

The motif of the body politic is present here among common images used by moralists in their fulminations against face painting. The reference to the 'stain'd honours' of the state is implicitly a cosmetic image pattern.[10] A sermon preached by Roger Edgeworth during the reign of Henry VIII declares that, if a woman paints her face, then the 'figure of her face is stained or polluted'; Edgeworth goes on to say that, if a woman continues to paint herself, she will not be able to see God because 'the devil's craft hath dyed and stained' her face. Significantly, in the trial scene of *The Revenger's Tragedy* the Duke chooses not to pardon Junior for his actions, because they have 'stain'd' the royal family, sullying their reputation. The Duke's actions are purely superficial, resting upon a concern for appearances. The language in these early scenes constructs an attitude to cosmetics as conventionally negative and moralistic. Yet this is not the only function it serves. It also highlights the utility of cosmetic metaphors in the drama of the period to comment on the visual attractiveness of paint. The audience would have understood these references; a painted face carried more significance in early modern England than it does today. Conversely, Lussurioso, the Duke's own son and heir, argues that showing 'mercy' to Junior will prove to be as morally unsound as women who paint their faces:

> for offences
> Gilt o'er with mercy show like fairest women,
> Good only for their beauties, which wash'd off,
> No sin is uglier.
>
> (I, ii, 28–31)

Lussurioso's suggestion in the preceding passage proves to be ironic insofar as his own sexual deviance brings about his demise. After the trial, by means of a parallel revenge plot, the Duchess vows to take revenge on the Duke for the lack of mercy he has shown to her son: 'I'll kill him in his forehead, hate there feed; / That wound is deepest though it never bleed' (I, ii, 108–9). Recalling the Duke's earlier reference to his 'stain'd' forehead and his anxiety about his reputation, the Duchess decides to have an affair with her stepson Spurio in order to worsen the 'stain' on the 'forehead' of the state. Here, the fusion of death, sexual and cosmetic imagery brings into focus the corruption that is at the core of the court, the corruption that the characters are attempting to conceal at every turn, but that Vindice masterfully exposes in the central action of the play when he actually does kill the Duke 'in his forehead' with the cosmetically poisoned skull of Gloriana. He thereby reverses the moralistic meaning of cosmetics constructed in the early acts of the play.

Vindice's hatred for courtly vices such as lasciviousness, excessive wealth and display is apparent in many of his speeches and asides as he rails against cosmetics, which for him is tied to dressing:

> Any kin now next to the rim o' th' sister
> Is man's meat in these days, and in the morning,
> When they are up and dress'd, and their mask on,
> Who can perceive this, save that eternal eye
> That sees through flesh and all?
>
> (I, iii, 65–9)

None but the 'eternal eye' can see through the 'vanity' of the court, whose impenetrability is figured in ostentatious clothing and cosmetics, epitomised in this speech by a 'mask'. Anatomical dissection in early modern Europe and England revealed that the human body consists of layers, making it fundamentally impossible to read the soul. Only God 'sees through flesh and all', the 'all' referring to the system of layers piled on to the surface of the body. In his opening soliloquy, Vindice proudly wields the skull: 'Advance thee, o thou terror to fat folks, / To have their costly three-pil'd flesh worn off / As bare as this' (I, i, 45–7). The 'three pil'd flesh' alludes to the expensive three-piled velvet available to the elite of society in Elizabethan England. Jacobson observes that the phrase 'three pil'd flesh' suggests 'a sense of ostentatious, voluptuous luxury'.[11] But Vindice also makes correlations between skin and clothing, both of which conceal. The relationship between flesh and textile is a link between human corporeality and external materiality generally, illustrating how, in a society motivated by the attraction to 'worldly goods', cosmetics and brave clothing are perceived as acquisitions used to deflect the gaze from the inner self. The relationship between the human body and its prosthetic attachments is ultimately theatrical. Humans perform selves that are necessarily disparate from the inner selves. Clothing and, more so, cosmetics are crucial elements in creating this disparity. When we paint our faces we are one step further away from our inner self, as the newly created image has the potential to make one unrecognisable to others and, as polemicists complain, to God.

Thus, cosmetics are as crucial to the theatrical design of *The Revenger's Tragedy*, as is clothing. Covering, concealing, rubbing over, masking either with fabric or paint are cosmetic actions in which the body takes precedence over the mind. Disguise not only forces one to take on a new physical appearance, it facilitates the assumption of a different identity. Peter Stallybrass and Ann Rosalind Jones have argued that items of clothing in theatrical accounts suggest 'the ability of the clothes to absorb the very identity of the actors',[12] thus widening the gap between their inner and outer selves. By this account, in *The Revenger's Tragedy* and *The Second Maiden's Tragedy* the virtuous identities of Gloriana and the Lady are transported via the paint to the Duke and Tyrant respectively through the cosmetic kiss. It is in fact their purity that proves toxic to their ravishers, and cosmetics in both plays enable this transference of identity.

Another set of image patterns in *The Revenger's Tragedy* is associated with hot irons and heat. In *The Anatomy of Melancholy* Robert Burton insists that women ought to 'have their cheeks stigmatized with a hot iron, I say, some of our *Jesabells*, instead of painting'.[13] This type of imagery in *The Revenger's Tragedy* is tied to blushing and redness: 'The blush of many women, whose chaste presence / Would e'en call shame up to their cheeks' (I, iv, 6–7); here Hippolito aligns shame with the natural flush that should appear in a woman's face when she is humbled by the presence of virtue. Castiza, Vindice's virtuous sister whom he tests, slaps and reddens his face when he (in disguise) tempts her on behalf of Lussurioso: 'Bear to him / That figure of my hate upon thy cheek, / Whilst 'tis yet hot, and I'll reward thee for 't' (II, i, 34–6). Eventually, both Gratiana and Vindice test Castiza's modesty, but with chaste defiance she responds: 'I have endur'd you with an ear of fire, / Your tongues have struck hot irons on my face' (I, ii, 230–1). The heat imagery gains momentum in Lussurioso's blatant admission that he wants Castiza to be won over through cosmetic means: 'Hast thou beguil'd her of salvation / And rubb'd hell o'er with honey?' (II, ii, 20–1). While Jacobson acknowledges that 'the image of blushing, and the sense that it brings both a red 'glow' and accompanying heat to the face, is conveyed through images of fire and searing heat', he doesn't acknowledge the association of heat with the poison of cosmetics.[14] As I have mentioned previously, Richard Haydocke's translation of Lomazzo's *A Tracte Containing the Artes of curious Paintinge Carvinge & buildinge* exposes vividly the corrosive effects of poisonous compounds while it emphasises the burning sensations of mineral cosmetics; for example, the 'oyle of Tartare', 'if it be used about the face, it will worke the like effects in the same, by scorching and hardning it so'.[15] Also, rock alum 'is a very pearcing and drying mineral' and when it is put on the skin, 'burneth and shrivleth, and parcheth it'. Equally, 'camphire' is 'so hott and drie' that it burns anything it touches; 'this being applied to the face scaldeth it exceedingly, causing a great alteration by parching of the skinne, and procuring a flushing in the face'.[16] The heat and blushing imagery in Middleton's play anticipates the cosmetic masques of revenge, and both together point to the damaging physical effects of poisonous cosmetics.

In her study of poison, Tanya Pollard points out the link between cosmetics and theatre. Pollard argues that 'the painted women dramatized in plays are often closely affiliated with theatricality itself'.[17] She goes on to say that 'as standard stage props, face paints were a deeply entrenched part of theatrical production: early theater company records include accounts such as: "Pay'd to the painter for paynting the players facys, iiijd" '.[18] Shirley Nelson Garner speculates that 'women's heavily made-up face gave a highly artificial, mask-like appearance. If so, women may have found a pleasure in making up akin to that of playing a part, acting'.[19] This inevitable connection between cosmetics and theatre is referred to in *The Revenger's Tragedy* and *The Second Maiden's Tragedy*. Many critics have argued that the theatricality of *The Revenger's Tragedy* is apparent not only in the masques of the play, but also in the characters themselves: Vindice is like an artist, 'and likes to see himself as dramaturge, even as writer of his own play'.[20]

Scott McMillin argues that the entire play 'is virtually an exercise in theatrical self-abandonment', and that the skull of Gloriana is an actor; 'through costuming and illusion it gains its double identity in the scene where the hero gains his personified name'.[21] The ties between the stage and cosmetics are touched upon by Tanya Pollard; however, she does not explore thoroughly the historical basis for the parallels between cosmetics and the stage. Anti-cosmetic moralists often argue that face painting and attending plays are two similar activities in that they are both symptomatic of excessive pride and an almost pathological addiction to display. Roger Edgeworth preaches: 'let the dressings of your heads, and the apparellings of your bodies be chaste, clean, and after a sober fashion, not like players disguised after any wanton manner'.[22] For Edgeworth, what players and women have in common is their love of disguise and the sexually charged performances of the body. Barnabe Rich makes similar connections between cosmetics and theatre by suggesting that one activity inevitably leads a woman to the other:

> on her way, perhaps to the *Tyre makers shoppe* where she shaketh out her Crownes to bestow upon some new fashioned *Attire*, that if we may say, there be deformitie in Art, upon such artificiall deformed *Periwigs*, that they were fitter to furnish a *Theater*, or for her that in a *stage* play, should represent some Hagge of Hell.[23]

Writers like Rich make such links because clothing, makeup and wigs serve a socially performative function in addition to their material lives as stage properties. John Earle's character of 'A Player' compares an actor to 'painting gentlewomen, seldom in his own face, seldomer in his cloaths; and he pleases the better he counterfeits'.[24] In *The Revenger's Tragedy*, the language of performance is thus located within a socially familiar cosmetics discourse, which identifies the body as a site of theatrical exchange.

In Act III Vindice dresses and paints his primary stage property, the skull of Gloriana: 'I have took care / For a delicious lip, a sparkling eye' (III, v, 31–2), and he proudly boasts about his backstage makeup artistry:

> Art thou beguil'd now? Tut, a lady can
> At such all hid beguile a wiser man.
> Have I not fitted the old surfeiter
> With a quaint piece of beauty?
> (III, v, 50–3)

The use of the *danse macabre* to enact the revenge allows Vindice to be entirely in control of the sequence of events to follow. The use of the revenge masque also uncovers the anti-theatrical anxiety about the effect plays may have had on their vulnerable auditors. Tanya Pollard argues that the parallel between face paint and the theatre lies in the 'invasive' threat of both.[25] It is the use of painted props and perfume that create a sense of cosmetic mystification, signifying the political mystification endured by the citizens of the Duke's realm. However, these materials on the stage, while registering certain Puritan anxieties, nevertheless reflected more the cultural attraction to cosmetic sexuality and power.

Annette Drew-Bear's contention that 'pride, lust, deceit, and devilish temptation are repeatedly expressed visually by the painted face' is not entirely applicable to *The Second Maiden's Tragedy*, because the Wife's cheeks, which are *naturally* red, seem to incite sexual desire in Votarius more dramatically.[26] The numerous visual images in the play remind us of the Renaissance notion that love is engendered in the eyes. As Richard Brathwait explains, 'it is the eye that conveys love to the heart';[27] 'a pleasing Object to the eye, improved by the apprehension of fancy, [is] conveyed to the heart by the Optick part'.[28] This theory of love would certainly have been complicated by face painting on one level, but on another, painted beauty was an expectation at court and cosmetics were crucial to courtship and the fashioning of femininity. There are many instances in the period's drama in which painted portraits compel one to love or lust, for example Bassanio's worship of Portia's portrait in *The Merchant of Venice*, or the painted/toxic portrait of Arden's wife in *Arden of Faversham*.[29]

The use of art in *The Second Maiden's Tragedy* has been explored by various critics, including David Bergeron who argues that 'the failure of art within this play is very much the subject of the play'.[30] But art proves to be instrumental in the destruction of tyranny. Bergeron sees the Tyrant as attempting to be the 'artist' who directs his own play: 'the Tyrant is a would-be dramatist unable to control his increasingly intractable material'.[31] The Tyrant is not a dramatist; rather, in this play, the Tyrant becomes a victim in the masque of revenge. Like Vindice in *The Revenger's Tragedy*, Govianus is the disguised 'artist' in this play, who uses 'art' in the form of painting to reclaim his political power. Such manipulation for political means points to the Tudor mandate of creating a visible presence of monarchy, and Elizabeth Tudor's painted body was a material property of the realm, reproduced and proliferated through paint.

Cosmetic Revenge Tragedy

The knowledge of the poisonous ingredients in many cosmetic recipes in early modern England should suggest that such ingredients were not in use. But the price of beauty is high, as many in our own society who have had disfiguring cosmetic procedures know. Cosmetics on the Renaissance stage provide us with a heightened sense of the dangers of certain ingredients in cosmetic recipes, namely lead and mercury. In both tragedies the male protagonist uses the painted corpse, or fragments of the painted corpse of a dead lady, in order to murder a tyrant in the name of revenge. Such sensational scenes on the stage spoke directly to the misogynistic terror of contamination by the female body but, paradoxically, in *The Revenger's Tragedy* and *The Second Maiden's Tragedy* the painted ladies are not morally impure, though their bodies prove toxic. In *The Revenger's Tragedy*, Vindice's growing cruelty reaches its peak in his deception of the Duke in the *danse macabre*, the masque at the end of Act III. Vindice combines his acting skills and his knowledge of makeup artistry with his lust for revenge and murder. Because of his theatrical involvement with the cosmetic (disguising, acting, dressing up), Vindice becomes metaphorically contaminated (a contamination, which runs parallel to the physical contamination of the Duke by the cosmetic) and evolves from a revenge hero into a villain who is punished and executed at the end of Act V.

Vindice even seems to recognise early on that he is becoming infected by his obsession with the skull: 'And now methinks I could e'en chide myself / For doting on her beauty' (III, v, 68–9). In Act III, scene v, Vindice enters '*with the skull of his love dressed up in tires*' (stage direction). He addresses the skull, imagining it as a decayed but active agent: 'A poor thin shell, / 'Tis the best grace you have to do it well. / I'll save your hand that labour, I'll unmask you' (III, v, 46–8). He then reveals the skull and describes its role as a man trap, recalling the contemporary association of a painted lady with a snare:

> Have I not fitted the old surfeiter
> With a quaint piece of beauty? Age and bare bone
> Are e'er allied in action: here's an eye
> Able to tempt a great man–to serve God;
> A Pretty hanging lip, that has forgot now to dissemble
> Methinks this mouth should make a swearer tremble,
> A drunkard clasp his teeth, and not undo 'em
> To suffer wet damnation to run through 'em.
>
> (III, v, 51–8)

As I mentioned earlier, traps were a popular metaphor for painted ladies. One playwright who indulges in this stock association with cosmetics is Barnabe Barnes. In *The Devil's Charter*, Lucretia is trapped by the adulterated cosmetics with which she paints herself. She calls for her 'mixtures' and 'dressing boxes'; two Pages enter bringing in mirrors and

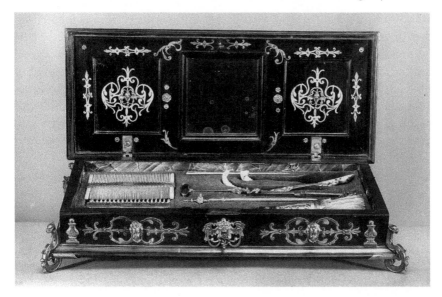

Figure 3.1   Cosmetics box (c. 1610), V & A Images/Victoria and Albert Museum.

'a box with combes and instruments' (Figure 3.1). After Lucretia 'corrects these arches with this mullet' (IV, iii, 62), she smells her death: 'I feele a foule stincke in my nostrells, / Some stincke is vehement and hurts my braine. / My cheeks both burn and sting; give me my glass' (65–7). Here we have an instance of a woman being trapped by her own cosmetic materials. Reflecting these dramatic spectacles in his fulminations against pride, William Prynne insists that face painting is the devil's invention and *'peculiar unto none but audacious Whores and Strumpets, or persons desperately wicked: as a baite, a Snare . . . as an art that offers violence unto God'.*[32] Lucretia, by Prynne's standards, got what she deserved because of her treacherous behaviour, but more importantly, the cosmetics and cosmetic instruments as stage properties engage our attention as objects used to rid the political body of a contaminative element.

The skull of Gloriana is Vindice's painted springe and serves that function effectively, while ironically purging the court of a corrupt Duke. Before Vindice uses the skull, like Hamlet, he questions the value of artificial beauty:

> Does every proud and self-affecting dame
> Camphor her face for this? And grieve her maker
> In sinful baths of milk when many an infant starves
> For her superfluous outside, all for this?
>
> (III, v, 83–6)

Here Vindice rehearses some of the anti-cosmetic arguments located in the contemporary debates. The idea that a painted woman neglects her household duties and her children is a common one, and is most likely due to the extensive lists of culinary ingredients in cosmetic recipes. John Bulwer says, 'the more curious she is about her face, the more carelesse about her house'.[33] Regardless of Vindice's rejection of cosmetics on moral grounds, he will use them to cleanse or 'rubbe' out the 'stain' on the forehead of the body politic, evoking the type of cosmetics popularly used to rid the complexion of spots.

Vindice boldly states that the skull will function as his weapon, a weapon that has a motive all its own:

> This very skull
> Whose mistress the Duke poison'd with this drug,
> The mortal curse of the earth, shall be reveng'd
> In the like strain and kiss his lips to death.
> (III, v, 101–4)

Vindice poisons the skull's mouth and covers it with a mask as he prepares to 'crowd' 'nine years vengeance . . . into a minute!' (III, v, 121). The Duke enters expecting to have a young lady brought in for his pleasure. When the Duke asks Vindice/Piato for his woman, Vindice tells his brother to 'raise the perfumes' (139). The Duke kisses the skull and immediately senses the poison: 'O't'as poisoned me' (148). The terror increases as Vindice stamps on his victim, who progressively describes the effect of the poison on his mouth: 'My teeth are eaten out' (156); 'O my tongue!' (160). Vindice cruelly responds: 'Your tongue? 'Twill teach you to kiss closer, / Not like a slobbering Dutchman' (161–2). The use of perfume, another cosmetic, serves to establish further the deception that is taking place in the scene; it disorientates the Duke and allows Vindice to spin yet another cosmetic web with which to entrap and murder his victim. In fact, the perfume does little to mask the true 'beastliness' of the entire scene.[34] The cosmetics have served a dual purpose, though, in that they are being used to show their inherent dangerousness, while cleansing the court of corruption and guile through a marvellous dramatic spectacle of murder and revenge.

Similarly, in *The Second Maiden's Tragedy*, Act V, scene ii when Govianus appears disguised as an artist, the Tyrant instructs him to

> Let but thy art hide death upon her face,
> That now looks fearfully upon us, and but strive
> To give our eye delight in that paler part . . .
> (81–3)

The use of the word 'art' in these lines underscores the fact that all forms of painting were referred to as 'art'; sometimes 'art' referred to aesthetics and other times it meant craft. In this context the Tyrant seems to conflate the two meanings by employing an artist not an artisan to paint his dead lady with the craft of cosmetic beauty. While Govianus prepares his weapon, by painting the face and body of the Lady, the Tyrant is distracted by his own lewd thoughts, as he wishes he could hire a workman to rekindle the heat *within* the Lady's breast. After the Lady is painted, the Tyrant is struck by the semblance of life on her face: 'O, she lives again!. . . . Does she feel warm to thee' (V, ii, 114–17). The Tyrant in this play falls victim to the trap that Govianus has laid for him; the Tyrant declares: 'Our arms and lips / Shall labour life into her. Wake sweet mistress! / 'Tis I that call thee at the door of life' [*He kisses the body*] (117–19). Ironically, the kiss that was meant to be the 'door of life' becomes the door to death for the Tyrant: 'I talk so long to death, I'm sick myself. / Methinks an evil scent still follows me' (120–1); Govianus responds: 'Maybe 'tis nothing but the colour, sir, / That I laid on' (122–3). At this point Govianus, like Vindice removes his disguise.

The editor of the 1978 edition, Anne Lancashire, argues that the play is a hagiographical Protestant allegory, positing the Lady as a virgin martyr, and the Tyrant as the embodiment of Catholicism, who paints, ornaments and worships the Lady's body as if she were an icon. However, the representation of cosmetics in this play suggests that it does more than promote Protestantism. It, in fact, dramatises the varied social views of cosmetics: the moralistic abhorrence of mineral cosmetics and the attraction to artistically painted beauty and it recalls the painted image of the late Queen of England. While this dramatic sequence teaches its audience that the use of cosmetics is dangerous and duplicitous, it nevertheless allows the cosmetics to function as an intriguing remedy for the restoration of morality and political stability. Celia Daileader reveals that 'the body of a dead martyr or a member taken from the body held both the power to heal the faithful and the power to harm an infidel'.[35] This appears to be what is happening in Middleton's play. The face paint is the tool, however, which destroys the corrupt Tyrant, and leaves the 'faithful' individual, Govianus, unharmed. Although Govianus has committed a murder, unlike Vindice he does not become contaminated by the poison and artifice. Govianus's revenge 'is a furtive murder, questionable until we remind ourselves that he is, after all, the legitimate prince'.[36] Significantly, his act is legitimised by the presence of the Lady's spirit, even though Govianus's hand did tremble at the act.

Michael Foucault describes a kiss as 'very highly valued as a physical pleasure and a communication of souls despite the danger it carried'.[37]

This dangerous 'communication of souls' is embodied in the poisoned kiss sequence, which was a popular trope. As Pollard observes, 'the idea of cosmetics as invasive poisons, reinforced by the material properties of their chemical ingredients, offered a forceful way to articulate links between face-paints and lips, tangible forms of transgression and contamination'.[38] Even more significantly, the fact that the medium that transfers poison to the lips of a victim is a woman reflects the contemporary belief in the physical unreliability of women and their bodies, thus pointing to the reasons for such heated debates about cosmetics. Additionally, the poisoned kiss motif stems from the popular notion that the tongue was a dangerous member of the body, specifically the female body. The relationship of the tongue, as a mendacious device, to cosmetics seems to be registered in poisoned kiss sequences of *The Revenger's Tragedy* and *The Second Maiden's Tragedy*. Abernathy, the Bishop of Cathnes, in *The Poisonous Tongue* (1622) says that the organ 'is both in it selfe poisoned, and a poysoner of others'.[39] This metaphorical rhetoric reminds us that for early modern audiences the poisoned kiss is a crucial element in the acts of revenge that take place in both tragedies, and a cultural register for the misogynistic notion that female sexuality is dangerously powerful.

'Dainty preserved flesh': Fetishising the Painted Body

'The touchstone of artistic genius was the ability to suggest a pulsating life beneath the marble or painted surface'.[40] The erotic appeal of such artistic representations dates back to the story of Pygmalion, and features in *The Revenger's Tragedy* and *The Second Maiden's Tragedy*. Both plays dramatise a culture that is addicted to artifice, while commenting upon the contemporary fixation on the body. In Jacobean tragedy an effeminate body is subject to the male gaze, to interrogation and judgement. Moreover, in the two tragedies being discussed here, it is the dead body of a female character that acts as a 'site of conflict' and erotic fetishism.[41] John Harrington's Epigram 58, 'Of the Same to the Ladies', about a naked statue which was to stand in Lord Chamberlain's gallery, conflates the images of a painted statue and a painted lady:

> Her face unmask't, I saw, her corps unclad,
> No vaile, no cover, her and me betweene:
> No ornament was hid, that beauty had,
> I blusht that saw, she blusht not that was seene
>> With that I vow'd never to care a rush,
>> For such a beauty, as doth never blush

The erotic tone of the poem is suggestive of the provocative fusion of art and feminine beauty. However, the final judgement of the poem's closing lines reveals that the male reaction (blushing) to such painted bodies is a response to the figure's passive seductiveness. The paint paradoxically lays the female body open for exposure. This is not an instance in which paint conceals, but where it lays bare. This is art, not cosmetics. But the materials to construct both are the same, so under what circumstances can cosmetic beauty be viewed as artistic?

In *The Winter's Tale*, Shakespeare answers this question with the painted statue of Hermione. She is painted in the likeness of her 'former' self. However, she is *not* dead, and although nature triumphs in this scene, Leontes attributes the vitality upon her face to art: 'The fixture of her eye has motion in't, / As we are mocked with art' (V, iii, 67–8). Curiously, in this episode of *The Winter's Tale*, there is a poignant message about artistic production. The paint on Hermione's face does not conceal her age: 'Hermione was not so much wrinkled, nothing / So aged as this seems' (V, iii, 27–8); hence, the paint actually enhances and makes visible the maturation in Hermione's face, which Leontes finds aesthetically pleasing. In *The Revenger's Tragedy* Gloriana's skull is one example of a fetishised object, even though it is no longer the beautiful, living body of his love:

> Thou sallow picture of my poison'd love,
> My study's ornament, thou shell of death,
> Once the bright face of my betrothed lady,
> When life and beauty naturally fill'd out
> These ragged imperfections,
> When two heaven-pointed diamonds were set
> In those unsightly rings–then 'twas a face
> So far beyond the artificial shine
> Of any woman's bought complexion . . .
>   (I, i, 14–22)

When she was alive, Gloriana was clearly not a painted lady, at least not according to Vindice's account; this is evident from line 17, when he tells us that her face was 'naturally fill'd out', and in the last two lines of the passage, where he simultaneously condemns the use of cosmetics and refers satirically to the 'artificial shine' and 'any woman's bought complexion'.[42] However, Vindice uses memory figuratively to paint the face of the skull, recalling her 'bright face' and her eyes, which were 'heaven-pointed diamonds'. In this way he fetishises the skull, projecting his own nostalgic perception of the 'bony' lady's face on to it. Later in the same scene, Vindice's brother, Hippolito, tells us that Vindice has been 'sighing o'er Death's vizard' for quite some time (I, i, 49). The characterisation of the two revengers in *The Revenger's Tragedy* and *The Second Maiden's Tragedy* differs in that Vindice is presumably the one who exhumed Gloriana's tomb and emptied it of her remains, which he paints and uses as a material weapon against tyrannical lust. In *The Second Maiden's Tragedy* it is the Tyrant (not Govianus) who performs the horrid deed of emptying the Lady's tomb, and it is the Tyrant who privately and publically fondles the Lady's body after it has been painted.

The chorus in *The Second Maiden's Tragedy* is heard early on in Act V, which devalues cosmetics and the addiction to artifice, while commenting upon the contemporary fixation with the exterior body:

> O what is beauty, that's so much adored?
> A flatt'ring glass that cozens her beholders.
> One night of death makes it look pale and horrid;
> The dainty preserved flesh, how soon it moulders.
> To love it living bewitcheth many,
> But after life is seldom heard of any.
> (V, ii, 14–19)

Critics have long acknowledged that Renaissance culture saw intimate connections between death and sexuality, and these connections are vividly represented in this play. Carnal imagery in the period's drama reveals a morbid curiosity about the spectacle of the body; coupled with this, 'a religiously motivated iconophobia seems to have heightened . . . awareness of the dangerous power of all images, especially those with a high degree of versimilitude and three-dimensionality'.[43] Specifically, in *The Second Maiden's Tragedy*, the visual embodiment on the stage of the fetishistic objectification of painted beauty is exemplified when the Tyrant exhumes the Lady's body from her tomb, dresses her up in iconic clothing and attempts to have her painted to maintain the appearance of life, ultimately turning her into a sexualised artefact, a painted statue:

> I'll clasp the body for the spirit that dwelt in't,
> And love the house still for the mistress' sake.
> Thou art mine now, spite of destruction
> And Govianus, and I will possess thee.
> (IV, iii, 110–14)

His desires are projected on to the 'house' or body of the Lady. But, deluded by his notions of ownership and power, the Tyrant imagines the Lady to be a piece of art, contained within a manageable spatial frame-work, void of spiritual substance. The Tyrant's corporeal obsession with the Lady increases immediately after her death, when she occupies the liminal space between recent death and imminent decay. This is the point at which the Lady is viewed purely as a painted statue: in this space, 'the feminine body appears as a perfect immaculate aesthetic form because it is a dead body, solidified into an object of art'.[44]

The Lady's body is an object used as a medium for the enactment of the Tyrant's sexual fantasies and, curiously, Govianus's domestic fantasies; for after the Tyrant dies from the poisoned kiss, the Lady's body is still on stage when Govianus insists: 'Here place her in this throne; crown her our queen, / The first and last that ever we make ours' (V, ii, 200–1). The Tyrant's desire for the dead Lady and Govianus's 'marriage' to the corpse and spirit are interesting when one considers the penchant for the dead or dying mistress in early modern England. The 1633 portrait of Venetia, Lady Digby (Figure 3.2) painted by Van Dyck was commissioned by her husband Kenelm Digby two days after her death:

> Digby recounts that Venetia's waiting-women 'brought a little seeming color into her pale cheeks' by 'rubbing her face'; since there was no circulation of blood, this can only mean that rouge was applied . . . Venetia is hardly likely to have gone to bed in her pearls; Van Dyck presumably added these . . . the picture is designed not as a truthful document but as an elegy.[45]

Figure 3.2 *Venetia Stanley, Lady Digby on her Deathbed*, Sir Anthony Van Dyck (1633), by permission of the Trustees of Dulwich Picture Gallery.

Apparently, cosmetics were applied to the dead Lady Digby's face and then she was imitated and embellished through art. There is a curious doubling of artistic representation here, in that Venetia's dead body is painted with cosmetics and immediately afterwards her image is painted on to a canvas. Digby himself experimented with alchemy and cosmetics and it is rumoured that one of his cosmetic concoctions may have unintentionally killed his wife.[46] He may have caused her death 'through a concoction of viper's blood to preserve the beauty of her complexion'.[47] Digby later erected an effigy of his wife, 'designed to stand forever as a replacement for the social body', and as 'a reminder of the living form of the natural body' of the woman whom he continued to worship in death.[48]

Catholic Ritual and Cosmetics

Painted beauty reminded many Puritan moralists of Catholic idolatry: 'Beauty that is painted, resembles an idole, and hee that worshipeth it is an idolater'.[49] Tanya Pollard rightly says that 'not only were women who painted their faces seen by both supporters and detractors as seeking to be idolized, they were also idolaters themselves'.[50] Thomas Tuke declares that 'a painted face is not much unlike an Idoll'.[51] He adds that 'artificiall favour and beautie becomes only artificiall creatures, as statues, images, & the like'.[52] George Gascoigne's satire characterises some priests as false: 'one of these will paint out worldly pride . . . / . . . Shrinke not to say, that some do (Romainelike) / Esteme their pall, and habyte overmuche'.[53] The fascinating link between cosmetics and Catholicism is evident in the adoption of cosmetic pigments in 1467 by Pope Paul II, who 'adopted the scarlet produced by the use of imported kermes or galls as the official colour for cardinals' robes'.[54] Kermes are insects crushed and translated into a red dye, which is 'formed by action of acetic acid on copper . . . used not only in the dying of textiles but in artists' paints, and in cosmetics',[55] later replaced by the South American import, cochineal.[56] In *The Second Maiden's Tragedy*, before the painting scene takes place, the Lady's spirit appears to Govianus, who is praying at her tomb, to tell him about the defilement to which her body is subject:

> I am now at court
> In his own private chamber. There he woos me
> And plies his suit to me with serious pains
> As if the short flame of mortality
> Were lighted up again in my cold breast;
> Folds me in his arms and often sets

> A sinful kiss upon my lip;
> Weeps when he sees the paleness of my cheek,
> And will send privately for a hand of art
> That may dissemble life upon my face
> To please his lustful eye
>
> (IV, iv, 67–77)

She then goes on to tell him: 'I leave 'em to thy thought, dearest of men. / My rest is lost; thou must restore't again' (78–9). Govianus does indeed 'restore' her body to her tomb after he *restores* her complexion with colour. The spirit of the Lady is dressed in white, reflecting her luminescent neo-Platonic beauty; she stands for, at this point, purity and feminine modesty. In essence, she is a saint. The fact that this play was first performed at the Blackfriars Theatre also resonates with symbolism. The candlelit space would create a cosmetic spectacle with the overtones of Catholic worship.[57]

The Tyrant worships images and one can quickly see the predictable charge that this play is a Protestant allegory with the Tyrant the chief idolator and Govianus the champion of the Protestant ethic of modesty and restraint. But what fascinates me is the role cosmetics play in bodying forth this popular iconic imagery on the stage and in theory, and how this particular stage picture seems to resurrect the memory of the late queen of England. According to the manuscript of the play, the Lady was played by Richard Robinson, a boy actor with the King's Men; his body is brought out upon a chair through the central opening of the stage at Blackfriars and the Globe to highlight her raised status in the play. The stage directions for Act V, scene ii require the body to be '*dressed up in black velvet which sets out the paleness of the hands and face, and a fair chain of pearl 'cross her breast, and the crucifix above it . . . he himself makes a low honour to the body and kisses the hands*'. Lancashire's Protestant allegory theory is indeed applicable here as Middleton indulges in satirising Catholic ritual. However, this dramatic presentation of the Marian cult of worship echoes more closely the cult of worship surrounding Queen Elizabeth I. In Spenser's *Faerie Queene* Una is described below:

> A louely Ladie rode him faire beside,
> Vpon a lowly Asse more white than snow,
> Yet she much whiter, but the same did hide
> Vnder a vele, that wimpled was full low,
> And ouer all a blacke stole she did throw,
>
> (I, i, 4)

Joan Fitzpatrick says 'Una is dressed in white and black which were, as Roy Strong has shown, Elizabeth's personal colours worn by champions in the tiltyard and by dancers in court masques'.[58] This stage picture of the dead Lady evokes Queen Elizabeth I to demonstrate the political agency of painted beauty.

Conclusion

The makeup in the ritual sequence of *The Second Maiden's Tragedy* is a signifier of performativity, female sexuality and papal ceremony; it also points to the link often made in Puritan pamphlets between the scarlet Whore in the *Book of Revelations* and painted Catholic idolatry:[59] 'And the woman was arrayed in purple and scarlet colour, and decked with gold and precious stones and pearls, having a golden cup in her hand full of abominations and filthiness of her fornication'.[60] Simon Shepherd comments: 'before our eyes he [the Tyrant] manufactures an image of the false church, the painted and literally scarlet woman – which costs a kingdom'.[61] Annette Drew-Bear argues that a painted face on stage is meant to signal the internal corruption of the individual painted. While in many cases, this might be true, in *The Revenger's Tragedy* and *The Second Maiden's Tragedy* the only painted faces are those of virtuous women. What is particularly appealing about these two tragic heroines is their refusal to suffer sexual violation at the hands of a perverse usurper of bodies. Equally liberating are the cosmetics in both plays, which in their signification of female political power, cleanse the court of the stain upon it, and allow the Lady and Gloriana to escape subjectivity.

Notes

1. Tuke, *A Treatise Against Paint[i]ng*, Sig. B3r.
2. Pollard, *Drugs and Theater*, p. 91.
3. Anonymous, *A Closet for Ladies*, Sig. C1v.
4. Jeamson, *Artificiall Embellishments*, p. 31.
5. Pollard, *Drugs and Theater*, p. 94.
6. Fitzpatrick, 'Spenser's nationalistic images of beauty, p. 14.
7. Polland, *Drugs and Theater*, p. 94.
8. Jacobson, *The Language of The Revenger's Tragedy*, pp. 100, 150.
9. Rich, *The Excellency of good women*, p. 16.
10. In *The Comedy of Errors* Adriana's emotional plea to Antipholus illustrates her anxiety about her position as an honourable wife: 'Wouldst thou not spit at me, and spurn at me, / And hurl the name of husband in my face, / And tear the stained skin off my harlot brow' (II, ii, 134–6).
11. Jacobson, *The Language of The Revenger's Tragedy*, p. 37.

12. Stallybrass and Jones, *Renaissance Clothing*, p. 177.
13. Burton, *The Anatomy of Melancholy*, p. 97.
14. Jacobson, *The Language of The Revenger's Tragedy*, p. 96.
15. Lomazzo, *A Tracte Containing the Artes of curious Paintinge*, p. 131.
16. Ibid. p. 132.
17. Pollard, 'Beauty's poisonous properties', p. 192.
18. Ibid. p. 199.
19. Garner, ' "Let Her Paint an Inch Thick" ', p. 133.
20. Foakes, 'The art of cruelty', p. 28.
21. McMillin, 'Acting and violence', pp. 275, 284.
22. Welsby (ed.), *Sermons and Society*, p. 50.
23. Rich, *The Honestie of this Age*, p. 8.
24. Earle, *Microcosmographie*, p. 68.
25. Pollard, 'Beauty's poisonous properties', p. 187.
26. Drew-Bear, *Painted Faces*, p. 17.
27. Brathwait, *Ar't Asleepe Husband*, p. 8.
28. Ibid. p. 17.
29. The anonymous author of *Arden of Faversham* (1592) interrogates painted idolatry through the main plot, in which Arden's wife and lover plan to murder him. They employ a painter to paint a portrait of the wife, so that when Arden looks upon it, the poisonous vapours will infect his eyes and eventually kill him.
30. Bergeron, 'Art within *The Second Maiden's Tragedy*', p. 180.
31. Ibid. p. 183.
32. Prynne, *The Unlovelinesse of Love Lockes*, p. 2.
33. Bulwer, *Anthropometamorphosis*, p. 266.
34. 'Howsoever thou perfumest thyself, yet cannot thy beastliness be hidden, or overcome with thy smells and savours' (Edgeworth, 'A Sermon Against Excess of Apparel', in Welsby (ed.), *Sermons and Society*, p. 62).
35. Daileader, *Eroticism on the Renaissance Stage*, p. 178.
36. Bushnell, *Tragedies of Tyrants*, p. 156.
37. Foucault, *The History of Sexuality*, p. 41.
38. Pollard, 'Beauty's poisonous properties', p. 192.
39. Mazzio, 'Sins of the tongue', p. 56.
40. Sawday, *The Body Emblazoned*, p. 97.
41. Stallybrass, 'Patriarchal territories', p. 123.
42. Thomas Tuke echoes this phrase when he claims that 'a vertuous woman needs no borrowed, no bought complexion' (*A Treatise Against Paint[i]ng*, p. 21).
43. Tassi, 'Lover, poisoner, counterfeiter', p. 132.
44. Bronfen, *Over Her Dead Body*, p. 5.
45. Egerton, 'Catalogue', p. 251.
46. One recipe manual contains a recipe entitled 'Another more Precious Cosmetick or Beautifying Water, by Sir Kenelm Digby': '*This water smooths, whitens, beautifies and preserves the Complexion of Ladies. They may wash their Faces with it at anytime, but especially Morning and Evening*' (Hartman, *The True Preserver*, p. 338).
47. Egerton, 'Catalogue', p. 252.

48. Llewellyn, *The Art of Death*, p. 101.
49. Gainsford, *The Rich Cabinet*, p. 7.
50. Pollard, *Drugs and Theater*, p. 90.
51. Tuke, *A Treatise Against Paint[i]ng*, p. 2.
52. Ibid. p. 37.
53. Gascoigne, *The Steel Glas*, pp. 165–8.
54. Jardine, *Worldly Goods*, p. 120.
55. Linthicum, *Costume in the Drama of Shakespeare*, p. 5.
56. Stallybrass and Jones, *Renaissance Clothing*, p. 45.
57. For the relationship between indoor performance, candlelight and cosmetic beauty, see Karim-Cooper, 'To glisten in a playhouse', pp. 184–200.
58. Fitzpatrick, 'Spenser's nationalistic images of beauty', p. 14.
59. The Prologue of *The Devil's Charter* warns the audience that Lucretia's tragedy is evil and bloody: 'Behold the strumpet of proud Babylon / Her cup with fornication full' (Prologue).
60. Carroll and Prickett (eds), Revelations 17.4, in *The Bible*, p. 313.
61. Shepherd, *Amazons and Warrior Women*, p. 124.

Chapter 4

John Webster and the Culture of Cosmetics

John Webster's contributions to the 1615 edition of Overbury's *Characters* includes a 'fayre and happy Milke-mayd', whom Webster describes as

> a Countrey Wench, that is so farre from making her selfe beautifull by Art, that one looke of hers is able to put all *face-physicke* out of countenance . . . the lining of her apparel (which is her selfe) is farre better than outsides of *Tissew*: for though shee bee not arrayed in the spoyle of the *Silkeworme*, shee is deckt in *innocence*, a farre better wearing . . . the *Garden* and *Bee-hive* are all her *Physicke & Chyrurgery*, & she lives the longer for't.[1]

Character devising was primarily a rhetorical exercise, a chance for writers to flex their wit and satirical muscles. Webster describes the milkmaid's beauty and charm within an anti-cosmetic context. She does not use art to make herself beautiful, instead she is 'decked with innocence' and her labour provides her with the health and vitality that would draw beauty to her cheeks. Webster seemingly participates in an anti-cosmetic discourse in this example, by raising nature above art, but it is a rhetorical exercise whereby, skillfully, he surpasses the anti-cosmetic polemicists by using wit, literary form and metaphor to address the issue of beauty within a fairly new genre. Similarly, in his dramatic works, Webster seems to denigrate cosmetic embellishment; for example, in *The Devil's Law-Case*, painting is described as 'odious' and women described as 'creatures made up and compounded / Of all monsters, poisoned minerals, / And sorcerous herbs that grows' (IV, ii, 291–3). While, on the surface, Webster appears to agree with anti-cosmetic moralising, cosmetics nevertheless would have held for the dramatist a degree of ambiguity. Early modern playwrights recognised the value of cosmetics and the crucial role they had in theatrical representations. Webster lifts the subject of cosmetics out of its usual context even as his characters repeat moralistic clichés against them. Dramatic representation liberates the subject of cosmetics, and, like Middleton, Webster saw the theatrical and poetic potential in cosmetic metaphors and materials, exploiting this potential with rigourous energy in *The White Devil* and *The Duchess of Malfi*.

In these two plays Webster constructs female characters as heroic within an atmosphere of misogynistic condemnation; these bold women, unlike his Overburian milkmaid, wear cosmetics and fashion not only their physical appearances, but also their own lives. Secondly, he weaves cosmetic images together with complex discourses of a theological or supernatural nature (Catholicism vs. Protestantism, witchcraft), which provides his drama with linguistic richness and significant cultural resonances. Finally, he also takes advantage of cosmetic materials, allowing ingredients from contemporary recipes to permeate his plays linguistically and literally, ultimately, giving their enactments more tragic vitality and theatrical intensity.

Beautified and Heroic: Webster's Painted Ladies

In Webster's intriguing play *The White Devil*, the character of Vittoria Corombona has been deemed 'vicious and virtuous, bold and coy, magnificent and cheap'.[2] Vittoria is a woman who is relatively ambiguous, embodying the binary opposites of the traditional portrayals of women throughout Western literature. Vittoria is the wife and the 'whore' all in one. The language of the play vividly constructs her as deceptive, indiscreet, promiscuous, devilish even, and this construction is embedded in anti-cosmetic and misogynistic discourse. But if, as I am arguing, early modern dramatists sought to legitimise the use of cosmetics, at least within the masculine worlds of drama and poetry, then perhaps it can be argued that painted women on the stage are somehow revalued as well. However, this revaluation is entirely conditional: first upon the fact that they are played by boys (so are not women at all), and secondly, upon the fact that they are confined to the stage and the language of the drama that constructs their identities. Nevertheless, Webster's Vittoria Corombona and his Duchess of Malfi are heroic female characters who are painted, and one (the Duchess), at least, is seen at her dressing table, meditating upon her beauty and its eventual loss. How should we approach this contradictory construction of femininity within Webster's plays? Perhaps we can reconcile it in the same way that we accept Elizabeth I's ability to inspire love and honour even in the wake of her decaying body and crumbling painted complexion. In 1603, Queen Elizabeth – the most visibly and theatrically painted body – had died, rendering the painted face on the Renaissance stage a living artefact and thereby a functioning memorial of recent political history.

Her death inspired plays that would make cosmeticised bodies central to dramatic action (as we saw with *The Second Maiden's Tragedy*), and I believe that this aspect of the queen's legacy has some bearing upon Webster's construction of Vittoria and the Duchess. Cosmetics were troubling because many of them were poisonous even while they made a woman beautiful. The fact that lots of Renaissance men were attracted to painted beauty made them vulnerable to seduction and entrapment, according to early modern polemicists. This is the double edge that cosmetics had to offer early modern society. Yet, dramatists were deeply attracted to this curious contradiction, the paradox of cosmetic beauty, and this is why characters like Vittoria and the Duchess are so complex.

In *The White Devil* Vittoria is having an affair with the Duke Brachiano. Flamineo, her brother who promotes her infidelity, reassures Brachiano that his sister actively deceives and manipulates him, creating a sexual dynamic in which she has the upper hand:

> What is't you doubt? Her coyness? That's but the superficies of lust most women have. Yet why should ladies blush to hear that named, which they do not fear to handle? O they are politic . . .
>
> (I, ii, 17–19)

The impression we get of Vittoria is that she is manipulative ('politic') and deceptive, common allegations thrust at women who paint their faces. Isabella, Brachiano's wife, evokes our sympathy as the scorned wife who contributes to the play's condemnatory construction of Vittoria's character; in the following passage, Isabella targets the source of Vittoria's power, her beauty, indicating that as easily as it was made, her beauty should be destroyed:

> To dig the strumpet's eyes out, let her lie
> Some twenty months a-dying, to cut off
> Her nose and lips, pull out her rotten teeth,
> Preserve her flesh like mummia, for trophies
> Of my just anger; hell to my affliction
> Is mere snow-water.
>
> (II, i, 245–50)

Isabella insinuates that Vittoria's beauty is cosmetic, artificial when she puns on the word 'dying', meaning to dye the complexion, to die and to climax sexually. The accusation is framed by the precarious relationship between women. The relationship is fragile and it is beauty that threatens. In *The White Devil*, Isabella's fury is directed at Vittoria's false beauty and is inspired by her sexual jealousy. Thomas Jeamson would have it that those who rail against cosmetics are jealous and he instructs women to paint anyway: 'Be not banisht company for want of Beauty, when Art affords a innocent supply'.[3]

During her trial scene, the Cardinal attempts to shape our perceptions of Vittoria. Monticelso takes charge of the proceedings and tells Vittoria that he will be 'plainer with you, and paint out / Your follies in more natural red and white / Than that upon your cheek' (III, ii, 51–3). Here Monticelso bluntly tells the audience that Vittoria is painted even as he proceeds to participate in a type of verbal painting when he accuses her of being a whore:

> You see, my lords, what goodly fruit she seems;
> Yet like those apples travellers report
> To grow where Sodom and Gomorrah stood,
> I will but touch her and you straight shall see
> She'll fall to soot and ashes.
> (III, ii, 63–7)

Monticelso's comparison of a painted lady to 'goodly' but deceptive fruit seems to conform to the trite, moralistic discourse that repeatedly made similar comparisons between painted ladies and deceitful objects. Monticelso continues his verbal assault against her character when he paints out a description of a whore. He uses cosmetic language once again, as he constructs for us the character of Vittoria:

> I'll give their perfect character. They are first,
> Sweet-meats which rot the eater; in man's nostril
> Poisoned perfumes. They are cozening alchemy,
> Ship wrecks in calmest weather! What are whores?
>   What's a whore?
> She's like the guilty counterfeited coin
> Which, whosoe'er first stamps it, brings in trouble
> All that receive it.
> (III, ii, 79–82, 98–101)

In these passages Monticelso recalls his earlier image of Vittoria as hollow fruit, when he refers to whores as 'sweet-meats which rot the eater'; the perfumes that poison men's 'nostrils' remind the audience of the poisonous elements in cosmetics, including perfume. K. H. Ansari also detects the cosmetic undercurrent in Monticelso's 'Character', noting that Vittoria 'is one of the whores that are deceptive by nature – sweetmeats that rot the eater, shipwrecks in the calmest weather, flattering bells that have one tune at weddings and funerals, and counterfeit coins which deceive by their gilt'.[4] Monticelso's description of a whore as a 'shipwreck' is not a terribly obvious cosmetic image; nonetheless, it is one often used by anti-cosmetic moralists to describe the attention and time spent on the 'rigging' up of a woman's body. Barnabe Rich rails against harlots and their 'amorous glances, these yielding gestures and these inticing tricks', but finds that it is a great deale of charge and to very little purpose that is bestowed on some ships in superfluities in the paintinge of *Caage workes* like the painting of womens faces that being worne of with wind and weather leaves loathsomnes behind to those that do behold it and then what *Flags* what *Ensignes* what *Streamers*, and what *pendants* that serveth for no use but for pride and bravery.[5]

A whore is like a 'shipwreck' because her painted face is 'worne of with wind and weather' implying that her sexual activity has adverse affects on her complexion. In Jonson's *The Devil is an Ass* (1616), this sentiment is satirised in the exchanges between Wittipol or 'the Spanish Lady' and the Ladies Tailbush and Eitherside. Wittipol tells the ladies that fucuses are 'dangerous' to the 'fallen' women, who make a living 'with their sweat': 'For any distemper / Of heat and motion may displace the colours / And if the paint once run about their faces, / Twenty to one they will appear so ill-favoured' (IV, iv, 41–3). Webster relishes in comparisons like this, because he enjoys the imagistic and metaphorical richness that anti-cosmetic rhetoric had to offer, and in the trial scene of *The White Devil*, he forces us to see the irony of the superficial Cardinal speaking out against temptation and deception. Vittoria is elevated by this very discrepancy, and by the fact that she recognises his hypocrisy and dares to speak out against it in her own defence: 'Terrify babes, my lord, with painted devils; / I am past such needless palsy' (III, ii, 147–8). Claiming that 'beauty and gay clothes, a merry heart, / And a good stomach to a feast' are all she is guilty of, Vittoria releases herself from the social labels attached by moralists to painted whores. Ultimately, what she is saying is that being beautiful and painted does not make her a murderer, which contradicts the popular notion, voiced by Thomas Tuke's anti-cosmetic treatise, that painting leads to poison and murder. Vittoria is not necessarily innocent, but like Gertrude in *Hamlet*, she is suitably ambiguous enough to be given the benefit of the doubt when it comes to murder.

> Art turns people into objects. We gaze at pictures; they cannot move, though they may move us.[6]

Pictorial worship was common in early modern culture. Samuel Schuman contends that 'allegorical civic pageantry, emblem books, symbolic figures as motif in decorative arts, and numerous other stimuli that created and encouraged an awareness of the potential "meaningfulness" of pictures was pervasive'.[7] Drawing upon the heightened significance attributed to pictures, Webster valorises female suffering and stages cosmetic rituals as acts of heroic resistance by framing them both within a dramatic stage picture. Samuel Schuman defines a 'stage picture' as 'a dramatic allegorical tableau – a static or dynamic grouping on the stage of actors with props, costumes, and setting for an instant or a sharply limited duration'.[8] In Act III, scene ii of *The Duchess of Malfi* Webster creates a curious stage picture for his audience. The reflection of the Duchess in her mirror is half of the image; the other half consists of those accompanying her in her closet. At first she is joined by Cariola and Antonio, and in the second half of the scene, Ferdinand approaches from behind. Antonio and Cariola banter playfully while the Duchess beautifies herself, the scene beginning conventionally, with the Duchess commanding her maidservant to 'Bring me the casket hither, and the glass' (III, ii, 1). The scene continues as the Duchess becomes flirtatious with her husband, while preparing her hair and face in the mirror. This intimate exposure of the private space of the Duchess recalls the many dramatic scenes that take place inside a woman's closet; particularly in *Hamlet*, we are given access to Gertrude's chamber and the symbolism of the objects one might find there (a subject I will return to in Chapter 8). The relationship between private and public spaces is crucial to Webster's play and there is a seamless connection between the female interior, cosmetics, and public display. Bosola's description of a woman's chamber as 'a shop of witchcraft' is driven by his hatred of cosmetic materials. Bosola's judgement and the Duchess' heroism seem at odds, when we consider that one of the most poignant moments in the play is her beautification scene. In this particular stage picture, Webster asks us to withhold judgement of a lady who beautifies herself.

Appropriately in this scene, the Duchess and Antonio discourse upon beauty and the vanity of women. Antonio asks: 'I do wonder why hard-favoured ladies / For the most part, keep worse-favoured waiting-women / To attend them, and cannot endure fair ones' (III, ii, 45–7); the Duchess responds, pointing to the analogous relationship between face painting and canvas painting:

> Did you ever in your life know an ill painter –
> Desire to have his dwelling next door to the shop
> Of an excellent picture-maker? 'Twould disgrace
> His face-making, and undo him.
>
> (III, ii, 49–52)

Here Webster emphasises the aesthetic product of both types of craft; they create a picture. Moralists referred to painted women as pictures, and Iago calls Venetian women 'pictures out of doors'. Sir John Harrington's *Epigrams* contain a satirical poem entitled 'Of a painted Lady', in which he blurs the distinctions between the real woman and her painted copy: 'I saw dame *Leda's* picture lately drawne . . . / That

I had been long with her acquainted, / Did think that both were quick, or both were painted'. This telling poem points to the inextricable links between aesthetic materials and the materials found in face paint. If I may digress for a moment, the ambiguity of the word 'picture' and the notion of 'pictures' is exploited in Webster's tragicomedy *The Devil's Law-Case*. The plot is significantly lighter than the tragic plots of *The White Devil* and *The Duchess of Malfi*, and we are also confronted by a different social group of characters, namely, lawyers and merchants. The petty character, Leonora, is in love with one of her daughter's (Jolenta) suitors, Contarino, who asks permission to marry Jolenta: he asks Leonora 'to bestow your picture on me' (I, I, 136). He uses the term 'picture' to refer to her daughter, a conventional idea that a child is a picture of the parent's youth. Leonora misreads this meaning of the word 'picture' and speaks of painted portraits:

> With what a compelled face a woman sits
> While she is drawing. I have noted divers
> Either to feign smiles, or suck in the lips
> To have a little mouth; ruffle the cheeks
> To have the dimple seen, and so disorder
> The face with affectation, at next sitting
> It has not been the same. I have known others
> Have lost the entire fashion of their face
> In half an hour's sitting.
>
> （I, i, 47–57）

Leonora suggests that a woman would actively use canvas painting to misrepresent herself, much in the same way as she uses face painting. Leonora, who cannot extricate one art from the other glides easily into a discussion of cosmetically painted faces:

> 　　　　　In hot weather,
> The painting on their face has been so mellow,
> They have left the poor man harder work by half,
> To mend the copy he wrought by.
>
> （I, i, 159–62）

Leonora points out the grotesqueness of the effect of hot weather on face paint, and notes comically how it frustrates a portrait painter, who has to keep mending the 'copy'. Again, Leonora blurs the distinction between the two arts. This moment is highly satirical because, traditionally, it is the painted portrait that is always valued above the painted flesh of a woman, but in Webster the opposite is true. In *The Duchess of Malfi* Webster's stage picture is of a heroine who re-creates her *own* face, a picture within a theatrical tableau.

　　Curiously, Antonio and Cariola decide to leave the Duchess's closet secretly so that she will continue speaking to them without realising their absence. The Duchess is left alone only briefly, at which time she reflects upon her physical beauty, and seemingly exhibits pride, especially in her desire to be the most beautiful and youthful looking woman at court: 'Doth not the colour of my hair 'gin to change? / When I wax gray, I shall have all the court / Powder their hair with orris, to be like me' (III, ii, 58–60). There is one object in this scene that is crucial to Webster's construction of the Duchess as heroic and that is the looking glass. As I have mentioned already, looking glasses had a variety of signifying functions in early modern culture: the one metaphorical meant for spiritual reflection and the other is literal, the type of looking glass that would be found in a harlot's closet. But the Duchess is no harlot and she does meditate upon her moral condition even as she is reflecting upon her changing hair colour. Antonio tells us early on that the Duchess's beauty stems from her virtue; in this scene, her outward gestures of correcting her beauty also symbolise her internal beautification. Although she appears to be full of pride, the dignity of the Duchess remains intact, undermining the orthodox anti-cosmetic critique that characters like Bosola recite in the play. This stage picture of this Duchess engaged in self-beautification serves as a counter discourse to the moral cliché upheld by most of the male characters that painted ladies are whores.

The sexual tenor of the scene changes when Ferdinand appears with his poniard pointing at the Duchess. The scene shifts dramatically here as we move from the intimacy of married love and discourse on beauty to a darker, more sinister exchange between the avenging Ferdinand's naked poniard reflected in the Duchess's looking glass and the picture of the Duchess herself. For Ferdinand, the picture of a woman looking into her glass recalls what he perceives are her sexual crimes; therefore this image is a dangerous one for him and aggravates him further. Frances Dolan comments upon the motif of the woman gazing into her glass, who, 'absorbed in self-transformation, threatens the boundaries between creator and creation, desiring subject and object of desire, masculine and feminine, self and body, gentlewoman and prostitute – boundaries on which social order and sexual ideology depend'.[9] Ferdinand is concerned about the social order, but his extreme need to control his sister's sexual activity perverts him. The pictorial motif of the devil behind a woman at her looking glass was a popular one in early modern Europe and England (Figure 4.1); what soon becomes clear is that, in this dramatic moment, Webster inverts the traditional associations of the devil in the glass by elevating the status of the Duchess. She paints her face even while she attempts to fashion her own life, which Ferdinand perceives as lacking moral virtue: 'Virtue, where art thou hid?

Of Pride.

When daintie dames hath whole delight : with proude attyre them selues to raye
Pirasmos shineth in the sight : of glittering glasse such fooles to fray.

¶ The signification.

¶ 'He woman signifieth pride : the glasse in her hand flatte-
ry or deceate : the deuill behinde her temptation : the
death head which she setteth her foote on, signifieth forget-
fulnes of the life to come, wherby commeth destruction.
H.iij.   Take

Figure 4.1   'The Sin of Pride', *A Christall glasse of Christian reformation*, Stephen
Bateman (1569) c. 37.d. 2, by permission of the British Library.

What hideous thing / Is it that doth eclipse thee?' (III, ii, 73–4). H. T.
Price rightly contends that, here 'Webster trusts the idea of appearance
and reality to show that Ferdinand . . . cannot recognize virtue when
he sees it in its most beautiful form'.[10] The Duchess's use of the looking

glass and cosmetics, however, such as 'orris powder' suggests that she is not the traditional emblem of virtue, at least not by seventeenth-century standards. She is forced into dissimulation by her brothers, but Webster reverses the symbolism of cosmetics in this scene, which do not indicate her fallen sexuality; instead they serve, paradoxically, to illustrate her alluring moral superiority.

Rethinking Webster's Imagery

Mid to late twentieth-century criticism of Webster was largely focused on imagery. H. T. Price's study of the 'function' of Webster's imagery argues that it serves to reveal 'character, it does the work of argument, it emphasizes mood, and it prefigures the events to come'.[11] Price substantiates his claim by observing that 'Webster especially uses imagery to convey the basic conflict of his drama, the conflict between outward appearance and inner substance or reality'.[12] He also connects poison, in Webster's imagery, to the idea of 'fair shows and foul truth'.[13] Yet Price's argument pays little attention to Webster's indulgence in cosmetic metaphors and his references to cosmetic materials. He could not have seen the pointed links between the dramatist's use of linguistic cosmetics and material cosmetics on the stage; critical trends saw little need for Price to provide any historical basis for the popularity of such imagery. My interest in Webster's cosmetic imagery is that it has an epistemological basis; images of art, Catholicism, witchcraft, traps, food, death, disease, medicine, skin, the body, colour, ships, tombs and effigies, nature, and animals, all of them are images that in some way speak to the contemporary discourse on cosmetics. Most of these subjects are areas of learning in themselves and have their own deliberate discourses. When Francis Bacon refers to the cosmetic arts in *The Advancement of Learning*, he is making a space for the beautification of the body within a legitimising framework; Webster does the same by giving prominence to the theme of cosmetics and by demonstrating their relationship to the ideological concerns of the day.

Ralph Berry's study of Webster's language in the early 1970s distinguishes between the strands of images in Webster, and separates them into categories of their own: 'sixty-six images, in all, treat of sickness and corruption, physic and physicians'; he goes on to argue that witchcraft images are related to 'the macabre, grotesque tone that Webster loves to invoke'.[14] But I see an interconnectedness between the many objects and ideas evoked by Webster's imagery. Eloise K. Goreau's 1974 study of Webster's dramatic imagery cleverly infers that 'in the tradition of allegorical imagery, "painted" means more, however, than simply deceptive. The deceiver is the devil, and the painting is his means of ensnaring victims by making temptation of the world alluring'.[15] I agree with Goreau's contention that if we simplify Webster's language by labelling his images merely 'deceptive', we gain very little from a reading of his plays. But like most critics who write about cosmetics on the Renaissance stage, Goreau suggests that the dramatist reinforces moralistic anti-cosmetic sentiments. But why would any dramatist do so exclusively, when cosmetics are practically synonymous with theatre?

Critical studies of Webster do at times acknowledge the references to cosmetics in the plays, but on the whole they do not imagine that such references may be central to the verbal, visual and theatrical structure of the plays. Many studies only comment on the few blatant references to cosmetics in *The White Devil* and the famous diatribe against the Old Lady's cosmetic arts by Bosola in *The Duchess of Malfi*. In his analysis of Webster's tragedies, K. H. Ansari discovers that 'there are masks, vizards, curtains and clothes to cover the real nature of the characters'.[16] Webster does indeed perceive power as a system of layers, with the top layers as the most deceptive. His Duchess is deceptive and the cosmetics in some ways materialise this even while they materialise the blatant deception of the boy actor who is pretending to be a Duchess on the stage. But the Duchess deceives her brothers who threaten her sexuality and love, her dignity and her life; therefore, her deception becomes an act of heroic defiance, as she attempts to rescue herself from them. Catherine Belsey sees the Duchess of Malfi as innocent, and insists that the only function of the Old Lady and Bosola's attack on her painting is 'to reinforce the Duchess's purity'.[17] However, there is nothing in the text to suggest that the Duchess is not a painted lady herself. In fact Bosola's tirade against the old lady could be taken as displacement. Meanwhile, Ralph Berry argues that 'we do not, of course, need to take too seriously the obscure caricature of womanhood that the Old Lady represents'.[18] Kathleen McLuskie calls Bosola's raillery against the Old Lady a 'generalized "meditation" on the decay of the flesh and the folly of human pride', and she goes on to argue that Bosola is 'mouthing the clichés of medieval complaint but these are shown to have no particular application to the events or the characters of the play'.[19] However, the argument that the old lady is merely a catalyst for Bosola's conventional, malcontented outburst against women lacks insight into contemporary culture, the discourse about cosmetics and the role that culture and discourse play in Webster's complex construction of images.

Cosmetics and Catholic Imagery

Thomas Tuke frequently cites the early Church fathers' admonitions to women about their cosmetic practices, including those of St Chrysostom whose rage against cosmetics adopts Eucharistic language to shame women into religious guilt:

> And wilt thou, whose head is Christ, who art a beleever, wilt thou allow of the inventions of Satan? Wilt thou not remember that water, that was sprinckled upon they face, nor the Sacrament, which beautified thy lips, nor the blood, which made red thy tongue?[20]

St Chrysostom recommends beautifying the spirit using the rituals of Catholic worship as cosmetics themselves, the holy water, the Sacrament and Christ's blood should be enough to make a woman beautiful. Yet Protestant moralists appropriated the anti-cosmetic stance and used it to simultaneously reject the trappings of the Catholic church, by repeatedly drawing upon anti-Catholic sentiments; the comparison between the Whore of Babylon and the Pope, the satirical representation of Eucharistic rituals, the worship of relics and the relationship between European cosmetic habits and Catholicism are most common. Such polemics denigrate the worship of painted images, idols and saints, giving the anti-cosmetic argument a theological undercurrent. Protestant moralists were already busy denigrating the Catholic indulgence in ostentation, such as brightly coloured vestments, incense (perfumes), painted idols, time-consuming ritual and overwrought ceremony. In 'An Homilie against Peril of Idolatrie, and superfluous deckyng of Churches' the homilist describes the 'corruption' of the times, which 'hath brought into the Church infinite multitudes of images, and the same, with other parts of the temple also, have decked with golde and silver, paynted with colours, set them with stone & pearle, clothed them with silkes and pretious vestures.' He also sees 'the seekyng out of images' as 'the begynnyng of whooredom'.[21] This perception of idolatry as a type of painting or 'deckyng' of the church (the religious body, figuratively) is reflected in Webster's use of iconoclastic language and his portrayal of Catholic clergy. Cosmetic metaphors and materials prove useful to a playwright who seeks to dramatise the corrosive potential of ecclesiastical hierarchy.

The Cardinal in *The White Devil* typifies the Italian, Catholic man of the cloth, whose murderous aims and sinister methods speak directly to Protestant anxieties in early modern England. In Act IV, scene iii, the Conclave elect Monticelso as Pope, who has until now demonstrated with Machiavellian rigour, his almost nihilistic ambition. Likewise, in *The Duchess of Malfi* the Cardinal plays a significant part in Webster's exploration of the relationship between anti-Catholic and anti-cosmetic imagery. In Act III, scene v, the dumb show demonstrates the Cardinal's metamorphosis from religious official to military official. The Cardinal's ceremony involves divesting himself of the trappings of religious office and trading them for the trappings of war. The song is perhaps the most interesting element of this dumb show:

> *Lay aside all those robes lie by thee,*
> *Crown thy arts with arms, they'll beautify thee.*
> *O worthy of worthiest name, adorned in this manner,*
> *Lead bravely thy forces under war's warlike banner.*
> (III, iv, 16–19)

The words 'beautify' and 'adorned' call to mind cosmetic discourse, since definitions of the word 'beautify' mostly refer to cosmetic embellishment. Webster's use of cosmetic signifiers (materials and metaphors) in relation to his female heroines seems to elevate the status of cosmetics above that of poisoning materials, but when applied in this way, Webster can evoke contemporary discourse and reintroduce the notion that cosmetics are morally corrosive; hence, the meaning of cosmetic embellishment changes as it moves from noble characters to those who abuse their power. The song above suggests that the distance between ritual and violence is a short one as it anticipates the Cardinal's murder of Julia with the poisoned Bible.

Tragically, Julia probes the Cardinal for his deepest secrets, hoping to force out a confession of his part in the Duchess's murder, an act he is attempting to conceal; here we see more of Webster's relentless disclosure of the hidden. The Cardinal warns Julia about the dangerous burden of his secret: ''tis a secret / That, like a ling'ring poison, may chance lie / Spread in thy veins, and kill thee seven year hence' (V, ii, 260–2). Finally, however, the Cardinal admits the truth, and it does prove to be poisonous to Julia; for while he has unburdened himself in a type of confession, Julia is the one to suffer the penance. She admits that she cannot conceal such a secret, so the Cardinal makes her swear upon the Bible by kissing it: 'thou'rt poisoned with that book; / Because I knew thou couldst not keep my counsel, / I have bound thee to't by death' (V, ii, 274–6). The literal use of religious doctrine for murder is meant to expose the corruption of Catholic clergy, who were poisoning scripture figuratively, in the view of Elizabethan and Jacobean Protestants. Significantly, the Cardinal uses poison, death and religion as cosmetics in order to conceal the spiritual hollowness beneath the scarlet robes. He is the Jezebel in the play. Thomas Adams's sermon entitled 'The White Devil' insists that Jezebel's paint 'is a complexion for lust, who, were she not painted over with a religious shew, would appeare as loathsome to the world, as she is indeed'.[22] However, having been the henchman of both the Aragonian brothers, Bosola tells the Cardinal that he cannot hide his crimes from him: 'And wherefore should you lay fair marble colours / Upon your rotten purposes to me?' (V, ii, 293–4). Bosola gives voice here to the notion that painted tombs have rotten bones beneath, which became a popular metaphor in the period for describing the increasing dependence upon ostentation and was picked up by anti-cosmetic writers who saw decided links between painted ladies and effigies. Webster and Middleton both saw the added advantage of combining both anxieties within a dramatic framework. Michael Neill assumes that in the Vault scene of *The Duchess of Malfi*, 'Webster must have intended to make use of a specially adapted version of the tomb-property which the King's men had already employed in *The Second Maiden's Tragedy*'.[23]

The analogical relationship between tombs and cosmetics is even more pronounced in John Weever's *Ancient Funerall Monuments*, cited by Neill:

> The very Latin name for a tomb, he claimed, pointed to its double aspect, since *sepulchral* was to be derived from *semi*-pulchra – 'half fair and beautiful: the external part of superficies thereof being beautified and adorned, and having nothing within, but dreadfull darkness, loathsome stink, and rottenness of bones'.[24]

Funerary images have long been an important artistic response to death and grief, as have idols and statues. Fascinatingly, the medieval cult of images was implicitly cosmetic: 'the dressing-up of statues with clothes and jewels, if it did not excite wonder (or envy) of poor working-women, by contrast with their own drab garb, helped to encourage the belief that the female sex was particularly involved in this activity'.[25] In the seventeenth century, even Queen Elizabeth I's effigy was beautified in such a way, recalling the Catholic adornment of saints and idols, and so it becomes clear that the adornment of the Queen's body did not cease after her death. The effigy in 1603 is said to be decked in 'her ermine-edged *white* mantle and combined an ermine-cuffed traditional furcoat with a large up-to-date ruff. There was no head-dress, but the hair was plaited and coiffed'.[26] After Queen Elizabeth's death, painted faces on the stage became living artefacts, producing a similar effect to monumental effigies. Cosmetics worried Protestant moralists because the lines between Catholic and Protestant become blurred in a figure like Queen Elizabeth I, for example. But in Webster's play, in the wooing scene, the Duchess emphasises her vitality even while she attempts to divest herself of her memorialistic function: 'This is flesh, and blood, sir; / 'Tis not the figure cut in alabaster/ Kneels at my husband's tomb' (I, i, 443–5).

Although the Duchess appears to show more concern for her private needs than her public duty, it is because the public world oppresses her natural desires and inclinations as a woman. This tension between the private and the public is acted upon the Duchess's body. Nigel Alexander observes that 'the reference to the body as a tomb is a traditional proverb and an equally traditional part of puritan psychology that regarded the entire world of the senses as a deceitful marriage'.[27] However, there is something visionary about the Duchess's extraordinary belief that love and family are more important than public duty. This belief and her resulting actions fly in the face of polemical assumptions that painted women make terrible wives and mothers. The Duchess 'stains the time past, lights the time to come' (I, i, 200). Webster exposes her extraordinary character even while he shows her breaking free from traditional homiletic assumptions about women who beautify their appearances.

Cosmetics and Witchcraft

According to Nancy Etcoff, 'a law was passed by the English Parliament in the late eighteenth century which attempted to impose on women the same penalty for adornment as for witchcraft, freeing up the husbands who had married them under such false pretences'.[28] In the early modern period witches were feared because they had an invisible power; they made potions, using a wide range of organic and mineral ingredients, including animal parts, fats and blood. It was believed witches could transform themselves into anything they wanted to deceive men. To bewitch was to charm, seduce, and entrap, to render a man powerless against the materials and methods of the darker arts. Women who used cosmetics were often placed in the same category as witches. From the quotation above, it is perfectly clear that well beyond the Renaissance period, the fear of witchcraft translated easily into a fear of cosmeticised ladies. There is some validity, I might add, to the perceived intersections of these two crafts. Some of the ingredients located in cosmetics recipes suggest why it was seen as an art as ominous as witchcraft. The witches in *Macbeth* use 'leopard's bane', 'the juice of toad, the oil of adder' (IV, i, 53, 55–6) to conjure the prophetic images that will predict Macbeth's tragic narrative. Ingredients such as these bear a striking resemblance to some of the ingredients found in varied cosmetic recipes. Giovanni Battista Della Porta's collection of recipes translated in 1653 contains some gruesome instructions: to make a black dye for long hair, one would have to 'take a green lizard, and cutting off the Head and Tail, boyl it in common Oyl, and anoynt your Head with it'.[29] The use of reptiles and the word 'anoynt' would undoubtedly conjure up the practices of witchcraft. Similarly, Giovanni Ruscelli's book of recipes calls for birds in the ingredients to make a face look fair and smooth:

> Take a young Crow even out of the nest . . . kill him and flawe him, breaking the flesh into small peeces: then take leaves of a Mirtle tree, and lay one ranke of them, and another of the little peeces of the Crow, in some great viol of glasse, poudred and strewed over with the pouder of Talchum, stamped with oyle of sweet Almonds.[30]

The use of powders, animals and oils for cosmetics or any other type of concoction was cause for suspicion and anxiety in post-Reformation England. John S. Mebane has argued that early modern witchhunts were a response to the potential threat of subversion posed by witchcraft: 'those who wished to defend the status quo associated witchcraft with rebelliousness and discontent among the lower classes and/or among those who dissented from government-sanctioned religion and natural philosophy'.[31] The anti-witchcraft treatises and anti-cosmetic treatises would have readers believe that the biggest threat posed by both is bodily and spiritual contamination. It was also believed in early modern England that witches had as much access to poison as did women who painted their faces. In *A Treatise Against Witchcraft*, Henry Holland fears that witches' 'greatest practise is by poison & powders, which the devil teacheth them it hurt withall'.[32] Anxiety about contamination in the Renaissance period, as I mentioned in my discussion of Middleton's plays, is part of the reason why many writers were rabid about face paints, perfumes and powders; this fear is also detectable in the writings pertaining to witchcraft. Reginald Scot's famous *The Discoverie of Witchcraft*, published in 1584, argues that witches 'kill with poison', and the title of the tenth chapter of his book reflects the fear of female contamination: 'The bewitching Venome conteined in the bodie of an harlot, how hir eie, hir toong, hir beautie and behavior bewitcheth some men . . . '; Scot argues in this section that a harlot's 'toong, hir gesture, hir behaviour, hir beautie, and other allurements poison and intoxicate the mind'.[33] Conflating the practices of cosmetics and witchcraft, this reference speaks to the literal threat of syphilis posed by painted harlots, but even more pointed is the fact that women of all levels of society used cosmetics, including Queen Elizabeth, Mary Queen of Scots and Queen Anne of Denmark. In some ways discourses of this nature are politically subversive. There is the latent suggestion that female monarchy may prove to be a poisonous threat to the commonwealth. Robin Briggs's study of witchcraft and fear indicates that men believed witches avenged the wrongs done to them, and 'they most frequently did this by physical means, employing the powders, poisoned sticks and similar weapons' that the devil 'had provided'.[34] Witches were perceived mainly as female tyrants, deceptive, demonic and unstable. The concept of the cosmeticised queen had the potential to create enormous anxiety and this is pointedly registered in Webster's *The Duchess of Malfi*: 'For they whose faces do belie their hearts / Are witches, ere they arrive at twenty years' (I, i, 299–301).

The fearful practice of skin flaying, considered barbaric and frightening within early modern discourses about witches and demons, was also a medical practice, taking place in Europe's anatomy theatres. In Figure 4.2 the view of the Leiden anatomy theatre from the early seventeenth century shows a theatre in the round with a woman on the periphery inspecting a flayed human skin. Skin flaying was also a cosmetic practice (and still is). An essay by Montaigne – 'That the taste of goods or evils depend on the opinion we have of them' – discusses the concept of 'pain' and the lengths women will go to in order to improve their appearance: 'Who hath not heard of her at Paris, which only to get a fresher hew of a new skin, endured to have her face flead

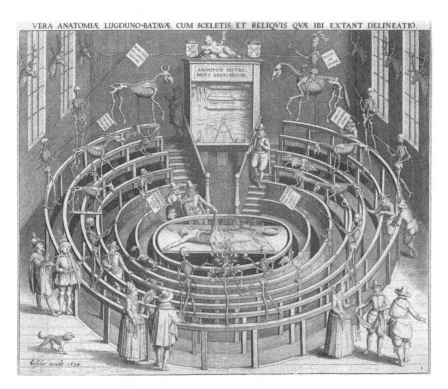

Figure 4.2   View of Leiden anatomy theatre (1610), University of Leiden Library.

all over?'[35] Other treatises reveal that skin flaying was a popular activity amongst women in early modern Europe. One section of Lomazzo's artistry tract entitled 'Of scaling or Plume-Alume' defines 'Plume-Alume' as a type of stone with which 'some use to rubbe the skinne off their face, to make it seem red, by reason of the inflammation it procureth'.[36] Some women used mercury sublimate to remove the top layer of their skin in order to rid their complexions of blemishes or spots. However, by removing this 'outer layer of skin', they 'slightly' consume 'the layer of flesh underneath . . . causing a recession of the gums'.[37] The notion that this method actually worsened, rather than improved the complexion, is central to the contemporary opposition to it. Lomazzo claims that those women who think they will look beautiful, many times 'become disfigured, hastening old age before the time'.[38] Later on in the seventeenth century, Thomas Hall argues that some of these methods only 'deceive themselves, getting deformity instead of beauty, losing that true beauty which they have by nature, by their Medicines and Mineralls, oft making their faces to wrinkle, their colour pale . . .'[39] Reginald Scot says that witches hide their secrets in their 'haire, in their privities, and betweene their skinne and their flesh', for which, he argues, they should indeed be flayed before they are burned.[40] The terrifying link between contemporary cosmetic practices and the cruel punishment for witchcraft cannot be missed in Webster's tragic drama.

In Act II, scene i of *The Duchess of Malfi*, Bosola tells the story of a woman who flayed her skin. Apart from introducing a type of grotesque humour into his play, Webster uses this moment to undermine the anti-cosmetic tenor of the play's misogyny by having Bosola speak out against this cultural practice in a way that suggests that the male anxiety about transformation is the issue continuously bubbling under the surface of the play:

> Why, from your scurvy face-physic. To behold thee not painted inclines somewhat near a miracle. These, in thy face here, were deep ruts and foul sloughs the last progress. There was a lady in France that, having had the smallpox, flayed the skin off her face, to make it more level; and whereas before she looked like a nutmeg-grater, after she resembled an abortive hedgehog.
>
> (II, ii, 21–5)

Here, Bosola recalls a story about a woman in France; it is likely that this anecdote was pulled from the essay of Montaigne cited earlier. The Old Lady asks Bosola if he thinks skin flaying is painting. He replies: 'No, no, but careening of an old morphewed lady, to make her disembogue again. There rough-cast phrase to your plastic' (29–30).

Trading in the ship-as-painted-lady image for one of an old boat, Bosola argues that flaying the face is like turning a boat over for cleaning and scraping before it can be put out to sea.

There are many references throughout the play to the Duchess as a blemish on the state or as a skin infection. When Ferdinand discovers the Duchess has lied and remarried, he feels the need to soothe his 'wildfire'(or skin disease) and immediately calls for 'rhubarb', a common herb used for medicinal purposes, to purge bile. The metaphor of skin disease is tied closely to the increasing instability of Ferdinand's mind and his association of his sister with witchcraft. He sees his sister only in physical terms, first as a sexualised body, then as an infectious blot on the body of the political state:

> Apply desperate physic –
> We must not now uses balsumum, but fire,
> The smarting cupping-glass, for that's the mean
> To purge infected blood, such blood as hers.
>   (II, v, 23–6)

'Balsumum' is a balm used to sooth skin ailments; Ferdinand insists that a balm would be too gentle; the Duchess needs to burn, like all witches. Ferdinand's rage sounds too like contemporary threats to painted ladies: '*God shall smite thee, thou painted wall*: and wash off they vermillion dye with the rivers of brimston'.[41]

Bosola's diatribe against the Old Lady's cosmetic practice incorporates the same images of witchcraft, animals and disease. The Old Lady observes that he seems to know a great deal about her 'closet', meaning every woman's cosmetic chamber; he says he does and proceeds to disclose the secrets of such suspicious arts, while creating a parody of the feminine domestic interior:

> One would expect it for a shop of witchcraft, to find in it the fat of serpents, spawn of snakes, Jew's spittle, and their young children's ordures, and all these for the face. I would sooner eat a dead pigeon, taken from the soles of the feet of one sick of the plague, than kiss one of you fasting.
>   (II, i, 32–5)

Kate Aughterson suggests that Bosola's remarks to the Old Lady are 'exaggerated', because he creates a 'fantasy, imagining her makeup as excretion and body fluids'.[42] In actual fact, Bosola's tirade is not necessarily 'fantasy' nor is he really 'imagining' her makeup to consist of exaggerated materials. While these ingredients seem likely to be located in witches' brews, some are also cosmetic ingredients. Lomazzo's tract tells us that women use '*ointments* of diverse sorts; *pouder, fattes, waters* and the like'.[43] And we have already seen Porta's instructions for cutting up a lizard and making a dye, and Ruscelli's advice on killing and flaying crows in order to smoothe and whiten the complexion. Thus the relationship between witchcraft and cosmetic practice has a material basis as well as a metaphorical one. But what Webster does is suggest that the anxiety about these female practices stems primarily from social and sexual insecurity. Ferdinand's own fears about lycanthropy (transforming into a wolf) register his fundamentally unstable identity. His sexual perversion manifest in his incestuous desire to dictate the Duchess' sexual behaviour underlies his eventual destruction of the Duchess and his fear of what she might turn him into. Because of his sexual insecurities, Ferdinand has already metamorphosed into what he fears most. Thus the anxiety of transformation is one of the crucial strands of this tragedy, and cosmetic and witchcraft imagery help in its construction.

Conclusion

Webster dramatises the fear of transformation with a self-reflexivity common to early modern drama. Disguise, cosmetics, metamorphosis – these are the methods and materials of theatre, and Webster captures brilliantly the relationship between theatre, cosmetics and witchcraft. The many references to wolves in both tragedies illuminate the belief that witches could not only transform their own shapes, but also transform the shapes of others, especially men. In *The White Devil* Brachiano fears that Vittoria's love or desire for him has changed when he reads a letter to her by Francisco. He accuses her of being changeable and calls her a whore: 'Thy loose thoughts / Scatter like quicksilver. I was bewitched, / For all the world speaks ill of thee' (IV, ii, 97–9). Ironically, he proves to be more changeable, when moments later he repents his words: 'I have drunk Lethe, Vittoria? / My dearest happiness? Vittoria?' (126–7). When Brachiano finally dies from the poison in his helmet, he regrets his relationship with the 'white devil' whose face, he perceives, is a 'maske for treason, whose shop full of poisons, pistols, daggers . . . would easily be spied out, had hypocrise left them bare-faced'.[44] Brachiano goes a step further than Bosola when he imagines Vittoria as a type of cosmetic assassin with a face for treason and whose 'shop' is full of not only poisons, but pistols and daggers. He is making the clichéd leap from cosmeticised lady to hypocritical murderess. The men in these two plays fault the women for their own maniacal and sometimes psychotic behaviour. The anti-cosmetic and misogynous tenor of the plays is subverted by Webster's construction of femininity.

The notion and practice of beautification are given added significance and value when Webster demonstrates the ways in which cosmetic metaphors and materials link themselves neatly to contemporary epistemological discourses, thus providing an intellectual framework for his theatrical and artistic expression.

Notes

1. Webster, 'The Characters', in *The Complete Works*, p. 30.
2. Brooke, *Horrid Laughter*, p. 47.
3. Jeamson, *Artificiall Embellishments, Sig.* A4v.
4. Ansari, *Imagery*, p. 60.
5. Rich, *The Excellency of good women*, p. 14.
6. Mullins, *The Painted Witch*, p. 85.
7. Schuman, *The Theatre of Fine Devices*, p. 4.
8. Ibid. p. 73.
9. Dolan, 'Taking the pencil out of God's hand', p. 236.
10. Price, 'The function of imagery', p. 734.
11. Ibid. p. 720.
12. Ibid. p. 720.
13. Ibid. p. 720.
14. Berry, *The Art of John Webster*, pp. 63, 92.
15. Goreau, *Integrity of Life*, p. 139.
16. Ansari, *Imagery*, p. 18.
17. Belsey, 'Emblem and antithesis', p. 126.
18. Berry, *The Art of John Webster*, p. 42.
19. McLuskie, 'Drama and sexual politics', p. 114.
20. Tuke, *A Treatise Against Paint[i]ng*, p. 27.
21. Anonymous, 'An Homilie against Peril of Idolatrie', p. 33.
22. Adams, 'The White Devil', p. 45.
23. Neill, *Issues of Death*, p. 331.
24. Ibid. p. 342.
25. Aston, *England's Iconoclasts*, p. 108.
26. Cunnington and Lucas, *Costumes for Births*, p. 177.
27. Alexander, 'Intelligence in *The Duchess of Malfi*', p. 101.
28. Etcoff, *Survival of the Prettiest*, pp. 102–3.
29. Della Porta, *Natural Magick*, p. 235.
30. Ruscelli, *The Secrets of Alexis*, p. 70.
31. Mebane, *Renaissance Magic*, p. 105.
32. Holland, *A Treatise Against Witchcraft, Sig.* B4r.
33. Scot, *The Discoverie of Witchcraft*, pp. 33, 304.
34. Briggs, *Witches and Neighbours*, p. 105.
35. Montaigne, *Essays*, p. 285.
36. Lomazzo, *A Tracte Containing the Artes of curious Paintinge*, p. 131.
37. Woodforde, *The History of Vanity*, p. 51.
38. Lomazzo, A Tracte Containing the Artes of curious Paintinge, p. 130.
39. Hall, *The Loathsomenesse of Long Hair*, p. 102.

40. Scot, *The Discoverie of Witchcraft*, p. 30.
41. Adams, 'The White Devil', p. 47.
42. Aughterson, *Webster*, p. 123.
43. Lomazzo, *A Tracte Containing the Artes of curious Paintinge*, p. 129.
44. Adams, 'The White Devil', p. 45.

Chapter 5

Jonson's Cosmetic Ritual

In a satirical poem called 'A Paradox of a Painted Face', written in the mid-seventeenth century, the author demonstrates the multivocality of the cultural attitude towards cosmetics by emphasising the contemporary attraction to painted faces, while using terms like 'cunning', 'deceive' and 'fraud' to demonstrate their association with hypocrisy:

> The *Fucus* and *Cerusse* which on thy face
> Thy cunning hand layes on to add more grace,
> Deceive me with such pleasing fraud, that I
> Find in thy Art what can in Nature lye.[1]

It is a familiar paradox that painted beauty is alluring, but the attraction to artifice is slightly dubious on religious as well as on poetical grounds. A desire for deception, is implicit in the attraction to painted faces, and in Elizabethan and Jacobean England, painted artifice was a powerful material reminder of the human need for aesthetic pleasure. Thus there is a dialogical relationship between aesthetics and deception, which means that face painting can be viewed as an art form unto itself. Ovid, read widely in the Renaissance, instructs ladies in his *Art of Love* to use cosmetics to correct their natural deficiencies, but he tells them that they must hide it from their suitors, suggesting that it is their deception or artifice to which the potential suitors are attracted: 'Why must I know the cause of the whiteness of your cheek? Shut your chamber door: why show the unfinished work? There is much that it befits men not to know; most of your doings would offend, did you not hide them within'.[2] There seems to be an implicit aversion to the material processes that a woman must undergo to arrive at the stylised version of herself; this is just one reason why authors of printed cosmetic recipes persistently refer to the recipes as secrets. Nevertheless, the marriage between the affect of art (including poetry and theatre) and deception places all art, like cosmetics, in a slightly morally unstable category. This issue is tackled by Ben

Jonson in his comedies *Epicoene, or the Silent Woman* (1609) and *The Devil is an Ass* (1616).

In *Epicoene* Ben Jonson rehearses some of the classical arguments for and against cosmetics, resurrecting the ideological questions about the desire for deception that held significant contemporary relevance. Jonson's attitude towards artifice is seemingly straightforward, but his own art tends to reconstitute cultural formulations of cosmetic embellishment. Generally, critics agree that 'Jonson retained a special animosity toward theatrical stuff, the stage objects and material practices that made the early modern theatre what it was'.[3] But I argue that Jonson's comedies are steeped in 'theatrical stuff', and I am particularly interested in the ways in which the material lives of cosmetics are mediated in these plays. Like the other dramatists discussed in this book, Jonson saw great theatrical potential in cosmetic metaphors and materials, but even more significant is the dramatist's meta-theatrical celebration of feminine cosmetic rituals. Plays like *Epicoene*, written for the Children of the Queen's Revels and later performed by the King's Men, and *The Devil is an Ass* (1616), also written for the King's Men, contain scenes in which a boy actor plays a male character who disguises himself as a woman. This particular configuration of crossdressing is important because the construction of gender becomes a doubly theatrical as well as prosthetic exercise. In this chapter, it will become clear that although Ben Jonson is morally opposed to women who paint their faces, he too appropriates the materials and metaphors of cosmetic adornment to serve his own dramatic purposes. Intriguingly, while doing so, he provides a social topography of the industry of cosmetics in early modern England. Jonson displays a curiosity about the rich tapestry of goods that the market economy of seventeenth-century London held, while at other times he appears furiously moralistic about the dubious technology of beauty and the wide range of prosthetic materials women attach to their bodies. Secondly, Jonson's comedies, in this light, register the contemporary fear of foreign infiltration: materially, textually (through the translated texts he uses as sources), and linguistically, but this fear is channelled through a discourse of ingredients: specifically, cosmetic ingredients.

'Pieced beauty': Cosmetics as Prosthetics

Critics in recent studies of materials for the stage and the body have used the term 'prosthetic' to refer to the ancillary attachments or objects useful or necessary for the construction of gender and the eventual display of the then gendered subject. Peter Stallybrass and Ann Rosalind

Jones comment on the ways in which clothing is constituted in pieces: 'clothing was a composition of detachable parts, so garments could be disassembled'.[4] They go on to recount that the inventories amongst Henslowe's papers speak to this detachability of clothing; thus, the prosthetic quality of dressing was crucially significant in the enactment of gender on the early modern stage.

When William Austin defines the standards of beauty in the early modern period, he argues that 'a good and proportionable agreeing coherence, and compacture of all the several parts of the body in one fairnesse' make for a beautiful woman.[5] The key words in this description are 'coherence' and 'compacture', which suggest, as the Introduction states, that symmetricality was crucial to female beauty; yet, there is also the latent suggestion in Austin's definition, that external symmetricality would be the natural reflection of a moral symmetricality, thus engaging this definition with the neo-Platonic reformulation of physical perfection.

Thus when raging against female beautification, to emphasise the lack of internal symmetricality, moralists dissect cosmeticised bodies linguistically. Anti-cosmetic sermons and pamphlets do not represent women as composites, but repeatedly reduce them, in long lists, to the parts of their bodies or the accoutrements that they might attach to their frames. For example, Hugh Latimer, preaching earlier in the period, insists that

> Their trimmed shoes, their nouches, brooches, and rings, their chains and pendents, their costly edges and precious habiliments shall come to naught. And then their pleasant odours of musk, civet, and of all perfumes shall be turned into stench.[6]

Similarly, Robert Burton asks:

> why doe they adorne themselves with so many colours of hearbes, fictitious floures . . . why doe they crowne themselves with gold and silver, use coronets and tires of severall fashions, decke themselves with pendants, bracelets, eare-rings, chaines, girdles, rings, pinnes . . .[7]

John Downame takes this process one step further as he catalogues the parts of women's bodies that correspond with their auxillary attachments:

> Some highly please themselves in those *artificiall eyes*, *hands*, leggs, noses, teeth, and *hair*, which makeup those breaches of the body, which age, or sicknesse, or other accidents have occasioned either to the inconveniency of *motion*, or of the deformity of their aspect.[8]

Downame emphasises the bodily inadequacies forcing women to try to compensate cosmetically; 'the deformity of their aspect', particularly, speaks to the contemporary custom of associating physical with moral deformity.

To view women in terms of their parts is to turn them into prosthetic beings. The passages cited above refer to the perceived inclination of a woman to construct her beauty by attaching to her body mineral and organic ingredients, paint and textiles, dyes and perfumes, jewels and stones, allowing her to compose a symmetrical identity through the systematic assemblage of material goods. In an analysis of supplementarity, David Wills coins the phrase 'prosthetic structure', which he defines as 'overreaching and compensating attempts at accommodation, a structural crisis and a contrived solution'.[9] Wills studies the nineteenth-century painting 'A Holiday at Mentone' by Charles Conder and interprets it theoretically in terms of amputation, suggesting that all the objects in the painting are somehow linked prosthetically to the human figures, posing a persistent threat. Noting Wills's theory that supplementarity is essentially threatening, one can apply this idea to early modern perceptions of feminine adornment. Wills argues that 'however much "prosthesis" refers to an apparatus alone, it cannot fail to imply the idea of the amputation—or a lack or deficiency'.[10] This implied absence of self is what undermines the female beautification process for contemporary moralists. It also added fuel to the fire of the anti-theatricalists who fumed against the crossdressing and painting of boys.

Cosmetics have a double prosthetic function on the stage: they are part of the wide array of objects necessary in the construction of femininity, but they are also stage props – 'propping up' the action of certain plays. In the introduction to *Staged Properties in Early Modern Drama*, Jonathan Gil Harris and Natasha Korda argue that the word 'prop' could be defined as ' "an object placed *beneath* or *against* a structure" ', which in turn 'resonates with the tendency to regard stage properties as theatrical prostheses, strictly ancillary to and "beneath or against" the main structure, the play text'. But they go on to argue that properties are not necessarily 'trifling' in their status as objects ancillary to the dramatic action.[11] I would argue, in fact, that in Jonson's two comedies to be discussed in this chapter, painted faces, cosmetic recipes and prosthetic women are not only the *objects* contained within, but they are also the *subjects* of the dramatic action, because cosmetics are crucial to the satire of *Epicoene* and to the staging of Wittipol's trick in *The Devil is an Ass*. By foregrounding this relationship between theatricality and cosmetic adornment, Jonson legitimises the rituals of feminine beautification even as he mocks cosmetic practices through his cynical portrayal of prosthetic, painted ladies.

The early modern trope of the scolded husband and his overpowering wife is exploited in one of Jonson's most famous dramatic couples, the Otters. Tom Otter cannot control his wife; thus, the portrayal of him is as satirical as the portrayal of his domineering spouse. However, in Act IV, scene ii, given a false sense of security by the fact that Mistress Otter is not within hearing distance, Otter dismantles her verbally, while he simultaneously exposes the secrets of her dressing table:

> O most vile face! And yet she spends me forty pound a year in mercury and hogs'-bones. All her teeth were made i' the Blackfriars, both her eyebrows i' the Strand, and her hair in Silver Street. Every part o' the town owns a piece of her.
>
> (IV, ii, 82–5)

Mistress Otter loses her mystique; the power of her own deceptive arts has been undermined when Otter takes her apart by cataloguing her cosmetic appendices: face paint, false teeth, eyebrows, and hair. The 'town owns a piece of her', but equally, her body becomes a cosmetic map of London, perhaps giving us some indication about the various locations of cosmetic industry. This diatribe also reflects the common complaint of husbands and moralists that the wife wastes her husband's money (or what Otter perceives as his money) on this ritual. Much of the anti-cosmetic argument hinges on re-empowering the husband and undermining the individuality of early modern woman within the emerging market economy of seventeenth-century London. For example, William Whately's *A Bride-Bush; or A Direction for Married Persons* (1619) reminds husbands that 'the wife hath not power over her owne body', while admonishing them not 'to make ostentation of their wealth'.[12] Equally, Barnabe Rich questions husbands: 'and what is it that doth make so many Citizens and tradesmen so commonly to play Banckrupt, but the excessive pride that is used by their wives?'[13] The author of the controversial crossdressing treatise, *Hic-Mulier*, warns gentlemen and citizens that 'your purses purchase these deformities at rates, both deare and unreasonable'.[14] Significantly, Otter's disparagement of his wife's prosthetic self-fashioning seeks to do the same, that is, undermine his wife's individuality, by emphasising not only the fact that she is piecing herself together artificially, but also that there is an absence at her core.

The prosthetic construction (or deconstruction) of Mistress Otter reinforces the nominal perception of her as less than human. Yet, she is not just, as her name suggests, linked with the animal world, but she becomes, through her cosmetic attachments, a type of machine assembled clumsily from disparate parts:

> she takes herself asunder still when she goes to bed, into some twenty boxes, and about next day noon is put together again, like a great German clock; and so comes forth and rings a tedious larum to the whole house, and then is quiet again for an hour, but for her quarters . . .
>
> (IV, ii, 87–91)

The boxing of Mistress Otter, in part, enacts her husband's fantasies about the dismemberment and containment of his wife, but it is also a grotesque caricature of the female rituals of undressing. The cosmetic ritual not only involves recreating the external body artistically, but also entails taking it apart at the end of the day, and putting the various parts into boxes. Tuke's 'Pictur' of a painted lady reveals that her '*last* care in the *euening* is to have her *box*, and all her *implements* ready against the next morning'.[15] It is Jonson's objective to lay open to mockery these boxes and reveal the secrets behind female beauty. William E. Slights observes that Mistress Otter does not exhibit brutality towards her husband until the secrets of her makeup rites are exposed.[16]

The relationship between secrecy and feminine adornment is a curious one for Jonson, who may indeed equate the two with female monarchy, albeit briefly. Later in the play, Truewit, who is of the opinion that women should keep their cosmetic alterations private, tells Clerimont a story redolent of a popular anecdote about Queen Elizabeth I: 'I once followed a rude fellow into a chamber, where the poor madam, for haste, and troubled, snatched at her peruke to cover her baldness and put it on the wrong way' (I, i, 117–19). To make matters worse, 'the unconscionable knave held her in compliment an hour, with that reversed face, when I still loked when shee should talk from t'other side' (122–4). This story is believed to be a parody of an actual incident that occurred towards the end of Queen Elizabeth I's life. The Queen, like most women, was known to have

> fabricated and protected the way in which she was perceived, in art, in lan-
> guage, and in life. Indeed she hid any signs of her mortality from even her
> closest confidantes. A well-known example links this defiance of age to the
> shattered vanity of an old woman: the Earl of Essex is said to have sealed
> his fate when he burst into the Queen's chamber and saw her: 'in a state of
> undress, her red wig still on its stand, her face bare of the elaborate makeup
> behind which it was not habitually concealed, and her grey hair in wisps
> about her temples'.[17]

Again, in this moment in the play, the Queen's dead body intrudes itself upon the early modern stage; this time it is within a grotesque parody of the crucially secretive preparatory nature of female beauty and, by extension, power.

Mocking the inherent prosthesis of female beauty rituals is, in actual fact, for Jonson a dramatic device. In Act I of *Sejanus, His Fall* (1603) the title character hearkens after the 'mysteries' of women, to which, he believes, Eudmeus (Livia's physician) is privy:

> Which lady sleepes with her owne face, a nights?
> Which puts her teeth off, with her clothes, in court?

Or, with her hayre? Which her complexion?
And, in which boxe she puts it?
                    (*Sejanus*, I, i, 307–10)

This passage does more than remind us of the prosthetic element of
cosmetic beauty, it actually points to Jonsonian dramatic practice. The
lines from *Sejanus* are a duplication of a speech, this time in prose, from
Cynthia's Revels (1600). Moira says she wishes she knew 'which lady
had her own face to lie with her a-nights and which not; who put off
their teeth with their clothes in court, who their hair, who their complexion; and in which box they put it' (*Cynthia's Revels*, IV, i, 127–9). It
appears, then, that Jonson's dramatic comedy is repetitively preoccupied
with female cosmetic rituals, but not just for satirical purposes. There is
an implicit suggestion in Renaissance cosmetic drama that the objects
of cosmetic prosthesis repeatedly find themselves on the stage, and this
is true for Jonsonian comedy. These objects are theatrically virile and
ideologically significant. Their geographical trajectories are practically
spelled out in Otter's outburst in *Epicoene* and in the lists of Italian and
Spanish recipes in *The Devil is an Ass*, both texts describing the journey of
these items and indicating the various meanings they acquire. By the time
Epicoene's Mistress Otter's makeup or the possible pots of ingredients in
The Devil is an Ass used to demonstrate the 'Spanish Lady's' recipes are
on the stage in both plays, their cultural biographies (to use Appadurai's
language) have endowed them with a specific social value that the male
characters attempt repeatedly to undermine.

There was no escaping London's crucial position within the emerging trade economy in the seventeenth century. The circulation of
objects from the cultural marketplace to the stage is often accounted
for within the language and imagery of these play texts. To return to
the 'German clock' image Otter uses to describe his wife, the passage
not only anticipates the cultural anxiety about the moment when 'the
body and technology are conjoined in a literal sense',[18] but it actually
belongs to a tradition of satire in which a woman is seen as a machine;
a conglomeration of marketable parts that fit together awkwardly. In
Love's Labour's Lost, Biron comments upon:

A woman, that is like a German clock,
Still a-repairing, ever out of frame,
And never going aright, being a watch
But being watched that it may still go right.
                    (III, i, 175–8)

The German clock image is cruelly satirical in both texts, but it does
more than characterise woman as 'a collection of moving parts, whose

one function when assembled is to make a loud noise'.[19] 'Still a-repairing' suggests a continuous cycle of cosmetic practice, beginning with the purchase of goods, the 'eye-brows' from Blackfriars, for instance, to the application of these goods, and finally to the display in the public domain (the Exchange, the playhouses), which would encourage the cycle to repeat itself. This is a viable economic cycle within which the beauty industry was beginning to construct itself. Barnabe Rich's diatribe allows us an historical insight into this burgeoning industry when he refers to 'new upstart companies', such as:

> *Attyre-makers* that within these 40 yeares, were not knowne by that name, and but nowe very lately, they kept their louzie commodities of *Perriwigges*, and their other monstrous *Attyres* closed in Boxes, they might not be seene in open show, and those women that did use to weare them, would not buy them but in secret.[20]

However, according to Rich, the days when these commodities were hidden away have given place to a time when merchants 'are not ashamed to sette them forth upon their stalles, such monstrous *May-powles* of *Hayre*, so proportioned and deformed . . . would have drawne the passers by to stand and gaze, and to wonder at them'.[21] Platter's *Travels* reveal that 'the exchange is a great square place like the one in Antwerp . . . where all kinds of fine goods are on show'.[22] Rich also claims that had St Peter 'walked but one turne through the *Royal Exchange* in *London*, he would have been put to his shiftes to have made a true repetition of the new invented vanities'.[23] Rich's statement and Jonson's representation of the college of Ladies demonstrate that the economy of London was being nourished by female consumerism at a powerful rate. Other remarks made by writers in the Renaissance period in England coincide with Rich's observations that all sorts of commodities were becoming increasingly visible in the market exchanges, and that a new phenomenon of voyeuristic shopping and commodity fetishism was beginning to arise.

Constructing Gender in Jonsonian Comedy

'For take away their painted cloaths and then they look like ragged walls; take away their Ruffs, and then they look ruggedly; their coyfes and stomachers, and they are simple to behold; their hair untrust, they look wildly'.[24] Joseph Swetnam argues here that once a woman is bereft of her prosthetic attachments of beauty, all that is left is a wild and rugged frame. But what is to become of her gender since it is essentially constructed via these parts? Anne Balsamo raises an important question about gender and fragmentation: 'what is the relationship between reconstructed body parts and gender identity?'[25] In the seventeenth century the relationship was a primary one, if one takes 'reconstructed body parts' to mean the cosmetic accessories that both Swetnam and Otter catalogue; these 'parts', when pieced together, articulate a specific gender identity. The desire to use makeup and dress fashionably in the early modern period, in some circles was viewed as transgressive behaviour. Furthermore, if a woman was to belong to a secret society, attend social gatherings unescorted, and wear clothing normally worn by men, she would be indulging not only in subversive behaviour, but also in a presumptuous attempt at masculinity; as a result, her 'gender identity' would become blurred, indistinguishable, thus destabilising the social order. Thomas Platter observed on his visit to England in the 1590s that the women here 'have far more liberty than in other lands . . . they often stroll out or drive by coach in very gorgeous clothes'.[26] Taking a much more critical standpoint, William Harrison regrets that 'it is now come to passe, that women are become men'; moreover, he finds that the clothes they wear show their bodies 'rather deformed than commended'.[27] Jonson represents the Lady Collegiates and Mistress Otter in *Epicoene* and Lady Tailbush and Wittipol as the 'Spanish Lady' in *The Devil is an Ass* as belonging to this category of mannish women; but he does so with the use of double prosthesis. They are boy actors, playing women; they will wear makeup to indicate their female roles.

We are introduced to the Lady Collegiates, specifically Lady Haughty in the first scene, through the 'boy's' frightened tale of his encounter with them:

> The gentlewomen play with me and throw me o' the bed and carry me in to my lady; and she kisses me with her oiled face and puts a peruke o' my head and asks me an I will wear her gown; and I say, 'no': and then she hits me a blow o' the ear and calls me innocent and lets me go.
>
> (I, i, 12–16)

Jonson's examination of the transgressed boundaries of gender hierarchy takes root in this scene, as we discover that the boy is painted by an oily kiss, bewigged, and almost forced to dress in women's clothing. It would be apt if the actor playing Clerimont's boy were the same actor who, playing Epicoene, is later dressed and painted like a woman. This would give the scene greater comic effect and sharpen the edge of Jonson's ironic point about the fluidity of gender. The scene also shows the lines between male and female to be malleable. This malleability is even more pronounced in the suggestion of an 'oily kiss', in which gender is feared to be transferred from the Lady to the boy because she stained his face with her oily paints. Literally on stage the actors are both boys. But it gives one pause to wonder how boy actors felt about having their faces painted. Like the famous story of Edward Alleyn's fears of conjuring the devil when he played Faustus, was there a fear on the part of boys of actually becoming women once they had donned the materials of femininity?

Exclusive feminine grouping creates anxiety for the wits of the play, who in turn use satire to guard against the potential threat of the Lady Collegiates. According to Slights, the collegiates are a source of 'tireless secret-making among the young men'.[28] Their sexual ambiguity allows Jonson to draw on a familiar trope in his portrayal of the ladies as monstrous, transgressive, unnatural and potentially grotesque: 'no beaste is prouder than a woman well apparelled'.[29] To add to this, William Averell argues that such women look like neither men nor women, they are 'but plaine monsters'.[30] Barnabe Rich is appalled at having seen some women 'whom *God* and *Nature* had adorned with beauty, with perfection, and with comeliness of personage, that have disguised themselves in that sort, with the deformities of fashion . . . they have transformed themselves to be most deformed and loathsome monsters'.[31] Jonson has Truewit inform us about the existence of such ambiguous Ladies:

> A new foundation, sir, here i' the town, of ladies that call themselves Collegiates, an order between courtiers and country madams, that live from their husbands and give entertainment to all the Wits and Braveries o' the time, as they call 'em: cry down or up what they like or dislike in a brain or a fashion with most masculine or rather hermaphroditical authority, and every day gain to their college some new probationer.
>
> (I, i, 67–74)

Truewit points out that these ladies are the fashion gurus of their time, setting trends and deciding what is 'in' or 'out'. Consequently, the ladies are described as 'hermaphroditical' because of their assertiveness; yet this paradoxical ascription sits uncomfortably with the fact that they are women indulging in womanly behaviour such as beautification. The 'School of vanity' that is the collegiate group provides training similar to the type that Fitzdottrel in *The Devil is an Ass* wants for his wife. However, these gatherings are also charged with the paradoxical combination of masculine assertiveness and feminine vanity. For example, Lady Haughty advises: 'ladies should be mindful of the approach of age, and let no time want his due use' (IV, iii, 36–7). She then argues that birth control is a necessity: 'How should we maintain our youth and beauty else? Many births of a woman make her old, as many crops make the earth barren' (IV, iii, 52–4). In seeking to liberate themselves from the deforming effects of childbirth, the Ladies can be seen to be 'mimicking masculine authority', as they 'transgress the boundaries of womanhood'.[32] These cosmetic meetings call to mind the society of ladies in Renaissance Venice that formed organisations designed to meet regularly, test new recipes and exchange cosmetic products. Jonson mocks this type of female grouping repeatedly, providing his audience with a burlesque of cosmeticised ladies that were fundamentally, for Jonson, the stars of his riveting and visually spectacular satirical theatre.

The anti-crossdressing pamphlets *Hic-Mulier* and *Haec-Vir,* both published in 1620, present a paradoxical picture of the opposition to transvestism. *Hic-Mulier: or, The Man-Woman* fulminates against women who exhibit masculine behaviour; however, the judgement of 'man-woman' is rather complex: 'You that are the gilt durt, which imbroders Play-houses; the painted Statues which adorne Caroches, and the perfumed Carrion that bad men feede on in Brothels'.[33] The masculine behaviour underlined here is the attendance at 'play-houses' and, generally, an overactive presence in the public domain; however, the author of this pamphlet sees face painting and the use of perfume as equally insidious, without distinguishing these practices as effeminate. The pamphlet continues in this vein: 'what can bee more barbarous, then with the glosse of mumming Art, to disguise the beauty of their creations?'[34] Similarly, in *Haec-Vir: or, The Womanish-Man,* which is set up as a dialogue between 'womanish-man' and 'man-woman', 'womanish-man' is interrogated for his seemingly effeminate practices:

> why doe you curle, frizell and powder your hayres . . . why doe you rob us of our Ruffes, of our Eareings, Carkanets, and Mamillions, our Fannes and Feathers, our Busks and French bodies, nay, of our Maskes, Hoods, Shadowed and Shapynas? not so much as the very Art of Painting . . .[35]

Both tracts make a statement about gender and the nature of its construction, but the art of face painting is given no gender ascription whatsoever. Paradoxically, according to the author(s) of these tracts, face paint is manly on a woman, but womanly on a man. However, in the following passage, Robert Burton echoes the moralists of the age who thundered against the effeminacy of men: 'in tricking up themselves men goe beyond women, they weare harlots colours and doe not walke, but jet and dance, hic mulier haec vir, more like players, Butterflies, Babboones, Apes, Antickes then men'.[36] Barbara Millard argues that whether the transgressor of the gender hierarchy is male or female, in *Epicoene* 'we are given the full sense that what is dressed up is base, corrupt, or false'.[37] However, while on the surface, this seems to be true, it is difficult not to observe Jonson's own dressing-up habits. His pageant of painted, hermaphroditic ladies, his boy actors with perukes and oily faces are the 'theatrical stuff' that elsewhere Jonson seemed to reject.

Jonson and the Cosmetics Debate

Neither *Epicoene* nor *The Devil is an Ass* contains stage directions that require someone to paint their face on stage; however, because cosmetics are so prevalent in the language of these plays, there are a variety of ways in which they can become material properties on stage. By describing the rituals of the beautifying process, satirising women who wear makeup and ostentatious apparel through the use of painted boy actors, listing the ingredients of various cosmetic mixtures and the prosthetic accoutrements that comprise fashionability, Jonson provides us with a wide range of possibilities for cosmetic drama. The exchange that takes place between Clerimont and Truewit, in which they present their preferences for either nature or art, reflects the wider social debate about the value of artifice. In *The Defence of Poesy* Sir Philip Sidney defines the 'art of imitation, for so Aristotle termeth it in the word *Mimesis* – that is to say, a representing, counterfeiting, or figuring forth – to speak metaphorically, a speaking picture – with this end, to teach and delight'.[38] Sidney's contention is that if the end of artifice is to 'teach and delight', then it can be praised. However, for some, painting faces differs greatly from writing poetry or painting canvases; for example, John Lyly is famous for his contributions to rhetoric in his elaborate prose work *Euphues*. However, the eponymous hero of *Euphues* argues that when it comes to beauty, the quality of the inward mind should be the cosmetic to beautify the outward form: 'if we respect more the outward shape than the inward habit – good God, into how many mischiefs doe we fall!'[39] Curiously, in an attempt to suggest a difference between cosmetics and aesthetics, Lyly has Euphues reveal the secrets of beauty rituals while blasting women who paint:

> here I could enter into discourse of such fine dames as being in love with their own looks make such coarse account of their passionate lovers; for commonly, if they be adorned with beauty, they be so strait-laced and made so high in the instep . . . Pardon me, gentlewomen, if I unfold every wile and show every wrinkle of women's disposition . . . Let not gentlewomen . . . make too much of their painted sheath . . .[40]

For Jonson, verbal painting, canvas painting and face painting are inextricably linked. In Act V of *Cynthia's Revels* Crites says: 'Then for your ladies . . . all disdaining but their painter and 'pothecary, twixt whom and them there is the reciprocal commerce, their beauties maintain their painters and their painters their beauties' (V, iv, 45–7). In *Epicoene*, Jonson has Truewit illustrate his sentiments about concealing the adornment process through a popular analogy, comparing a master artist to a cosmetic one:

'you see gilders will not work but enclosed. They must not discover how little serves with the help of art to adorn a great deal' (I, i, 107–9). The first scene of *Epicoene* has Clerimont express his utter contempt for ladies who falsify their beauty. As he presents one side of the debate, his personal resentment of Lady Haughty's sexual inaccessibility because of the time she wastes getting dressed resonates loud and clear; he is annoyed that cosmetics allow the Ladies to focus upon their own self-improvement, provide them with autonomy, and give them creative agency:

> A pox of her autumnal face, her pieced beauty: there's no man can be admitted till she be painted and perfumed and washed and scoured, but the boy here; and him she wipes her oiled lips upon, like a sponge.
>
> (I, i, 77–80)

Clerimont's anti-cosmetic judgments rehearse a routine argument against vanity: the time it wastes. John Hoskins's sermon lashes out at women who 'spend whole mornings in purging, powdering and perfuming themselves'.[41] Similarly, Richard Brathwait complains that a woman's 'day might easily be divided: she bestowed the forenoone on her skinne, but the afternoon on a play'.[42] Later, Clerimont's quaint piece of poetry acts as a type of chorus in the scene, while it operates ironically as a vehicle for an anti-cosmetic sentiment:

> Still to be neat, still to be dressed,
> As you were going to a feast;
> Still to be powdered, still perfumed:
> Lady, is it to be presumed,
> Though art's hid causes are not found,
> All is not sweet, all is not sound.
> Give me a look, give me a face,
> That makes simplicity a grace;
> Robes loosely flowing, hair as free:
> Such sweet neglect more taketh me,
> Than all th'adulteries of art.
> They strike mine eyes, but not my heart
>
> (I, i, 82–93)

Jonson has Clerimont inveigh artfully against 'th'adulteries of art', indisputably as a way of mocking the hypocrisy of rhetoricians who wrote tracts and poems opposed to cosmetics. Sandra Clark's study of Elizabethan pamphlets reminds us that pamphleteers often used artful language to make their 'ideas pleasing and persuasive' and that 'style was conceived of as an ornamentation to subject matter'.[43] But early modern rhetoricians and literary theorists tended to distinguish between genuine art and adulterated, cosmetic embellishment; Jonson tries to do the same, but ultimately is unable to escape the cosmetic attachments of dramatic representation. Jonas Barish believes that not just the song, but also the prose of *Epicoene* 'shows a high degree of artful balance, appropriate, perhaps, in a play that makes such a strong plea for artifice as against "naturalness" and simplicity'.[44] However, I would argue that *Epicoene* ambiguously reflects both sides of the moral discourse, the side that stood against the supposed pride and folly of female adornment, and the side that promoted male aesthetic production in all its forms.

Michael Shapiro observes that Truewit's aversion to 'unadorned nature' is ironic.[45] It is ironic because there is no textual evidence to suggest that Truewit believes what he says. He states:

> and I am clearly o' the other side: I love a good dressing before any beauty o' the world. O, a woman is then like a delicate garden; nor is there one kind of it: she may vary every hour, take often counsel of her glasse and choose the best.
>
> (I, i, 94–7)

When he says he is clearly on the opposite side of the debate to Clerimont, he is acknowledging the existence of the debate and his conscious participation in it. It should come as no surprise that occasionally, for pamphleteers, participating in debate was more a case of professing their skill in structuring arguments, perfecting the art of persuasiveness, and challenging equally skilful rhetorical responses. In some instances, the debate would take place within one tract, so that an author might express *both* sides of the argument, affording him the opportunity to flex his syllogistic muscles. John Downame's tract argues both sides of the argument. It begins with a woman asking another what she has against face painting; when the question is answered, the first woman refutes her:

> why may you not also by the same severity destroy and disallow all other things there expressed in that same tone and tenour; as dressing and decking your self with any costly and comely ornaments; all sweet perfumes, all sitting on rich and stately beds, with tables before them.[46]

The speaker in this passage makes an extraordinary suggestion, that there are various forms of cosmetic embellishment, not just the application of face paint; hence she asks why it is acceptable to indulge in one, but not another. One could raise this question about Jonson's artistic practice, his uses of one form of embellishment to speak out against another.

Jonson's incorporation of the cosmetics debate into his drama has a classical precedence. Truewit presents the Ovidian case, which is pro-cosmetics, and Clerimont voices the contempt for feminine adornment found in the satires of Juvenal. Jonas Barish contends that although Jonson exhibits a 'strong natural affinity with Juvenal', he nevertheless 'permitted Ovid's point of view to triumph'.[47] However, it is through

his imitation of Ovid's sentiments in the *Ars Amatoria* that Jonson col-
ourfully ridicules women's vain obsession with physical alteration and
appearance: 'if she have good ears, show 'em; good hair, lay it out; good
legs, wear short clothes; a good hand, discover it often; practise any art
to mend breath, cleanse teeth, repair eyebrows, paint, and profess it'
(I, i, 97–100). Truewit continues his verbal exposition of female dressing rites, but insists paradoxically, like Ovid, that it is necessary to keep
the cosmetic detail and techniques hidden away, so that a lover may
convince himself that his mistress is naturally beautiful. Thus at the
centre of this debate for Jonson is the attraction to deception, the need
for artifice and the dramatist's own conflicting attitude towards this cultural desire. Truewit admits that he has a preference for such deception:

> the doing of it, not the manner: that must be private. Many things that seem
> foul i'the doing do please, done. A lady should indeed study her face when
> we think she sleeps; nor when the doors are shut should men be inquiring;
> all is sacred within then. Is it for us to see their perukes put on, their false
> teeth, their complexion, their eyebrows, their nails?
>
> (I, i, 102–7)

Here Truewit foregrounds the prosthetic nature of beautification,
showing repugnance for the individual, synthetic parts of a woman,
which he uses to support his argument that they must keep it hidden
away. The Ovidian echoes are difficult to miss; in Book III of the *Ars
Amatoria* Ovid advises:

> let no lover find the boxes set out upon the table; your looks are aided by
> dissembled art. Who would not be offended by paint smeared over all the
> face . . . such things will give beauty, but they will be unseemly to look on:
> many things ugly in the doing, please when done.[48]

The art of beautification is fundamentally deceptive; but like for an audience attending a play, the knowledge of this beguilement is half of the fun.
What is ironic about these speeches is that there is an insistence that the
material processes of beauty remain undisclosed, they are simultaneously
revealed in these very detailed arguments that Jonson rehearses. Barish
suggests that Ovid conceals the makeup process, while Jonson 'merci-
lessly strips away the concealment, and in the very moment he seems to
be justifying the lady's preparations reduces them to absurdity by turning
them into a catalogue of grotesque appliances'.[49] Truewit does indeed
tell his audience that a woman's hair, teeth, eyebrows and nails are all
false; however, I disagree with Barish's analysis of Ovid's corresponding
speeches. Ovid's original text creates a vivid picture of the adornment
ritual when he reveals that paint is not just applied, but is 'smeared' on
the face. He also informs his reader that 'oil of wool', 'the juices drawn

from a sheep's unwashed fleece', is a strong cosmetic, and he disapproves of women 'openly taking the mixed marrow of a hind'.[50] Such a detailed account of not only the cosmetic method, but also ingredients used in various mixtures is hardly a 'concealment' of women's customs.

Ingredient Culture

Wittipol, as the Spanish Lady in *The Devil is an Ass*, is well versed in cosmetic recipes and technology. Such technical knowledge was quite common among the ladies of the court and more so among the gentle-women. William Harrison's *Description of England* informs us that older Ladies 'are skilfull in surgurie and distillation of waters, beside sundrie other artificiall practices pertaining to the ornature and com-mendations of their bodies'.[51] What fascinated Jonson, however, was the craft and lore of the recipes and instruction manuals, which Jonson read and which are an intertextual component of his drama. Through Wittipol, Jonson is able to display the fetish for jargon for which he is well known in other plays, such as *The Alchemist*.

Lady Tailbush, eager to know what the Spaniards are putting on their faces, pleads with 'the Spanish Lady' to reveal the secrets of her country's cosmetic potions; Wittipol responds with a recipe, taken from various popular tracts of the period, including *The Secrets of Alexis*. The recipe he cites calls for 'The crumbs o' bread, goat's milk, and whites of eggs' (IV, iv, 22), arguably three of the most common ingredients for a cos-metic face pack. It is likely Jonson obtained this list of ingredients from Giovanni Ruscelli's recipe manual, *The Secrets of Alexis of Piemont: Containing Many Excellent Remedies Against Divers Diseases* (1615), in which one can find a recipe to make the face appear younger; in addi-tion to 'calve's feet', the mixture calls for 'a pound of rice, & let it seeth with crums of fine manchet bread steeped in milk, two pound of fresh butter, and the white of new laid eggs'.[52] However, the crumbs and milk concoction had been around for centuries, and it was a common recipe among Roman women, as Jonson demonstrates in the cosmetics scene in *Catiline*.[53]

The parody of recipe manuals was common among satirists of the age. John Taylor's *Superbiae Flagellum* also satirises particular culinary ingredients: 'Some I have heard of, that have bin so fine, / To wash and bathe themselves in milk or wine, / Or else with whites of egges, their face garnish'.[54] Moralists saw something insidious in the tendency to use food in cosmetics that was meant to feed a husband and family, and Jonson mocks this foible through the series of ingredients listed tirelessly in many of his plays. When Lady Tailbush asks Wittipol about the methods of some of his recipes, he responds with a humorous answer, pointing out the absurdity of instruction manuals for women that call for food in the ingredients: 'Madam, you take your hen, / Plume it, and skin it, cleanse it o' the innards: / Then chop it, bones and all' (IV, iv, 43–5). The seventeenth-century physician, Nicholas Culpeper, also provides a recipe in which one is asked to 'take the decoction of chicken, capon, or hen'.[55]

Annette Drew-Bear argues that 'the hodge-podge of makeup ingredients and the incredible claims for cosmetic rejuvination parody the beauty pretences of the courtly ladies and mock the gullibility of both the ladies and their listeners'.[56] However, I see Jonson's fetishistic cataloguing of ingredients in *The Devil is an Ass* as having more than one satirical function. One, as I have argued, is to mock the household practice of women by making voluminous lists of culinary ingredients meant for purposes of adornment, while suggesting that painted ladies are incompetent housewives. The second function of the catalogues is to speak directly to the desire of English women to imitate 'foreign' fashionable trends. Wittipol claims that there is no fucus like that of the 'argentata of Queen Isabella' (IV, iv, 29).[57] Wittipol goes on to detail the ingredients:

> Your *alum scagliola, or pol di pedra*;
> And *zuccarino*; turpentine of Abezzo,
> Washed in nine waters; *soda di levante*,
> Or your fern ashes; *Benjamin di gotta*;
> *Grasso di serpe*; *porcelletto marino*;
> Oils of *lentisco*; *zucche*; *mugia*—make
> The admirable varnish for the face,
> Gives the right lustre; but two drops rubbed on
> With a piece of scarlet makes a lady of sixty
> Look at sixteen. But, above all, the water
> Of the white hen, of the Lady Estifania's![58]
> (IV, iv, 30–40)

Jonson mingles languages (Spanish, English, Italian) as well as synthetic and natural properties. The use of the conflated languages reflects the important influence European countries were having on the English economy and the individual's self-fashioning habits in the early modern period. Many tracts lash out at such foreign influence and pretension: 'in wearing *Dutch* Hats, with *French* Feathers, *French* Dublets, with Collers after the custom of *Spain*. *Turkish* coats, *Spanish* Hose, *Italian* cloaks'.[59] *The Devil is an Ass* expresses the fear that foreign dressing practices and vanity were not just necessary food for the English economy, they were elements that could infect the purity of the English language.

Significantly, the speeches in *The Devil is an Ass*, taken with the play as a whole, illustrate a topographically familiar London encroached upon by strange elements; specifically, the play reflects a linguistic invasion of foreign terms. Moreover, the mixture of synthetic and natural ingredients corresponds to the combination of Italian and English terminology, both mirroring the fearful fusion of elements in this play, such as the fusion of masculinity and femininity. It can also be argued that Jonson's fethisising of cosmetic terminology duplicates the contemporary cultural fetishising of commodities, especially foreign and cosmetic.

Jon Stratton's work on cultural fetishism focuses on capitalist practices in the nineteenth century. He contends that 'the male eroticisation of the female body is one example of a more general structure founded on a culturally produced aspect of male desire which is the product of male psychosexual fetishistic formation. I call this structure cultural fetishism'.[60] However, I see this process as being already under way in the sixteenth and seventeenth centuries. The construction of the Royal and the New Exchanges brought women out into the public more frequently. The cosmetic commodities provided a feast for female eyes, but the more visible the women, the more they were gazed upon – 'as the fetishistic order spreads, so all women become eroticised'.[61] Thus the pressures of 'looking good' increased. Such pressures encouraged women to spend money on the items that would benefit their physical appearance, thus creating a circle of economic, cosmetic and fetishistic behaviour. Such behaviour contributed to the success of the traders and retailers of artificial and foreign products and to the rise of the beauty industry as a whole.

The Devil is an Ass invites us to examine these social conditions closely. In his interrogation of the economic practices of London society, Jonson denounces the masculine industriousness of women, while undermining the 'exhibitionist' tendencies of the wealthy.[62] Merecraft explains to Wittipol his plans for a new project with Lady Tailbush: 'She and I now / Are on a project for the fact, and venting / Of a new kind of fucus (paint, for ladies)' (III, iv, 48–50); he also reveals that Tailbush 'hopes to get the monopoly / As the reward, of her invention' (53–4). Merecraft informs us that Lady Tailbush has employed her Gentleman Usher to oversee the ingredients and the account books for her new fucus project: 'And Master Ambler, is he named examiner / For the ingredients, and the register / Of what is vented, and shall keep the office' (59–61). Lady Tailbush admits later that she hopes to be the trend-setter in the town. She tells Lady Eitherside that because of her monopoly they will be 'The examples o' the town, and govern it. / I'll lead the fashion still' (IV, ii, 14–15). Lady Tailbush's self-professed desire for the fashionable, her financial cleverness and technical knowledge of cosmetics render her an autonomous, powerful woman, but in Jonson's dramatic world, she becomes a satirical figure and one parodied by Wittipol's disguise.

Conclusion

Lady Tailbush's and Lady Eitherside's exchanges with the 'Spanish Lady' tell us a great deal about the importation of continental cosmetic practices. Tailbush asks: 'But for the manner of Spain! Sweet madam, let us / Be bold now we are in: are all the ladies / There i' the fashion?' (IV, iv, 64–6). She then inquires whether the women wear 'cioppinos'; Wittipol answers that the shoes in Spain are gilded in gold, 'And set with diamonds: and their Spanish pumps / Of perfumed leather' (71–2). Jonson's satire of fashionable English women and their desire to emulate the fads of the Europeans is not unique. Barnabe Rich associates such tendencies with religious transgression: 'Sinne hath her *Merchants,* that will transport the commodities, and will returne backe againe *toies* and *trifles*'.[63] At the heart of all attacks on foreign pride is the apprehension that wearing foreign styles of clothing, using foreign face paints, or indulging in foreign commodities of any kind will eventually lead to a loss of English culture and identity. Cosmetic ingredients, foreign and domestic, could be bought from apothecaries and grocers, both of which may have furnished the playhouses with properties. For example, the contract for building the Rose, located among Henslowe's papers, shows that John Cholmley, a grocer, would be allowed to sell his wares at the theatre.[64] Curiously, Jonson's linguistic inclusion of cosmetic ingredients into his dramatic language and his requirement for cosmetic materiality on the stage, though satirically motivated, celebrates, paradoxically, the cultural diversity of the cosmetics industry, its geographical pervasiveness, and its usefulness to the industry of playing.

Notes

1. J. D., 'A Paradox of a Painted Face'.
2. Ovid, *The Art of Love*, p. 135.
3. Bruster, 'The dramatic life of objects', p. 87.
4. Stallybrass and Jones, *Renaissance Clothing*, p. 24.
5. Austin, *Haec Homo*, p. 120.
6. Welsby (ed.), *Sermons and Society*, p. 50.
7. Burton, *The Anatomy of Melancholy*, p. 96.
8. Downame, *A Discourse of Auxillary Beauty*, p. 44.
9. Wills, *Prosthesis*, p. 97.

10. Ibid. p. 133.
11. Harris and Korda (eds), *Staged Properties*, p. 1.
12. Whately, *A Bride-Bush*, pp. 14, 18.
13. Rich, *The Excellency of good women*, p. 15.
14. Anonymous, *Hic-Mulier*, Sig. C2*v*.
15. Tuke, *A Treatise Against Paint[i]ng*, p. 57.
16. Slights, *Ben Jonson*, p. 83.
17. Cerasano and Wynne-Davies, *Gloriana's Face*, p. 18.
18. Balsamo, *Technologies of the Gendered Body*, p. 21.
19. Leggatt, *Ben Jonson*, p. 53.
20. Rich, *The Honestie of this Age*, p. 24.
21. Ibid. p. 24.
22. Williams (ed), *Thomas Platter's Travels*, p. 157.
23. Rich, *My Ladies Looking Glasse*, p. 20.
24. Swetnam, *The Arraignment*, p. 25.
25. Balsamo, *Technologies of the Gendered Body*, p. 6.
26. Williams, *Thomas Platter's Travels*, p. 182.
27. Harrison, *Description of England*, pp. 170, 171.
28. Slights, *Ben Jonson*, p. 84.
29. Vives, *A very Fruteful and pleasant booke*, Sig. hi*v*.
30. Averell, *A Meruailous Combat*, Sig. B1*v*.
31. Rich, *My Ladies Looking Glasse*, p. 20.
32. Hallahan, 'Silence, eloquence, and chatter', p. 125.
33. Anonymous, *Hic-Mulier*, Sig. A4*r*.
34. Ibid. *Sig.* B1*r–v*.
35. Anonymous, *Haec-Vir*, Sig. C1*r*.
36. Burton, *The Anatomy of Melancholy*, p. 101.
37. Millard, ' "An acceptable violence" ', p. 145.
38. Sidney, *The Defence of Poesy*, p. 217.
39. Lyly, *Euphues*, p. 21.
40. Ibid. p. 22.
41. Welsby (ed.), *Sermons and Society*, p. 101.
42. Brathwait, *The English Gentlewoman*, p. 12.
43. Clark, *The Elizabethan Pamphleteers*, pp. 225, 257.
44. Barish, *Ben Jonson*, p. 149.
45. Shapiro, 'Audience v. dramatist', p. 415.
46. Downame, *A Discourse of Auxillary Beauty*, p. 16.
47. Barish, 'Ovid, Juvenal', p. 214.
48. Ovid, *Ars Amatoria*, p. 133.
49. Barish, 'Ovid, Juvenal', p. 215.
50. Ovid, *Ars Amatoria*, p. 133.
51. Harrison, *Description of England*, p. 272.
52. Ruscelli, *The Secrets of Alexis*, p. 65.
53. Juvenal's Sixth Satire reveals a recipe using such ingredients; mocking women who beautify themselves, he points out: 'She presents a sight as funny as it's appalling, / Her features lost under a damp bread-face pack, / Or greasy with varnishing-cream that clings to her husband's / Lips when the poor man kisses her', and: 'Now she freshens her complexion with asses' milk' (461–4, 469).

54. Taylor, *Superbiae Flagellum, Sig.* C6v.

55. Culpeper, *Arts Master-piece*, p. 16.

56. Drew-Bear, 'Face painting scenes', p. 400.

57. Peter Happé thinks this reference is to Isabella Cortese, an Italian recipe-book author (Happé (ed.), *The Devil is an Ass*, p. 171).

58. 'Lady Estifania' was a famous dealer in perfumes (Ibid. p. 172); she is referred to again in *The Staple of News*: 's good / Right Spanish perfume, the Lady Estifania's', I, ii, 97–8).

59. Anonymous, *England's Vanity*, p. 130.

60. Stratton, *The Desirable Body*, p. 1.

61. Ibid. p. 92.

62. Cave, Schafer and Woolland (eds), *Ben Jonson and Theatre*, p. 36.

63. Rich, *My Ladies Looking Glasse*, p. 13.

64. Foakes (ed), *Henslowe's Diary*.

Chapter 6

Cosmetics and Poetics in Shakespearean Comedy

Towards the end of his life, in the 1590s, an anxious Robert Greene warns his fellow university-educated playwrights about an 'upstart Crow, beautified with our feathers, that with his *Tygrs heart wrapt in a Players hide* supposes he is as well able to bumbast out a blank verse as the best of you'.[1] The usual commentary on this allusion to Shakespeare tends to overlook the use of the word 'beautified' in this ferocious piece of criticism. In early modern England this word was used to describe the process of making something or someone beautiful by artificial means: to 'make faire to the eie or eares' 'adourne', 'to be decked, garnished, dressed, trimmed'; John Florio defines 'to beautify' as 'to paint, to make faire' and his suggested synonyms include 'to furnish, to adorne, to decke, to store, to perfect, to supply. Also to garnish, to trap'.[2] Writers who dispensed recipes for cosmetics also use this term frequently, like Thomas Lupton who suggests seven whole eggs and vinegar to 'beautifie' the face.[3] Greene contends that Shakespeare is a plagiarist, a phoney, and he does so using language that describes cosmetic embellishment. The type of beautifying that Greene refers to is base and false, but also, the implication is that it is transparent. One would know that it is not a natural beauty, but merely beautified. Beautification is a cosmetic process, and most early modern writers would be aware of the contemporary resonance of the word. But in some circles, 'to beautify' also meant 'to honour with some authoritie or dignitie, or doe some honourable pleasure, to doe one worship & credit: to praise, extol, set forth, or commend'.[4] This counter-definition of 'beautifie' forces us to see the gaps being made between worthy and less worthy forms of art.

Greene's use of such a term is pointedly meant to devalue Shakespeare's art, and by doing so he participates in the contemporary debate about poetry. Greene's criticism of Shakespeare is an interrogation of imitative forms of art; but this view seems at odds with Sidney's interpretation of poetry as that which 'beautify[s] our mother tongue'.

Sidney's *The Defense of Poesy* defines poetry as 'an arte of imitation'.[5] Drawing upon what is already in nature to create a new image is the very basis of Renaissance artistic ideology and also underpins Shakespeare's own model of poetics. This concept seems fundamentally synonymous with beautification or cosmetic embellishment. Greene is attempting to devalue Shakespeare's art by evoking the language of cosmetics and he thus reinforces the popular notion that cosmetics are corrosive. Many authors seeking to redefine poetry also used cosmetic metaphors with this quality of cosmetics in mind. When Ben Jonson complains that 'nothing is fashionable, till it bee deform'd; and this is to write like a *Gentlemen*. All must bee as affected, and preposterous as our Gallants cloathes, sweet bags, and night-dressings: in which you would thinke our men lay in, like *Ladies*: it is so curious', he distinguishes between good art and bad art.[6] Jonson sees fashionability as destructive to aesthetic practice, deforming the physical and moral integrity of true art. The analogical richness of cosmetics convinced artists like Jonson that it was possible to draw distinctions between art and artifice. Similarly, in the anti-cosmetic discourse moralists struggle with being able to distinguish a good woman from a bad one:

> They are so paynted so be periwigd, so be poudered, so be perfumed, so bee starched, so be laced … that I cannot tell what mentall virtues they may have that they do keepe inwardly to themselves, but I am sure, to the outward show, it is a hard matter in the church it selfe to distinguish between a good woman, and a bad.[7]

Contemporary literary and artistic theorists who aimed to make sense of their own practices used the idea of paintedness as a defining principle. The distinctions between art and artifice, however, divided critics, some viewing rhetoric as false and effeminate, and others viewing it as a worthy ornament of language. Abraham Fraunce defines 'Eloqution' as 'the ordering & triming of speech'.[8] Similarly, Montaigne sees rhetoric as 'a false, a couzening and deceitfull art'.[9] In fact, he claims rhetorical flourish is a crime worse than face painting:

> those that maske and paint women, commit not so foule a fault; for it is no great losse, though a man see them not, as they were naturally borne and unpainted: Whereas these professe to deceive and beguile not our eies, but our judgement.[10]

Here cosmetics are represented in the traditional moralistic sense; the materials of cosmetic practice are trivialised, while the idea of painted language is deemed more dangerous than the actual poison found in cosmetic unguents.

However, Thomas Wilson, who coined the term 'prosthesis' in *The Arte of Rhetorique* in the middle of the sixteenth century, did so in the context of defining rhetoric as a valuable skill. His tract demonstrates his belief in ornamentation as an important principle in writing or oration. He talks about 'amplification', which 'helpeth forwarde and Oracion, and beautifieth the same with suche delightfull ornamentes'.[11] He then defines 'Exornation' as 'a gorgeous beautifyinge of the tongue with borrowed wordes'; Wilson evokes the counter definition of 'beautifie' when he suggests it is a worthy process enabling the true beauty of oration to come to light. In addition to seeing prosthesis as a valuable element of written and oratorical practice, Wilson promotes the use of 'colours' of rhetoric to 'beautifie' speech.[12] However, like many contemporary theorists, Sidney saw dangers inherent in over ornamenting a poetic text; he defines poetic diction as a 'honny-flowing Matron Eloquence, apparelled, or rather disguised, in a Curtizan-like painted affectation: one time with so farre fette words, that may seeme straungers to any poore English man'.[13] In addition to being deemed foreign, the painted word is gendered feminine, ultimately because of the ancient tradition of attributing affectation to femininity. Jacqueline Lichtenstein notes that 'when Cicero attempted to describe a simple style, he compared it to a woman "without trappings", whose naturalness "suits her well" '.[14] In *The Art of English Poesie*, Puttenham appears to condone the use of rhetorical tropes, 'figures and figuratiue speaches, which be the flowers as it were and coulours that a Poet setteth vpon his language by arte, as the embroderer doth his stone and perle . . . or as th'excellent painter bestoweth the rich Orient coulours vpon his table of pourtraite'.[15] But Puttenham warns that it is easily overdone; to ornament language excessively not only gives the work

> no maner of grace at all, but rather do disfigure the stuffe and spill the whole workmanship taking away all bewtie and good liking from it, no lesse then if the crimson tainte, which should be laid vpon a Ladies lips, or right in the centre of her cheeks should by som ouersight or mishap be applied to her forhead or chinne, it would make (ye would say) but a very ridiculous bewtie.[16]

This passage may be referring to a painter's 'ouersight' when painting a picture, or a woman's when painting herself. Either way, the ambiguity here indicates the intimacy of the relationship between cosmetic and aesthetic production. Even in his defence of poesy, Puttenham is able to use the cosmetic metaphor to define and set the limits of poetic practice, in much the same way as William Webbe, who argued that 'the ornaments of colours must not be too many'.[17] These authors use the term 'colours' to evoke specifically the materiality of the body of the text as well as the human body and the decorative hues used to adorn both. Aristotle's *De Anima* says that it is colour that makes the body visible, and throughout the Middle Ages and early modern period, humoral theory was based on principles of involuntary chromatics. Female beautification complicates this discourse because by painting, women are controlling their colour, thereby they are in control of their identities. Thomas Tuke rages that 'these mixtures and slubber-sauces that they have made their faces of a thousand colours'; a Homilie preaches that any woman 'who can paint her face and curle her heare, and chaunge it into an unnaturall colour, but therein dooth woorke reproofe to her maker, who made her'.[18] Equally, Thomas Nashe tells painted ladies that 'however you disguise your bodies, you lay not on your colours so thick that they sincke into your soules'.[19] Puttenham and Webbe allow the colours of rhetoric, seeing them as necessary elements in making poetic meaning visible to truth, but anti-cosmetic writers oppose women having control over their physical representation through a manipulation of cosmetic colours. Like 'beautifie', the term 'colours' changes meaning as it moves between discourses.

Frances Dolan's important study of the art and nature debate recognises that there are parallel discourses, 'one about poetry and the other about women's face painting', which Dolan sees as constituting 'a single debate that constructs complexly gendered limits on creativity'.[20] Dolan's emphasis in her article is that while male poets are seen to be reinscribing nature through art, women who paint their faces are counterfeiting nature. Dolan argues that 'poetry and face painting are presented as comparable forms of creativity in complex and shifting ways that can, for instance, implicate poetry as effeminate and debased or elevate face painting as a potent means of self-transformation'.[21] What early modern poets and dramatists had in common was their use of tropes to articulate meaning through their oratorical forms of art. Poets had the cosmetic metaphor, but dramatists like Middleton, Webster, Jonson and indeed Shakespeare had cosmetics not only figuratively at their disposal, but materially too. What I have been arguing throughout this book is that Shakespearean and Renaissance drama elevates cosmetics by reinvigorating their metaphorical uses as well as by dynamically reasserting their materiality on the stage.

In this chapter I focus on Shakespeare's use of cosmetic signifiers as ingredients on the stage and tropes on the page, in constructing his own dramatic art in two comedies: *A Midsummer Night's Dream*, and *Love's Labour's Lost*. To do this, it is important first to provide some background about the use of cosmetics in early modern theatre and their utility in staging particularly Elizabethan dramatic devices. Secondly, I will examine how Shakespeare, in these two plays, legitimates cosmetics in artistic terms, by evoking their materiality within a poetic and theatrical context.

Painting Players

While Henslowe's diary tells us a great deal about the repertory of the Admiral's Men, the authors who wrote for them, and the costumes and props required in their productions, it is silent on the subject of cosmetics. Some scholars have taken this to mean that cosmetics were never used on the Elizabethan stage; for example, Andrew Gurr, who has long held that actors wore masks or vizards as opposed to cosmetics, and Mariko Ichikawa have argued that 'some of the items we might expect to find in a modern theatre's wardrobe are curiously absent from the Henslowe lists. The wigs that were needed for the boys to play women, for instance, get no mention'.[22] Also missing from the lists are false beards, staves and cudgels. Gurr and Ichikawa explain this discrepancy by suggesting that 'such items belonged to individual players, or, in the case of women's wigs, to the boys' masters'. The authors have also observed that cosmetics are noticeably absent from the inventory. However, they come to the conclusion that, 'apart from the evidence for blacking up . . . there is little to suggest that using makeup of any kind was a regular custom'.[23] Surely, the same explanation Gurr and Ichikawa provide for the lack of reference to 'false beards, staves' and 'wigs' can be used to account for the absence of cosmetics in the Henslowe papers. Gurr's and Ichikawa's alternative explanation is that when the text suggests that cosmetics may have been used, for example, when Leontes observes that Hermione's wrinkles are absent, it is likely to be 'what Alan C. Dessen calls a "fictional statement" rather than a "theatrical" one, identifying a feature precisely because it is not there, and therefore needs to be specified in words if it is to be imagined'.[24] I would argue, however, that the many references to cosmetics in Shakespearean and Renaissance drama, particularly in plays like *The Second Maiden's Tragedy*, where cosmetics are crucial to the play's action, acknowledge their vital and spectacular presence on the stage rather than specify their absence. Apart from stage directions and linguistic signifiers, there is further evidence that cosmetics were used on the Elizabethan and Jacobean stage in anti-theatrical tracts. Philip Stubbes, for example, refers to actors as 'you masking players, you painted sepulchers, you double dealing ambidexters . . .'[25]

The wide use of cosmetics in early modern society, the anti-cosmetic writings and their close relationship to anti-theatrical tracts provide further evidence that cosmetics were actively used on the stage. As I have noted elsewhere, anti-cosmetic writers often compared painted ladies to plastered or rough-cast walls, suggesting a material link between the craft of painting and cosmetic embellishment. Anti-cosmetic writers like John

Gaule refer bitterly to painted women as 'painted walls', and declare that 'walls and not women have need of such plastering'.[26] Tuke refers to the beautification rituals of women as 'pargetting and rough-casting of their faces'.[27] Shakespeare deploys the same language in *A Midsummer Night's Dream* when he dramatises the rehearsal of the mechanicals' version of 'Pyramus and Thisbe': 'Some man or other must present a Wall; and let him have some plaster, or some loam, or some rough-cast about him to signify a "wall" ' (III, i, 57–60). Bottom suggests implicitly that to signify a wall a player must plaster himself with lime or symbolise this with lead-based paints, which means that Elizabethan actors painted their faces for a variety of significations.

What I am arguing is that material cosmetics were a part of and crucial to the art and design of early modern theatrical production. Actors painted their faces; the dramatists knew it and pointedly register this in the language and imagery they use to evoke cosmetics. Henslowe's diary records the payments to painters and purchases of paint for the walls of the playhouse; the players may have applied this very paint on to their faces (since the pigment would have been composed of the same materials) to signify a woman, a ghost, to portray twins or to dramatise, for example, the presence of both a character's body and spirit explicitly called for in *The Second Maiden's Tragedy*. The vivid picture of beauty that cosmetics produced on the Renaissance stage was demonstrated in the 2005 revival of the Globe Theatre's 2004 production of *Measure for Measure*: it was revived with an all-male cast. The actor playing Mariana was painted with a blend of chalk and almond oil, which was finished with a light dusting of crushed pearl. Not only was Mariana's feminine beauty emphasised, but the concoction also demonstrated that the outdoor amphitheatres of Elizabethan and Jacobean London required a vivid splash of paint on the actors' faces to create a spectacular image of privileged visibility.

Critics have acknowledged the importance of transformation and 'fashioning' in *A Midsummer Night's Dream*. Louis Montrose makes the remarkable suggestion that the play's 'calling of attention to its own artifice, its own artistry – analogizes the powers of parents, princes, and playwrights; the fashioning of children, subjects, and plays'.[28] Makeup contributes in some ways to the play's self-reflexive quality. The meta-theatricality of *A Midsummer Night's Dream* is an aspect of the play's appeal that has long been acknowledged by critics and theatrical productions alike. Judith Dundas claims that 'from antiquity, painting was considered synonymous with mimetic art'.[29] This is true also of the art of face painting, which, as I have shown, was viewed by many anti-cosmetic moralists as an appropriation of divine and male artistic privileges. As we know, drama too is mimetic, an art of imitation. Face painting, or making up is a mimetic art and is, by nature, a performative act. The episode of the rude mechanicals' performance treats dramatic art as comical and ridiculous, but even as it mocks, it simultaneously exposes the visual tricks of the theatre, and the materials of cosmetic construction that acting companies had at their disposal.

Beautifying Poetic Drama

When Hermia and Lysander plan to leave Athens and marry secretly, they hope to do it under the cover of night. Lysander devises their plans and articulates them through poetic imagery evocative of the materials of cosmetic practice and, because of her associations with the moon, of Queen Elizabeth I:

> Tomorrow night, when Phoebe doth behold
> Her silver visage in the wat'ry glass,
> Decking with liquid pearl the bladed grass –
> (I, i, 209–11)

Lysander attempts to 'beautify' their deception through his evocative imagery. The phrase 'wat'ry glass' suggests the instability of the reflected image,[30] suggesting the transience of beauty and perhaps the transience of love. The moon is an apt cosmetic image not just because of its associations with the queen, but also because its beauty or light is borrowed. Helen Hackett argues that in the Queen's old age, the moon became a 'symbol of mutability and fickleness', which was 'an apt means of representing both her decline towards mortality, and her perceived "womanish" irrationality and unpredictability'.[31] Roy Strong's term 'moon cult' describes the authors and painters who represented the Queen metaphorically as the moon.[32] 'Silver visage' is not an inaccurate way to describe the face of the painted Queen, which may well have resembled the moon in its shimmering glow. As some recipe manuals of the period reveal, silver was a desired colour for face paint since it would produce the desired lustre and shine in a woman's face. Della Porta's *Natural Magick*, for example, instructs women that 'with white cleer Silver-coloured Herbs, Shel-Fish, and Stones, the Face might be made white, polished and Silver-coloured'.[33] The reference to 'liquid pearl' also evokes cosmetic materiality, since pearl was known to be an ingredient in some recipes: Thomas Tuke tells us in his treatise that 'all painting or colouring of the face is not of one kind, nor by one meane. The more artificiall and sumptuous is by tincture, the skinne being dried and stained with artificiall colours. This the wealthier sort perform by the helpe of pearle'.[34] Shakespeare transposes the materials of cosmetic practice into the materials of poetic practice in this passage, enabling the shift in perception from one that sees cosmetics as morally corrosive to one that sees cosmetics as a linguistic and material resource for constructing poetry and beautifying language.

Shakespeare's famous borrowings from Ovid's *Metamorphoses* extend to the theme of love's capacity to transform human behaviour, appearance and perspective. The use of flowers in cosmetics was extremely common: some of the period's recipe manuals show an abundance of flowers as important ingredients for facial ointments and perfumes. For example, Thomas Cogan recommends a recipe for a 'sweet water' to wash and lighten the complexion:

> the buddes of red roses, Spike flowers, and Carnation Gilophers, or others, but most of roses, let them drye a day and a night, put to them an ounce of Cloves grosse beaten, and so distill them, after that Sunne the water certaine dayes close stopped . . .[35]

The love juice from the flower is the agent of transformation in the play. It is a symbol of the mystification of the origins of love and, significantly, once placed upon the eyes, it is also a cosmetic agent of mutability, since the play incorporates the belief that cosmetic alteration can influence the rituals of love and courtship. In 1594 Thomas Nashe questioned why women 'ensparkle they theyr eyes with spiritualiz'd distillations?'[36] This reference points to the practice of putting chemicals and waters into the eyes to enlarge the pupils, creating the big, dark eyes praised in neo-Petrarchan poetry.

In addition to using cosmetic metaphors in *A Midsummer Night's Dream*, Shakespeare also dramatises the relationship between love and cosmetic mutability. Helena acknowledges the frustrating necessity of physical alteration and conformity to the popular ideal when she discloses to the audience her self-loathing and envy:

> Call you me fair? That 'fair' again unsay.
> Demetrius loves your fair – O happy fair!
> Your eyes are lodestars, and your tongue's sweet air
> More tuneable than lark to shepherd's ear
> When wheat is green, when hawthorn buds appear.
> Sickness is catching. O, were favour so!
> Your words I catch, fair Hermia; ere I go,
> My ear should catch your voice, my eye your eye,
> My tongue should catch your tongue's sweet melody.
> Were the world mine, Demetrius being bated,
> The rest I'd give to be to you translated.
> O teach me how you look, and with what art
> You sway the motion of Demetrius' heart.
>   (I, i, 181–93)

Helena plays on the various meanings of the word 'fair'; to be 'fair' is to be white and glistening, and to be thus is to be beautiful; hence, to be 'fair' is to be beautiful according to Elizabethan convention. But, in the world of this play, these meanings are reversed. Hermia's dark beauty captures the hearts of both Athenian bachelors, and Helena is confused as to why her socially acceptable beauty is inadequate to attract the man she loves. She asks Hermia for her 'art', beauty tips which would help her to obtain the love of Demetrius, while acknowledging that she must metamorphose into a new ideal. Once she is alone on stage, flummoxed, she laments: 'Through Athens I am thought as fair as she. / But what of that?' (I, i, 227–8). Here Shakespeare powerfully demonstrates the psychological motivation for female beautification. Love, passion, acceptance and social mobility compelled women to take control of their physical attractiveness.

Kim F. Hall has analysed the paradoxical complexities inherent in the attraction to darkness at a time when whiteness was politically, socially, and sexually the desired ideal; she argues that 'the paradox of black beauty creates women who are "beamy black," with "golden hair," "coral lips," and "ivory eyebrows" – curious hybrids of black and white, flesh and jewel'.[37] Traditionally, in Shakespearean comedy the natural or pastoral world is often the place where worlds are freely turned upside down; however, in *A Midsummer Night's Dream* with regard to the normative values of beauty, the opposite is true. With the help of the menacing Puck, the Elizabethan standard of beauty is restored in the woods as both male lovers turn their eyes upon the superficial 'white' beauty of Helena, the 'painted maypole', an ascription which, according to Annette Drew-Bear, suggests that 'cosmetics help' Helena's beauty.[38] Similarly, in Shakespeare's *Sonnets*, the poet expresses his preference for dark beauty because of the taint of 'false art'. R. W. Dent argues that imagination is the chief element in determining the young lovers' 'love choices'. He argues that 'in love there is no art; imagination follows and encourages the mysterious dictates of the heart'.[39] However, this is not entirely true. Shakespeare is insistent, in this play and others, that art *does* accompany love on various levels, including the cosmetic. This should be evident enough in the author's depiction throughout the comedies of love's power to transform and the role that cosmetics play in such processes of conversion. The best example from the *Dream* would no doubt be Titania's comic attraction to Bottom: the magical and cosmetic love juice has blinded Titania to Bottom's deformity (in a cruel attempt by Oberon to control her sexuality) and indeed beautified him in her eyes. By drawing attention to ingredients, the materials that move humans to love, Shakespeare is reinstating their value to poetics and theatrical production. Stephen Greenblatt calls what happens to Bottom a 'comic transformation', but it is more than this.[40] It is a commentary on the power of materials in affecting and influencing human emotions. It is what scared many anti-cosmetic polemicists and it is the basis of the anxieties expressed in anti-theatrical tracts too. In *The Two Gentlemen of Verona* an exchange between Valentine and Speed also illustrates love's transforming power vividly. Valentine has fallen in love with Silvia, and comments on her beauty:

> *Val.* I mean that her beauty is exquisite but her Favour infinite.
> *Speed.* That's because one is painted and the other out of all count.
> *Val.* How painted? And how out of count?
> *Speed.* Marry, sir, so painted to make her fair that no man counts of her beauty.
> *Val.* How esteem'st thou me? I account of her beauty.
> *Speed.* You never saw her since she was deformed.
> *Val.* How long has she been deformed?
> *Speed.* Ever since you loved her.
>
> (II, i, 49–58)

Speed's contention is that Silvia's painted beauty is a commodity with little value in the eyes of those who believe cosmetic art devalues beauty. However, Valentine's love for Silvia has 'deformed' her (or perhaps 'reformed' her), hence his view of her is distorted; her painted beauty, though traditionally devalued, has moved Valentine to love her, and his love has transformed her further because it influences his perception of her beauty. As a result, what he sees is beautiful, albeit cosmeticised.

It is well known that *A Midsummer Night's Dream* dramatises female friendship as inherently unstable owing to the competitive nature of the rituals of love and courtship. Beauty has an important function, of course, in such competition, and Shakespeare playfully satirises this particular dynamic by demonstrating once again how the rituals of cosmetic practice can be translated into dramatic action. After Puck's mistaken use of the love juice, Helena is incapable, at first, of believing she is loveable, while Hermia is stunned that she no longer is. The result is that the two turn upon each other, insulting the most powerful determinant of their success: their beauty. After Lysander has 'recognised' his distaste for dark beauty, through racist slurs, he calls Hermia 'Ethiope' and 'tawny Tartar' (III, ii, 259, 264); the two women insult each other's physicality, devaluing their beauty by first pointing out their flaws, and secondly, by accusing each other of beautifying themselves. Helena attacks Hermia, referring to her as 'puppet', a term, in the Elizabethan period, that would imply that Hermia's beauty is painted or contrived, since anti-cosmetic writers referred to women as 'painted puppets'. Hermia sees this term, however, as a jab at her diminutive height. She consequently refers to Helena as a 'painted maypole' (297), which draws attention to Helena's tallness and her painted face. 'Painted maypole' would also call to mind festive rites in Elizabethan England. During the May festivals children danced around a maypole, which was usually painted with red and white stripes; additionally, face and body painting was a common practice in many festive rituals that marked the changing of the seasons. Linda Woodbridge writes that 'black-face, or faces reddened or whited appears in mummers' plays, morris dance and Maygames'.[41] Makeup has long been a tradition in English forms of representation and Shakespearean festive comedy implicitly evokes these rites in the language, while the painted actors on the stage would recall the material traditions of seasonal occasions. The relations between women are fragile, as the exchanges between Helena and Hermia show. Beauty and its cultivation are key weapons exploited by authors of anti-cosmetic polemics as well as those who published recipes for cosmetics, such as Thomas Jeamson. In his dedicatory epistle to *Artificiall Embellishments* Jeamson tells ladies that he has 'published these Cosmeticks, so Beautifying, that those who use them shall Diana it in company, and with a radiant lustre outshine their thick skind companions, as so many browner Nymphs'.[42] The racial tenor in this excerpt suggests that authors were aware of the privileging of 'fairness' over darker complexions and used it as a marketing strategy to sell their recipes.

Love's Labour's Lost is a play that through its failed unions registers an underlying disapproval of Elizabethan courtship rituals. The poetry that was immured in this cultural exchange is highly charged with the tropes and 'colours' or rhetoric and is, according to Shakespeare, abusive of these colours. Heather Dubrow argues that in his *Sonnets*, Shakespeare 'assails Petrarchism for strained comparisons and unoriginal rhetoric' and because this was traditionally the language of love, he does the same in his romantic comedies.[43] The parallel discourses discussed eloquently by Frances Dolan are set into motion in this play. The complexities sharpen as Shakespeare introduces, again, a racial element into the relations between women, beauty and courtship. The discourses about the colours of poetic expression and the colours of cosmetics are fundamentally and linguistically tied to the notion of race. Cosmetic tincture was an art that was linked to false colours; the lack of authenticity in a painted face gave rise to the notion that beauty no longer has value, particularly white beauty. Kim F. Hall writes 'that the assertion of the naturalness of whiteness is immediately undermined by the possibility of "painting", suggesting a certain unease about the reliability of whiteness as a stable register of value'.[44] This idea operates in Shakespeare's *Sonnets*, particularly 127; however, *Love's Labour's Lost* is devoted to undermining the notion that white beauty is the only visual stimulus to love and sexual desire. The fundamental premise this notion operates under is that white beauty is not true beauty because it is too easily imitated by cosmetic means. Affecting a white complexion is a form of plagiarism, which provides an analogue for the type of artistic criticism Robert Greene levelled at Shakespeare. The result of this type of reasoning is a counter-racist discourse, a competing narrative that suggests to be fair 'white and glistening' was not always the ideal.

Biron (or Berowne, possibly a pun on 'brown') uses this argument in defence of his beloved Rosaline's dark beauty. Initially, the three young lords and their king are bonded together in a commitment to give up love, ladies and luxury, to spend three years in intensive academic study. However, when the four men fall in love, their verbal intelligence is alchemised by their emotions into linguistic foreplay, cunningly using rhetoric and poetic devices to outscore one another. In Act I, scene i, Biron debates with the other men their flawed intention to sacrifice conversing with women until their three-year sabbatical is complete. He argues that their education would be beneficially supplemented with the help of a woman's eyes; Biron relates the neo-Platonic assumption that a man's visionary enlightenment cannot be achieved without looking into the eyes of a beautiful woman:

> Light, seeking light, doth light of light beguile;
> So ere you find where light in darkness lies
> Your light grows dark by losing of your eyes.
> Study me how to please the eye indeed
>   By fixing it upon a fairer eye,
> Who dazzling so, that eye shall be his heed,
>   And give him light that it was blinded by.
>   (I, i, 77–83)

The imagery of light and darkness anticipates the thematic importance of race in the construction of dark beauty and its defence as a rhetorical exercise in this play. In line 77 the word 'light' means life, knowledge, insignificance and beauty (which stems from the word 'fair'). In line 78, Biron continues punning with 'find where light in darkness lies', which means seeking to gain knowledge in ignorance, and also looking for beauty in a dark complexion. Very early on in the play, Biron's defence of black beauty is beginning to take hold, well before the ladies have come to court.

Shakespeare uses cosmetic signifiers in *Love's Labour's Lost* to explore contemporary formulations of poetic models and the correct uses of rhetorical language. Biron himself is a parody of writers who advocate feminine simplicity in a far from plain style. Walter Cohen points out that 'in defending Rosaline's dark beauty, Biron contrasts its naturalness with the cosmetics and false hair of the other ladies. Employing characteristic rhetorical artifice, he denounces female artifice, praising instead the plainness of black'.[45] However, in doing this, Biron reverses the ideal of beauty and confers upon blackness the same power that white once had, the power to inspire imitation:

> *King.*   By heaven, thy love is black as ebony.
> *Biron.*   Is ebony like her? O word divine!
>   A wife of such wood were felicity.
>   O, who can give an oath? Where is a book,
>   That I may swear beauty doth beauty lack
>   If that she learn not of her eye to look?
>   No face is fair that is not full so black.
> *King.*   O Paradox! Black is the badge of hell,
>   The hue of dungeons and the style of night,
>   And beauty's crest becomes the heavens well.
> *Biron.*   Devils soonest tempt, resembling spirits of light.
>   O, if in black my lady's brows bedecked,
>   It mourns that painting and usurping hair
>   Should ravish doters with a false aspect,
>   And therefore is she born to make black fair.
>   Her favour turns the fashion of the days,
>   For native black is counted painting now,
>   And therefore red that would avoid dispraise
>   Paints itself black to imitate her brow.
>   (IV, iii, 243–61)

Biron admits in the closing metaphor that 'red' 'paints itself black to imitate her brow'; it is fashionability, trendy beauty that will determine cosmetic practice according to this view. As long as women conform to the beauty standard, no matter what it requires, they will use artificial means to achieve it. William Carroll spots the paradox in Biron's argument: 'a flushed or naturally red complexion – is now considered painted, or artificial, and, ironically, those who have such complexions must now "paint" themselves black in order to avoid the charge of "painting" '.[46]

On the Renaissance stage a cosmeticised white face signified femininity (in addition to other significations, that is, ghost). The question may arise, then, what 'colours' did the boy actor playing Rosaline have on his face? And for that matter, how is Hermia represented? How did the Lord Chamberlain's Men decide to differentiate between Helena's painted white beauty and Hermia's tawniness? Dympna Callaghan has rightly made much of the uses of blackface and whiteface on the stage and how these material signifiers disclosed the underlying racial tensions inherent in such representations: 'the theatrical depiction of women through cosmetics . . . uncovers the pivotal role of white femininity in the cultural production of race'.[47] But on the early modern stage there are varying categories of race. Rosaline's dark beauty becomes synonymous with blackness, with a racialised beauty. But the actor playing her would nevertheless have a white face composed by cosmetics. The complex construction of racial identities is given added point by a dark beauty being played in whiteface. Was there a liminal mode of racial representation? What markers of racial difference were available to early modern theatre companies? In some recipe manuals of the period there are numerous suggestions for dyeing the hair and eyebrows black. Della Porta's *Natural Magick* recommends 'a decoction of Sage-Leaves, the green husks of Walnuts, Sumacts, Myrtle-berries, Black-berries, Cypress-nits' to make a black dye.[48] Christopher Wirtzung suggests that women should 'burn hasel nuts, as many as you please, in a luted pot, stamp them to powder them make them unto a salve with the tallow of a Bear or Goat; this doth not onely dye black, but maketh also the hair to grow'; alternatively, one can 'take the green shales of Walnuts, stampe them and seethe them, anoint the hair with it, and it will be as black as pitch'.[49] Other manuals, such as *A New Dispensatory of Fourty Physicall Receipts* and *A Precious Treasury of twenty rare Secrets*, contain recipes on 'How to make the Haire of any colour to become black'.[50] The use of dyes and cosmetic paints to wash the hair and eyebrows black allowed for a particular hybridity that provided theatre practitioners with the means to blur the differences between the two primary colours of beauty. Thus Rosaline, being in whiteface, but constructed verbally and poetically through a discourse of blackness, allows us to see the subtle transformations and instability of traditional formulations of beauty were undergoing.

Shakespeare was contributing to an alternative model of preference that was just beginning to take shape. In his 1575 publication of 'The Poesies', George Gascoigne delivers 'A Sonet written in prayse of the browne beauty, compiled for the love of Mistresse E. P. as foloweth':

> The tysing talk which flowes from *Pallas* pooles:
> The painted pale, the (too much) red made white,
> Are smiling baytes to fishe her loving fooles.
> But lo, when eld in toothlesse mouth appears,
> And hoarty heares in steede of beauties blaze:
> Then had I wist, doth teach repenting yeares,
> The tickle track of craftie *Cupides* maze.
> Twixt faire and foule therefore, twixt great and small,
> A lovely nutbrowne face is best of all.[51]

In this sonnet and in Shakespeare's work, the argument is the same: white beauty is too commonly imitated by cosmetics, so the poet must call upon a new 'fashion' of beauty. But 'nutbrowne' is midway between white and black, and suggests an earthy quality to the complexion. It is a natural, unrefined and unsophisticated beauty associated with a rural class. Richard Brome's play *The English Moor, or the Mock-Marriage* dramatises the paradoxical belief that black beauty is undesirable, yet a sign of chastity being a highly desirable trait in early modern love poetry and culture. To prevent suitors from cuckolding him with his wife, Quicksands devises a plan to paint her black with, as the stage directions read, '*A box of black painting*' (III, ii). At first the wife is horrified and asks why he would 'blot out / Heavan's workmanship'. However, in line with Shakespeare's and Gascoigne's argument, he suggests:

> Is not an *Ethiope's* face his workmanship?
> As well as the fair'st Ladies? Nay, more too
> Then hers, that daubs and makes adulterate beauty?
> Some can be pleas'd to lye in oils and paste,
> At sins appointment, which is thrice more wicked.[52]

Quicksands uses this argument to convince his wife that her beauty will stay intact, and that 'Thou does but case thy splendor in a cloud'.[53] As he romanticises the black face paint, Quicksands participates in the encomia to black beauty:

> Now Jewel up
> Into your Ebon casket. And those eyes,
> Those sparkling eyes, that send forth modest anger
> To sindge the hand of so unkind a Painter,
> And make me pull't away and spoyle my work,
> They will look straight like Diamonds, set in lead,
> That yet retain their vertue and their value.[54]

The 'Diamond' eyes 'set in lead' allude to cosmetic facial paint, but also remind us of portraiture. Another example of such poetry by John Collop plays with images of black and white to challenge accepted ideas of beauty:

> Black specks for beauty spots white faces need:
> How fair are you whose face is black indeed?
> See how in hoods and masks some faces hide,
> As if asham'd the white should be espi'd.
> View how a blacker veil o'respreads the skies,
> And a black scarf on earth's rich bosom lies.[55]

Here the intermingling of racial categories is even more pronounced. Darkness within a context of hybridity is idealised here. However, the darkness is beautified with the word 'fair', a word synonymous with the pale, glistening ideal, suggesting that the racially privileged position is still white.

'Fie, painted rhetoric!' Biron claims in his passionate defence of the woman he loves. His distaste for cosmetic beauty is expressed ironically, through his own 'painted rhetoric'; imagining cosmetic beauty as equivalent to rhetorically bedecked language, he advocates the plain style; however, he expresses his advocacy in beautified terms. Through Biron's and the other lovers' speeches it becomes apparent that the play hinges upon the controversy of textual production. Rosaline gives voice to the central analogy of the play when she fuses the art of face painting with the art of poetic inscription: 'O, he hath drawn my picture in his letter' (V, ii, 38). The Princess then asks whether Biron has shown skill in representing Rosaline accurately; she answers: 'Much in the letters, nothing in the praise' (40). What she means is that his writing resembles her, who is 'beauteous as ink' (41), but his poetic praise has exaggerated her beauty in the form of hyperbole, which is a form of cosmetic representation. Textual production is racially charged when looked at from a material perspective. Ink is black and the same materials used to make black ink (galls and alum) were used in some cosmetic preparations as well.

Writing about Aaron the Moor in *Titus Andronicus*, Dympna Callaghan makes an important observation that blackness, unlike whiteness, 'can neither be written on, nor can it be returned to white'.[56] When Rosaline imagines Biron writing her praise, she is also imagining that he is painting her face with words, implying a type of cosmetic inscription upon the surface of her body. But allegorically she cannot be written upon because of her darkness. In his famous anti-cosmetic tract Thomas Tuke makes the link between the female body and the poetic text:

> Her own sweet face is the booke she most lookes on; this she reads over duly every morning, specially if she be to shew her self abroad that day: & as her eie or cha[m]bermaid teaches her, sometimes she blots out pale, & writes *red*.[57]

Imagining the woman as text was not uncommon in early modern writing. The seventeenth-century writer Simion Grahame claims that '*Lady Rhetorick* ever haunts the mouth of a Lover, and with borrowed speeches of braver wits, doeth enlarge their deceit'.[58] In this quotation, the surface of the text becomes even more prescribed, as Grahame likens the *false* gloss of rhetoric to femininity. This was quite common among literary critics of the age and cosmetic language provides metaphorical strategies for distinguishing between writing of ideological substance and superficial glossing. In the same scene, Catherine's response to the Princess's 'beauteous as ink' is 'Fair as a text B in a copy-book', and Rosaline replies: 'Ware pencils, ho! Let me not die your debtor, / My red dominical, my golden letter. / O, that your face were not so full of O's!' (V, ii, 42–5).[59] Pencil was another name for 'paint-brush' in early modern England; Rosaline is again weaving together the imagery of cosmetics, painting and writing. She cleverly fashions the red and gold of Catherine's beauty into the markings in an almanac, giving her beauty a textuality, while alluding to the false nature of such beauty with the sexual suggestion of 'O's' in her face (which the Norton Shakespeare defines as 'pockmarks').[60] Dolan has argued that writers like Sidney and Puttenham fuse together the notion that women's bodies are texts with the idea that male poets are the privileged inscribers with artistic license; she writes, 'by blurring the distinctions between nature and art, between women's bodies and poetry, these texts introduce the possibility of desire between the poet (gendered masculine) and his creation (gendered feminine)'.[61] Biron is figured literally as the male poet and Rosaline as his blank slate; the problem for him, though, is that she is not blank. She attempts to assert and redefine her own value through a creative self-inscription that can only be compared to cosmetic painting. In this context female self-fashioning is revalued as it resists the rhetorical constructions of the male poet.

Love's Labour's Lost is a play in which the contemporary models of poetic praise are challenged and reformulated. Shakespeare uses cosmetic analogies to represent the opposing definitions within a dramatic context. George Gascoigne insisted that 'if I should undertake to write in praise of a gentlewoman, I would neither praise her crystal eye, nor her cherry lip. For these things are *trita et obvia*'.[62] In Act II, scene ii of the play, the princess voices the key concern of many contemporary literary critics, by arguing: 'my beauty, though but mean, / Needs not the painted flourish of your praise. / Beauty is bought by judgement of the eye, / Not uttered by base sale of chapmen's tongues' (II, i, 13–16). Shakespeare challenges the conventional forms of representing female beauty, and he does so within a poetic and highly theatrical context. It is not so much that his text disapproves of such 'painted flourish' (since it indulges in it too), but there is a concern about how poetic expression moves one to love. The materiality of the actor's painted faces give added emphasis to the linguistic narratives that seek to revalue cosmetic representation within an artistic sphere (Figure 6.1). William Carroll cites Bacon's view of Petrarchan conceits: 'it "braves" the value of things; it pumps up a false praise, which leads ultimately to a false or unperceptive poetry'.[63] But by 1610, the notion of what type of art praise needed to be is fundamentally cosmetic: Dudley North's dedication to Lady Mary Wroth instructs that 'verses of love should be verses of pleasure, and to please in love, the smootherfaced the better'.[64] It is around this time that Shakespeare was writing *The Winter's Tale* in which Hermione's body is rendered into art by the materialising agent of paint. The sight of the so-called statue moves Leontes so deeply that he feels compelled to kiss what he now thinks

Figure 6.1 Making up in the tiring house (2002), photo by John Tramper, Shakespeare's Globe Theatre.

is an artefact: 'As it now coldly stands' (V, iii, 36). The painted beauty of Hermione is seductive and humbling all at once, but Paulina has to remind Leontes that 'The ruddiness upon her lip is wet / You'll mar it if you kiss it, stain your own / With oily painting' (V, iii, 81–3). The humour in these lines would not go unmissed by the original audience, who knew that kissing painted ladies was sometimes a messy affair, and with plays like *The Second Maiden's Tragedy* and *The Revenger's Tragedy* already in the repertory of the King's Men by 1611 when *The Winter's Tale* was staged, Jacobean audiences would have been familiar with the popular motif of cosmetic kisses. However, Hermione is not made of stone: she is human and in the marvellous moment of her awakening, Shakespeare provides us with a fusion of art and nature, using beautifying paints to accentuate her patience and virtue: 'This is an art', says Polixenes earlier on in Act IV, 'Which does mend nature – change it rather; but / The art itself is nature' (IV, iv, 95–7).

Notes

1. Greene, *Greens Groats-Worth of Wit*, p. 144.
2. Florio, *Queen Anna's New World of Words*.
3. Lupton, *A Thousand Notable Things*, p. 97.
4. Thomas, *Dictionarium*.
5. Sidney, *The Defense of Poesy*, p. 217.
6. Jonson, *Timber*, p. 581.
7. Rich, *The Honestie of this Age*, p. 15.
8. Fraunce, *The Arcadian Rhetorike*, Sig. A2r.
9. Montaigne, *Essays*, p. 352.
10. Ibid. p. 352.
11. Wilson, *The Arte of Rhetorique*, p. 64.
12. Ibid. p. 94.
13. Sidney, *An Apologie*, Sig., K4v.
14. Lichtenstein, 'Making up representation', p. 78.
15. Puttenham, *The Art of English Poesie*, p. 115.
16. Ibid. p. 115.
17. Webbe, *A Discourse of English Poetrie*, p. 85.
18. Anonymous, 'An Homille Against Excesse of Apparel', p. 222.
19. Nashe, *Christ's Tears*, p. 71.
20. Dolan, 'Taking the pencil out of God's hand', p. 224.
21. Ibid. p. 229.
22. Gurr and Ichikawa, *Staging in Shakespeare's Theatres*, p. 55.
23. Ibid. p. 55
24. Ibid. p. 56
25. Stubbes, *The Anatomie of Abuses*, p. 64.
26. Gaule, *Distractions*, p. 86
27. Tuke, *A Treatise Against Paint[i]ng*, p. 43.
28. Montrose, ' "Shaping fantasies" ', p. 56.
29. Dundas, *Pencils Rhetorique*, p. 15.
30. Sir John Davies uses the image of the 'wat'ry glass' to illustrate the transience of beauty in a satirical verse on the vanity of a 'Lady fair' who turns into a cow as punishment for her pride and lust: 'At first with terror she from thence doth fly; / And loathes the watery glass wherein she gazed' (ll. 17–18) (Sir John Davies, 'Of Human Knowledge', in *The New Oxford Book of Sixteenth Century Verse*, ll. 17–18).
31. Hackett, *Virgin Mother*, p. 183.
32. Strong, *The Cult of Elizabeth*, p. 48.
33. Della Porta, *Natural Magick*, p. 239.

34. Tuke, *A Treatise Against Paint[i]ng*, p. 30.
35. Cogan, *The Haven of Health*, p. 81.
36. Nashe, *Christ's Tears*, p. 70.
37. Hall, *Things of Darkness*, p. 240.
38. Drew-Bear, *Painted Faces*, p. 103.
39. Dent, 'Imagination in *A Midsummer Night's Dream*', pp. 129–30.
40. Greenblatt, 'Introduction to *A Midsummer Night's Dream*', p. 808.
41. Woodbridge, 'Black and white and red all over', p. 27.
42. Jeamson, *Artificiall Embellishments*, Sig. A6v.
43. Dubrow, *Echoes of Desire*, p. 130.
44. Hall, *Things of Darkness*, p. 51.
45. Cohen, 'Introduction to *Love's Labour's Lost*', p. 738.
46. Carroll, *The Great Feast of Language*, p. 186.
47. Callaghan, *Shakespeare Without Women*, p. 84.
48. Della Porta, *Natural Magick*, p. 235.
49. Wirtzung, *The General Practise of Physick*, p. 62.
50. Anonymous, *A Precious Treasury*, p. 2.
51. Gascoigne, 'The Poesies', p. 332.
52. Brome, *The English Moor*, pp. 37–8.
53. Ibid. p. 38.
54. Ibid. p. 38.
55. John Collop, 'On an Ethiopian Beauty, M.S.', in Hall, *Things of Darkness*, 'Appendix', p. 279.
56. Callaghan, *Shakespeare Without Women*, p. 80.
57. Tuke, *A Treatise Against Paint[i]ng*, pp. 57–62.
58. Grahame, *The Anatomie of Hvmors*, p. 29.
59. Significantly 'copy-book' is defined as 'a book in which copies are written or printed for learners to imitate' (Schmidt, *Shakespeare Lexicon*, p. 246).
60. Cohen, 'Notes to *Love's Labour's Lost*', in *The Norton Shakespeare*, p. 780.
61. Dolan, 'Taking the pencil our of God's hand', p. 227.
62. Gascoigne, *A Primer of English Poetry* (1575), in Vickers (ed.), *English Renaissance Literary Criticism*, p. 163.
63. Carroll, *The Great Feast of Language*, p. 107.
64. North, *Against Obscurity in love poetry* (1610), in Vickers (ed.), *English Renaissance Literary Criticism*, p. 508.

Chapter 7

'Deceived with ornament': Shakespeare's Venice

Her forehead fayre is like a brazen hill
Whose wrinckled furrows which her age doth breed
Are dawbed full of *Venice* chalke for need[1]

In 1616 Barnabe Rich complained that 'we have spoyled the *Venetian Curtizans* of their alluring vanities, to decke our *English* women in the new fashion.'[2] Acknowledging the influence Venice had upon English self-presentation, Rich contributes to contemporary assumptions about the Italian city by aligning it with female sexuality and commerce. Rich also reminds us, in his reference to the Venetian courtesans, of the relationship within the English imagination between uncontrollable female desire and Venice itself that fuelled much of its dramatic representation. The painted courtesan embodies the connections between cosmetics, female sexuality and commercial exchange. One of the dedicatory poems on the opening pages of Lewes Lewkenor's 1599 translation of Contarini's *The Commonwealth and Gouernment of Venice* describes the city as a maiden that has been misled into vanity by the corruption of the age:

Now I prognositcate thy ruinous case,
When thou shalt from thy Adriatique seas,
View in this Ocean Isle thy painted face,
In these pure colours coyest eyes to please,
Then gazing in thy shadowes peerles eye,
Enamour'd like *Narcissus* thou shalt dye.[3]

Paradoxically, Thomas Coryat's criticism of the cosmetic practices of the Venetian courtesans is at times curiously detailed, giving English women the opportunity to emulate the rituals that are being denigrated. For example, Coryat's account of a particular cosmetic ritual of the courtesans in Venice allows him, inadvertently, to provide a recipe for dyeing the hair blond:

all the women of Venice every Saturday in the afternoone doe use to annoint their hair with oyle, or some other drugs, to the end to make it looke faire that is whitish ... first they put on a readen hat, without any crowne at all, but brimmes of exceeding breadth and largeness: then they sit in some sun-shining place in a chamber of some other secret roome, where having a looking-glass before them they sophisticate and dye their haire with the foresaid drugs, and after cast it backe round upon the brimmes of the hat, till it be thoroughly dried with the heat of the sunne: and last of all they curle it up in curious locks with a frisling or crisping pinne of iron.[4]

The sensuous oils and drugs, the looking glass and curling iron are the objects of the European cosmetics industry that were eventually trans-ported into England. Many recipe manuals printed in England, whether they are translations of Italian books, such as Girolamo Ruscelli's *The Secrets of Alexis*, or English books including Hugh Platt's *Delights for Ladies*, contained recipes for dyeing the hair blond, and this technique, originally a foreign custom, was no doubt well known in England and perhaps made more famous by Coryat's narrative. Fascinatingly, this method of hair dyeing is pictured in an illustration published before Coryat's book. Cesare Vecellio's collection of fashion plates, *Degli Habiti Antichi, Et Moderni* (1590), contains engravings that represent contem-porary fashions in sixteenth-century Italy, including one (Figure 7.1) that details a courtesan wearing a 'readen hat' with no 'crowne' through which her hair has been pulled; she is seen anointing her hair with the dyes or 'drugs' pictured in jars and pots at her feet. The wide-brimmed hat is known as a 'Solana' and the bleaching of the hair using saffron and lemon juice or rhubarb came to be known as 'the *arte biondeggiante*'.[5] The sun is breaking through the clouds to suggest that after she anoints her hair, the lady will sit leisurely in the sun for the 'afternoone'. Additionally, a looking glass hangs from the balcony wall, not only signifying vanity, but also evoking the multiple meanings attached to mirrors in Renaissance culture.

To many, a looking glass was a metonym for an instructional or reli-gious text intended for spiritual reflection. Rich explores the metaphori-cal meaning of mirrors in his seventeenth-century tract, *My Ladies Looking Glasse* (1616); he suggests that moralising texts act as spiritual looking glasses with a corrective function enabling a reader to 'survey the interior part of the soule'.[6] Materially, it is also a reminder of Venice's pre-eminence in the manufacturing of fashionable looking glasses: Contarini boasts that 'they make very cleare and goodly glasses, com-monly called Christal glasses, which are thence transported into al coun-tries'.[7] Nevertheless, it is interesting to consider that Coryat's description in *Crudities* could serve as a gloss on a picture engraved much earlier, and the possibility that during his visit to Italy, Coryat came across Vecellio's sixteenth-century fashion magazine rather than gaining access

Figure 7.1   Hair dyer, Cesare Vecellio, *Degli Habiti Antichi, Et Moderni* (1590)
810.i.2, by permission of the British Library.

to the secret cosmetic rituals of the Venetian courtesans. Additionally, there were many recipe manuals in Venice providing the same instructions as Coryat's description; for example, Giovanni Marinello, a Venetian physician, 'published a comprehensive book on female beauty and adornment containing, among hundreds of recommendations, more than two dozen recipes for making dyes to bleach hair blond'.[8]

Venice was an influential centre for trade and this was primarily due to its fortunate global positioning. Lewkenor's translation tells us that it was Venice's geographical situation that made it 'opportune & commodious to the aboundance of all thinges that are behoouefull to the citizens, as also for traffiqur of all sorttes of merchandise, in manner with all nations of the worlde'.[9] Venice was, as Jerry Brotton puts it, 'a commercial intermediary, able to receive commodities from . . . Eastern bazaars, and then transport them to the markets of northern Europe', suggesting that the city itself provided a type of alchemy whereby the value of foreign goods is refined or their meanings transformed through this commercial filtering system.[10] It is only natural that Venice would be a principal source for imported cosmetics such as hair dyes, oils and perfumes, and, reputedly, the best ceruse came from there; 'since the ceruse produced in England was generally adulterated with common whiting, the better apothecaries would only use the Venetian product'.[11] It was a venture in which women were actively participating; Venetian ladies even 'formed a society (and elected offices) for learning and testing new discoveries in the cosmetic arts'.[12] Such arts required a substantial knowledge of the principles and practicalities of science and alchemy as Isabella Cortese's copious recipe manual, *I Secreti della Signora Isabella Cortese* (Venice: 1591), would suggest. Cortese's popular manual went through seven printings between 1561 and 1677, according to Rudolph Bell, and contains over 200 'guaranteed potions for every need', including recipes for 'bleaching hair, skin and clothing'.[13] The cosmetics industry of Venice signified for English dramatists the alluring captivation of the world's gaze. Commercially the city merchants were beginning to fear the loss of Venice's global monopoly and therefore seemed actively to have been engaged in their own cosmetic strategies. Vecellio's engraving, then, can be taken as a pictorial metaphor for Venice itself, representing the city's use of foreign agents to enhance its own attractiveness and the economic viability of its body.

Another figure often associated with Venice is the mountebank who, as Coryat tells his reader, was a popular resource for cosmetic ingredients: 'the principall things that they sell are oyles, soveraigne waters, amorous songs printed, Apothecary drugs, and a Commonweale of other trifles'.[14] Ben Jonson's *Volpone* satirises this popular figure, who promised eternal beauty through the use of mysterious potions and powders. Volpone disguises himself as a mountebank at the window of Celia and flouts his cosmetic materials:

> it is the powder that, made Venus a goddess (given her by Apollo), that kept her perpetually young, cleared her wrinkles, firmed her gums, filled her skin, colored her hair . . . in youth it perpetually preserves, in age restores the complexion, seats your teeth, did they dance like virginal jacks, firm as a wall: makes them white as ivory.
>
> (II, i, 375–90)

Jonson has Volpone evoke the ancient and mysterious promises, the beauty 'secrets' and the exoticism of the East that was so closely linked to Venice in the early modern imagination. He simultaneously attempts to reveal to his audience the perceived corruption behind the industry of beauty as it stood in the Renaissance. This extract also contributes to the social narrative warning English women about the physical deterioration of their national identity. Without a doubt, cosmetics were significant in the formation of English perceptions of Venetian women, courtesans and the stage presence of Venice itself.

Cosmetic Materials in *The Merchant of Venice*

In Shakespeare's Venetian plays, Venice is the ever-present backdrop against which Shakespeare investigates the links between desire, economic greed, marriage and sexuality. Significantly, Venice emerges as a character with its own particularised set of associations with cosmetic production and consumption, deriving from its cultural reputation. Virginia Mason Vaughan points out that contemporary descriptions of Venice were part of a discourse, which created what she terms the 'myth of Venice'. The descriptions of the city's luxuriousness, wealth and ornament contributed to its bewitching quality, but also established Venice as a 'source of anxiety and tension'.[15] Furthermore, these associations are tied to Shakespeare's use of cosmetic signifiers in *The Merchant of Venice* and *Othello*. Shakespeare provides his audience with a gleaming picture of a city in which beautification is not confined strictly to feminine practice.

Shakespeare's plays challenge the moralistic discourse on cosmetics by evoking the materiality of cosmetics, while cosmetic signifiers function on the linguistic and metaphorical levels as well. Cosmetics unlock the cultural anxieties and fantasies about self-fashioning, an activity that was inextricable from global trade in early modern England, and the European ingredient culture of the sixteenth and seventeenth centuries is reflected in the Shakespearean representation of Venice, where the commercial ambitions of the Venetian elite, and the desire for external transformation converge. This representation is achieved in part through a discourse of domestic engineering, specifically, the terms of measurement found in early modern recipes, words like 'dram' and 'pound', used in these plays within social and legal contexts.

The most repeated phrase in *The Merchant of Venice* is 'pound of flesh', which, I am suggesting, may gesture toward the materiality of cosmetic production and consumption. When exchanged goods are consumed they are absorbed bodily; hence, metaphorically, flesh is what has been exchanged. Shylock brings this to light by seeking Antonio's actual flesh as interest. Viewed in this light, the commercial movement of cosmetic materials is literally the trafficking of female flesh, and cosmetics themselves can be viewed as a type of interest. To purchase 'beauty by the weight' is a commercial exercise for the purpose of adding value to a female body and therefore making it fundamentally more marketable. Bassanio is very much aware of this in the play, and this is evidenced by his blatant admission that it is Portia's wealth and beauty that motivates him to borrow money in the first place: 'In Belmont is a lady richly left. / And she is fair, and, fairer than that word, / Of wondrous virtues' (I, i, 161–3). Critics have yet to make the connection between the pound of flesh and beauty purchased by the weight and how this relationship is connected to a discourse of cosmetics in *The Merchant of Venice*.

An examination of the casket scenes, the caskets' associations with commerce and their material identities as ingredients in the cosmetic recipes of the period will bring to the foreground Shakespeare's use of cosmetic metaphors and materials to comment upon the material influences upon human relationships. The strategic placement of the casket scenes in Belmont allows us to glimpse the far-reaching arms of Venetian commercial and material interests, and, contrary to many critical accounts, demonstrates the interchangeability of the two cities in that both house communities engaged in corporeal trafficking. To understand how Shakespeare encodes *The Merchant of Venice* with cosmetic signifiers, we must examine carefully these scenes; even more importantly, we should determine what Shakespeare meant by 'casket'. While many critics have suggested that these caskets refer to boxes, perhaps resembling coffins, 'casket' was also a term referring to decorative containers for either perfume, jewellery, cosmetics or miniatures, shaped much like the one in Figure 7.2: this alabaster casket dating from the early seventeenth century is perhaps typical of the type of objects referenced in the play. If this is indeed the case,

Figure 7.2   The Dyneley Casket, silver-gilt alabaster (1600–10), V & A Images/
Victoria and Albert Museum.

then the casket scenes carry explicit associations with cosmetics at first glance. Curiously, the caskets are located behind a curtain on stage, recalling the contemporary practice of veiling art, and this suggests powerfully the impenetrable secrets of femininity that inspire anti-cosmetic rhetoric. The caskets operate as cosmetic signifiers and their placement behind curtains makes this, ironically, rather overt. Like cosmetics, one of the caskets actually contains Portia's image, and the contest becomes a quest as each suitor seeks to locate the painted image of Portia. But one by one they fail, including Bassanio because he is unable, at first glance, to discern the true Portia from her painted image when he dotes upon the miniature.

In his analysis of the ideology of objects, Slavoj Žižek argues that 'indi-viduals know very well that there are relations between people behind the relations between things'.[16] The way in which Bassanio relates to the lead casket and the lead-painted portrait within predetermines his eventual relation to Portia: it is marked by a physical adoration that is inspired by paint. The double function of cosmetics on the stage is important here. As I have said, cosmetics on an actor's face signal his staged identity, but even if a boy actor is painted, the woman he is playing may have natural beauty, like the Wife in the sub-plot of *The Second Maiden's Tragedy*. It is likely that Portia would indeed have been a painted lady given the per-vasive use of cosmetics among Venetian ladies (and no doubt ladies from

Belmont). In fact, Shakespeare provides multiple painted representations in Bassanio's casket scene: the painted actor, Portia as painted lady, and her painted miniature.

In the first casket scene, when Morocco deliberates upon his choice, the Prince makes much of hazarding all for lead:

> I will survey th'inscriptions back again.
> What says this leaden casket?
> 'Who chooseth me must give and hazard all he hath.'
> Must give, for what? For lead? Hazard for lead?
> This casket threatens. Men that hazard all
> Do it in hope of fair advantages.
>
> (II, vii, 14–19)

Insightfully, he is aware that the 'casket threatens'. The casket episodes have a lot more to teach us than we have previously believed and we can no longer ignore the encoded link between the lead casket and lead-based cosmetics. As I demonstrated in the Introduction to this book, some of the period's love poetry compares the faces of women to gold and silver, and there are cosmetic recipes requiring gold and silver as ingredients, which suggest an implicit relationship between these caskets and the cosmetic theme.[17] But why have we not examined more considerably the significance of the lead casket and its material operation in the play as a whole? Morocco claims:

> One of these three contains her heavenly picture.
> Is't like that lead contains her? 'Twere damnation
> To think so base a thought. It were too gross
> To rib her cerecloth in the obscure grave.
>
> (II, vii, 48–51)

By elevating Portia's status to that of a Petrarchan goddess, whose 'shrine' he has come to kiss, the Prince is unable to imagine that she would be so debased as to allow lead to 'contain her', even though it is more than likely that she is no doubt subtly painted with a blend of vinegar and white lead. Clearly, Morocco is unable to see Portia in other than idealised terms; it is this quality in the Prince that compels him to choose the gold. Morocco's praise of Portia contains more than a Petrarchan strain. John Manningham's diary voices the disenchanted view of such praise, while seeing it as an insidious cosmetic strategy for self-promotion and sycophancy: 'Prayse is a kinde of paynt which makes everything seem better than it is'.[18] But as we saw in Chapter 6, there were competing notions of how best to present encomia. In this context, however, apart from the racialised impulse behind Portia's private rejection of him, it is his desire to conform to the poetic practice of insubstantially idealising female beauty by endorsing its commercial value (seeing it as synonymous with gold) that disqualifies him from the contest.

What appears to be operating in the casket scenes of *The Merchant of Venice* is the old adage that gaudily painted surfaces have a double function: seducing and entrapping:

> All that glisters is not gold;
> Often have you heard that told.
> Many a man his life hath sold
> But my outside to behold.
> Gilded tombs do worms infold.
> (II, vii, 65–9)

Significantly, entrapment was one of the chief accusations anti-cosmetic authors levelled at painted ladies. Thomas Gainsford echoes this belief, and suggests that, when confronted with a painted harlot, a man's entire being is at stake, his spiritual, emotional self as well as the sensual, bodily self: 'Beauty of a curtisan is a meete trap to deceive one, and a worse danger: for the one peradventure catcheth but our goods, or bodies; but the other ravisheth both our senses and our harts'.[19] Curiously, while the gold and silver caskets trap those easily ensnared by the seemingly beautiful, the lead casket also traps Bassanio into disclosing his own proclivities to ornament as he gazes upon and seems to worship the counterfeit portrait of Portia. Annette Drew-Bear contends that 'the play exalts the virtuous plainness of the lead casket over the deceptive guile of the gold and silver caskets'.[20] And Jyotsna Singh contends that Bassanio's 'correct choice fulfils her [Portia's] expectation that "if you love me, you will find me out" (III, ii, 41)'.[21] Yet Bassanio's choice of lead, with its cosmetic associations, can be equally beguiling in its supposed simplicity, and this *trompe l'oeil* is one example of the seductive power of objects. Shakespeare's art here is indeed a beautifying strategy requiring metaphorical and theatrical properties that allude to the powerful material influences that shape human relationships.

By arguing that the caskets represent women, Freud's essay on the casket scenes in *The Merchant of Venice* confirms that the objectification of Portia is signified through material objects, specifically, here, gold, silver and lead, which are stage properties, cosmetic ingredients, and poetic images used to describe the beauty of women. Freud writes that the caskets are:

> women, symbols of what is essential in woman, and therefore of a woman herself, like coffers, boxes, cases, baskets, and so on. If we boldly assume that these are symbolic substitutions of the same kind in myths as well, then the casket scene in *The Merchant of Venice* really becomes the inversion we

suspected . . . we see that the theme is a human one, *a man's choice between three women*.[22]

He then traces this symbolic episode to another Shakespeare play, *King Lear*, seeing Goneril, Regan and Cordelia as representing the qualities within the caskets. Cordelia, of course, represents simplicity, plainness and virtue. However, Freud argues that she 'makes herself unrecognizable, inconspicuous like lead, she remains dumb, she "loves and is silent" '.[23] The lead casket *is* 'inconspicuous', as white lead-based cosmetic beauty was *meant* to be. Some writers instruct men how to discern a woman's painted face, leading us to conclude that although many cosmetic bases were thick in substance, some painted faces were undetectable. Thomas Lupton, writing in the early seventeenth century, recommends that 'if one hath eaten Garlick or comminseed, breath on the face of a woman that is painted, the colour will vanish away straight, if not: then her colour remaines as it did before'.[24] Humorous as this method of detecting a painted face is, it nevertheless suggests that some face paints were applied subtly, perhaps artfully. Further evidence of this comes from Della Porta's *Natural Magick*, which contains instructions similar to Lupton's: 'Chew Grains of Cummin, or a Clove of Garlick, and speak close by her; if it be natural, it will remain; but counterfeit with Ceruss or Quick-silver, it presently decays'.[25] Della Porta also offers a recipe for 'A Fucus that cannot be detected', which is 'cunningly made, that it will delude all men'.[26] And Tuke's tract reminds his readers of a story told by Erasmus:

> *Erasmus* telles a prittie tale of a company of gallants, that were met at a banquet, al of them having their faces painted, unlesse one *Phryne*, the fairest of them. It was thus; Their manner was at their feasts to make certaine sports or ieasts, and that whatsoever any of them began to doe, the rest must all of them follow. Now *Phryne* washt her face in a basin of water: and because her natural beauty was good . . . she lookt nothing the worser, but the better rather for it: whereas the rest doing the like, because they were al painted, they were all disgraced.[27]

This story is recounted elsewhere and has echoes in the banquet scene of *Timon of Athens*.[28] Clearly, there is a narrative pretext for the undetectability of the lead casket's cosmetic identity.

The silver casket is not only tied to money, but to cosmetics as well. Aragon's choice of silver establishes his attraction to externalities and physical wealth. Although he appears to show more wisdom than the unfortunate Morocco when he reads the message upon the golden casket – '"What many men desire"– that "many" may be meant / By the fool multitude, that choose by show' (II, ix, 24–5) – he chooses the bright silver. Believing that all people should have what they deserve, Aragon is seen to be a strong advocate for the social order, while implicitly calling to mind the Tudor sumptuary laws:

> Let none presume
> To wear an undeserved dignity.
> O, that estates, degrees, and offices,
> Were not derived corruptly, and that clear honour
> Were purchased by the merit of the wearer!
> (II, ix, 38–42)

Aragon's punishment is a 'blinking idiot', which tells him:

> Some there be that shadows kiss;
> Such have but a shadow's bliss.
> There be fools alive, iwis,
> Silvered o'er; and so was this.
> (65–8)

The term 'silvered o'er' denotes a cosmetic action. Aragon's choice illustrates the tendency in a commercial society to praise the burgeoning capitalist ideology, which insists that financial rewards are deserved by merchants and aristocracy, who exhibit a greed that is thinly veiled by exploration and enterprise. Silver was more than likely a hue used in indoor theatrical performances that were only lit by candlelight. The use of silver, gold or pearl would allow the face of the actor to glisten in dimly lit halls and was therefore associated with court masques, dances and interludes. Both Morocco and Aragon objectify Portia economically and poetically by imagining her as a gold or silver artefact. Her face would likely glisten with these hues reflecting her material correspondence to the caskets and thereby suggesting her raised status in the play. The complex irony, however, is that Bassanio objectifies her through his fixation upon lead, which was a baser ingredient, but one used by women of all social levels. Curiously, a white lead foundation might be brushed with a silver, gold or pearl powder, providing an analogue for a social intermingling that is made possible through the acquisition of worldly objects that made merchants wealthier than previously imagined.

This casket scene is contained within an artistic framework; Portia uses art to manipulate perception, giving her a creative agency her father could never have predicted. As Bassanio deliberates, Portia has one of her train sing a song:

> Tell me where is fancy bred,
> Or in the heart, or in the head?
> How begot, how nourished
>   Reply, reply.
> It is engendered in the eyes,
> With gazing fed; and fancy dies

In the cradle where it lies.
Let us all ring fancy's knell.
I'll begin it: ding, dong, bell
(III, ii, 63–71)

The song suggests that 'fancy' is the sensation one feels when initially attracted to outward beauty. The song is a subtle hint to Bassanio to choose the least of the showy caskets, as is the obtrusive rhyme in the first stanza of the song. The death of fancy occurs when one's gaze is able to penetrate a painted surface, and love the body and soul beneath. We are slyly led to believe that this is just what Bassanio will do. Freud suggests that Bassanio's choice of lead is a result of his attraction to truth or 'plainness'.[29] But how, in a culture that is well aware of the use of lead in cosmetics, can lead be synonymous with truth? As we have seen, many writers and clergymen spoke out against the lies that they believed cosmetics told. Bassanio's understanding of the attractiveness of painted beauty may well guide his hand towards the lead, as much as Portia's musical clues. In his aside Bassanio laments the fact that 'the world is still deceived with ornament' (III, ii, 74), which is rich coming from one who has borrowed the trappings of wealth to make him seem the perfect suitor. In order to compete in an economic system that violates Biblical laws against usury and greed, however, Bassanio has had to subscribe to the practices that are a by-product of the commercially-minded society Shakespeare indicts. Shylock's open business practices and unapologetic advocacy of interest are then clearly seen in direct opposition to the 'Christian fools with varnished faces' (II, v, 32).

The rest of Bassanio's speech stems from this indictment. Marginally conscious of his own deceptive appearance, Bassanio bemoans the social pervasiveness of cosmetic gloss, conventionally reflecting the anti-cosmetic diatribes of the age. Equally, Bassanio confirms my argument that forms of beautification intrude inviolably upon the systematised structures of early modern society: textual, social, religious, professional, legal and commercial:

In law, what plea so tainted and corrupt
But, being seasoned with a gracious voice,
Obscures the show of evil? In religion,
What damned error but some sober brow
Will bless it and approve it with a text,
Hiding the grossness with fair ornament?
There is no vice so simple but assumes
Some mark of virtue on his outward parts.
How many cowards whose hearts are all as false
As stairs of sand, wear yet upon their chins

The beards of Hercules and frowning Mars,
Who, inward searched, have livers white as milk?
And these assume but valours excrement
To render them redoubted. Look on beauty
And you shall see 'tis purchased by the weight,
Which therein works a miracle in nature,
Making them lightest that wear most of it.
So those are crisped, snaky, golden locks
Which makes such wanton gambols with the wind
Upon supposed fairness, often known
To be the dowry of a second head,
The skull that bred them in the sepulchre.
Thus ornament is but the guiled shore
To a most dangerous sea, the beauteous scarf
Veiling an Indian beauty; in a word,
The seeming truth which cunning times put on
To entrap the wisest.

(III, ii, 75–101)

The phrase 'beauty purchased by the weight', signalling the economic materiality of cosmetics, resonates with the repeated phrase 'pound of flesh', suggesting a complex network of associations between cosmetic materiality, the Venetian mercantile economy and the relationship between female beauty and commercial exchange. The practice of usury, charging interest on an existing product, adds to its value, giving it a prosthetic quality. Cosmetic beauty is a type of usury in this regard. This system of associations indicates that Bassanio's speech does more than evoke a clichéd distrust of outward show; instead, it uncovers the consumptive hypocrisy of the Venetian characters in the play. By denigrating the cosmetic facades of the social world – the exotic, beauty 'purchased by the weight'– Bassanio attempts to suggest his own distrust of such devices, and that he has the wisdom not to choose the glistering gold or the attractive silver casket. Instead, he opts for the lead, which had a deep cultural register in its material connection with cosmetic paint. 'Ceruse' is a mixture of white lead and vinegar, which, fascinatingly, was produced most efficiently and effectively in Venice.

Freud points out that some editors have Bassanio say 'Thy *plainness*' when he chooses the lead casket instead of 'Thy paleness moves me more than eloquence' (106).[30] Yet, 'paleness' is a more accurate qualification here, given that it is the desired result of face painting with lead. Shakespeare, reflecting the ambiguous cultural attitudes towards cosmetics, uses cosmetic encryption himself in order to fool the suitors with *all* three caskets. Most critics, like John Doebler, maintain that 'gold is too often mere ornament, silver too often associated with commerce; therefore, Bassanio chooses humble lead and wins the lady'.[31]

However, Bassanio does not pass the test until he is able to penetrate *all* painted surfaces and finally settle upon the corporeal Portia:

> What find I here?
> Fair Portia's counterfeit. What demi-god
> Hath come so near creation? Move these eyes?
> Or whether, riding on the balls of mine,
> Seem they in motion? Here are severed lips
> Parted with sugar breath. So sweet a bar
> Should sunder such sweet friends. Here in her hairs
> The painter plays the spider, and hath woven
> A golden mesh t'entrap the hearts of men
> Faster than gnats in cobwebs. But her eyes –
> How could he see to do them? Having made one,
> Methinks it should have power to steal both his
> And leave itself unfurnished. Yet look how far
> The substance of my praise doth wrong this shadow
> In underprizing it, so far this shadow
> Doth limp behind the substance.
>
> (III, ii, 115–29)

When he discovers the counterfeit face hidden beneath the surface of lead, Bassanio is captivated by the aesthetic potency of the work and reveals the power of painted beauty, (more lead-based paints) to ensnare his own eyes, a moment reminiscent of Leontes's wonder at Hermione's painted statue. Painted art is imagined here as something magical in its ability to imitate reality and capture beauty so vividly. But more pointedly, the painted face acts as a living artefact. Bassanio is, at first, more attracted to the painted miniature than he is to the painted lady standing next to him. But fundamentally, it is Portia who can materialise his fantasies. She is the living painted face that can kiss him back. By aligning the caskets with cosmetic ingredients, Shakespeare forces Bassanio to accept his attraction to deception, even as he enables us to recognise the crucial role materials have in the formation of social and sexual identities. Bassanio's emotional response to the portrait hidden in the veiled casket points to Shakespeare's reassertion of the pre-eminence of art, the allure of cosmetic beauty and the beautifying power of lead.

Cosmetic Symbolism and *Othello*

The Venetian setting of *Othello* particularises the play's concern with obfuscation and its relationship to female sexuality, as a result of the city's own contribution – literal and mythological – to the production and consumption of cosmetics in the Renaissance. It also teases out the contemporary inclination to associate secretiveness with female rituals, domestic, sexual and cosmetic. However, cosmetic symbolism in *Othello* does not simply highlight the play's construction of women as threatening, secretive and externally unreliable, it also more powerfully suggests that there is an even greater threat amongst the community of men. It is the men who do the obfuscating, the 'blackening', as they wrongly accuse women of conspiring with the painted, effeminate city to obliterate love and to deconstruct the relationship between truth and beauty.

The setting itself is synonymous with painted femininity, as I suggested in the opening to this chapter, but even more curious is Iago's identification with contemporary perceptions of femininity in his dangerous admission that his purpose is obfuscation; it is what he stands for as a 'sign', and he establishes his link with moralistic notions of cosmetics when he confesses his role in the first scene:

> Though I do hate him as I do hell pains –
> Yet for necessity of present life
> I must show out a flag and sign of love,
> Which is indeed but a sign.
> (I, ii, 156–8)

Iago exhibits a rhetorical refulgence that Shakespearean drama simultaneously repudiates and celebrates. Yet, by aligning Iago with prescriptive moralism, Shakespeare uncovers the hypocrisy attributed to anti-cosmetic authors who beautify their language to suit their own purposes. I want now to consider the significance of the moment in the play when Iago establishes his relationship to the stage, to the audience and to Othello as a 'sign'. Of course, he is punning on his status in the army, but more importantly he wants us to recognise that he is a signifier. First, Iago tells us that he will signify love to Othello. As a sign of false love, then, Iago creates a gulf between truth and beauty. The relationship between the separation of truth and beauty and the fear of female sexuality becomes clear when we consider contemporary anxieties about cosmetic embellishment. Secondly, Iago is a cosmetic signifier himself. Evoking traditional, moralistic perceptions of cosmetics, he stands for outward show; he is figuratively like the decorative white pearl that hangs in Othello's ear and that paints corruption on to Desdemona's face racially figured as blackness. But equally, Iago is a compelling dramatic character, who may very well have his own face painted to highlight his role as a cosmetic signifier, or an epitome of seductive deception.

Phrases that gesture toward the universal and pervasive theme of appearance versus reality and the stock complaints about female cosmetic ritual that Shakespeare's text simultaneously echo and contradict can be re-examined in a much more complex fashion. For example, in Act I, scene ii, Brabanzio, seeing his daughter's marriage as incredible, uses the language of ingredients when he refers to the witchcraft he believes Othello has used on Desdemona. He insinuates that his daughter has been bewitched in the same way that anti-cosmetic polemicists argue women bewitch men with their cosmetic glazes: 'thou hast practiced on her with foul charms, / Abused her delicate youth with drugs and minerals / That weaken motion' (I, ii, 74–6). Racist inferences can readily be drawn from Brabanzio's allegation, which is also peppered with cosmetic signifiers. Brabanzio contends that Desdemona is 'abused' and 'corrupted / By spells and medicines bought of mountebanks' (I, iii, 61–2). The associations with the cosmetic are made clear by the references to 'mountebanks' (a common source of cosmetics in Venice) and to witchcraft. As we saw in Webster's plays, witchcraft was in many ways synonymous with cosmetics, especially, since the ingredients used in both arts often intersected, and since both were associated with secrecy and femininity. The fear that women who use cosmetics may have the same access to poison as witches is compounded here in *Othello* by the anxiety about foreigners and their own cultural rituals. Typically, such fears focus upon female practice but, curiously, in *Othello* the men are linked to secrecy, ritual and witchcraft, and I think this is precisely because of the dramatic representation of Venice, which embodies the seductive allure of painted female sexuality while simultaneously harbouring the masculine privileges of patriarchy, war and authority.

When Brabanzio accuses Othello of bewitching his daughter with his cunning ingredients, he is transferring the label of painted whore on to him, demonstrating the intersections of race and female sexuality. In *The Discoverie of Witchcraft* (1584), Reginald Scot warns men about the 'bewitching Venome conteined in the bodie of an harlot, how hir eie, hir toong, hir beautie and behavior bewitcheth some men'.[32] Brabanzio does not want to hear Othello's 'unvarnished tale' nor does he believe Othello has a 'perfect soul'; instead, he undermines the Moor's protestations of purity and 'fairness' by suggesting again that 'with mixtures powerful o'er the blood, / Or with some dram conjured to this effect, / He wrought upon her' (I, iii, 104–6). The language recalls *The Merchant of Venice* when the Duke asks for a 'dram of mercy'; but here, 'dram' is not one drop but an entire concoction used to enchant Brabanzio's daughter, suggesting the copiousness and uncontrollability of Othello's resources (physiological or external, depending on whether one reads the sexual register in the line). Nevertheless, the speech resonates with cosmetic signifiers, which cannot be denied because of the very intimate connections between witchcraft and cosmetics, two arts that are practically synonymous in early modern misogynistic discourse.

The cosmetic theme in this play is of course racialised. Othello's darkness is the key issue and the actor's painted black face is the material signifier that brings this issue literally to the forefront. According to Michael Neill, 'blackness is not only the apparent sign of sin and death', it can also stand for a vicious hiddenness – as, for example, when Aaron the Moor in *Titus Andronicus* mockingly proclaims its superiority to the 'treacherous hue' of white skin 'that will betray with blushing / The close enacts and counsels of thy heart' (IV, ii, 117–18). 'Thus, blackness proves to be oddly like death, a disfiguring exposure so absolute that it becomes a "great disguiser" '.[33] But Othello is repeatedly referred to as 'fair', a construction of his identity that deepens the racial implications of the play because it negates his blackness and privileges 'fairness' as socially superior.

Othello's paradoxical 'fairness' has a cultural precedent. Writing about beauty, Thomas Buoni provides a defence of blackness on aesthetic terms, asserting that Moors, 'though they are blacke, doe many times bewray a strange kinde of *Beauty* in them'.[34] Othello 'bewrays' this 'strange kinde of *Beauty*' when he speaks masterfully. But when others speak of him it is through a discourse of apologetics: first when Desdemona tells us she sees Othello's 'visage in his mind' (I, iii, 251); next when the Duke tells Brabanzio, 'If virtue no delighted beauty lack, / Your son-in-law is far more fair than black' (I, iii, 289–90). Both of these testimonials to Othello's 'fairness' actually participate in a cosmetic discourse in which Othello's darkness, a source of shame, is painted white in defensive acts of concealment. Othello thinks he too has to hide his darkness and his reputation, which 'is not begrimed and black' (III, iii, 392). According to Ewan Fernie, shame is what begs concealment, and Iago conceals himself too because he lives in fear of 'the gaze of others'.[35] The twisted and tragic thing is that Othello did not need painting white because, as Neill says, Iago's purpose is to convince us all that Othello's blackness is 'the sign of Othello's inherent corruption, the secret viciousness beneath his noble Venetian persona'.[36] Instead, his darkness would have 'bewray[ed]' a 'strange kinde of *Beauty*' because it is truth (for the character, not the actor, of course). Again, we witness the separation of truth and beauty. It is Iago who constructs the discrepancy between Othello's facial appearance and moral worth: 'Men should be what they seem' (III, iii, 132) because women never are. Acutely conscious of similar discrepancies in his social world, he bitterly embodies it himself. Because Iago knows that there is no such thing as reality, only perception, he is able to become a macabre artist of death, playing with his metaphorical black and white paints and assuming the role of cosmetic dramaturge like Vindice in *The*

Revenger's Tragedy. His plan is to paint Desdemona black, so that 'She'll find a white that shall her blackness fit' (II, i, 136).

The fear that Iago embodies is embedded in contemporary anxieties about foreign infiltration, a fear that Jonathan Gil Harris has suggested 'led to a heightened attention to the margins, orifices, and gaps of the social organism'.[37] Venice is the appropriate site upon which to explore the consequences of intersecting races because of its commercial interest and geographical position. In England there were fears that a consistent exotic presence would annihilate the concept of the Other. In an anonymous tract entitled *England's Vanity*, the author refers to Stowe's Chronicle, which reveals that 'from one *Spanish Ewe* brought over and placed among other Sheep, there followed so strange a *Murrain* that most of the Flocks of *England* dyed'.[38] This passage indicates that the reference to black rams and white ewes in the opening scene of *Othello* points to the fear of miscegenation. The term 'dyed' in its double meaning of 'die' and 'dye' articulates a fear of the disappearance of true racial whiteness.

The notion of black beauty pointed out by Kim Hall's study of race and gender stems from a loss of faith in white beauty because it is easily imitated and, hence, contaminated. Dympna Callaghan details Queen Anne's controversial request for Ben Jonson to write a masque that would require her and other aristocratic ladies to paint themselves black. Callaghan points out the inextricability of cosmetics from such theatrical portrayals: 'both negritude and whiteness are, on the Renaissance stage, the cosmetic, though far from superficial, surfaces of difference'.[39] This, of course, would remind us that the actor playing Othello, Richard Burbage would be painted with black cosmetic paint; thus he becomes at once a cosmetic signifier, both on the stage and in the play. His social significance as a representation of the Other is further enhanced by his cosmetic appearance, which serves to emphasise the darkness of his social and sexual insecurities which Iago so skillfully brings to the surface.

Race, cosmetics and secret female spaces are linked in *Othello*, and the contemporary knowledge of Venice as a multiracial society invites these links. In her essay on Shakespeare, race and women, Joyce Green MacDonald says that secret female power is an overwhelming force in the play and it is evoked by the absent women: Desdemona's mother's maid, Othello's mother and the Egyptian charmer. MacDonald writes,

> these three non-white women's association with secret female power – if only the power to grieve – is overwritten within the action of the play by the patriarchal authority on display (in crisis mode) in Brabantio's fear and in the cool adjudication of the elopement by the Venetian signiory.[40]

What is also true is that the threatening materialism of female sexuality is appropriated by the male characters in the play as they exhibit a powerful threat themselves, and the danger they pose is projected on to the female characters. This appropriation is registered in the cosmetic signifiers used by Iago, Brabanzio and Othello. When Brabanzio warns fathers 'from hence trust not your daughters' minds / By what you see them act' (I, i, 171–2), he reintroduces the separation of truth and beauty. This statement resonates with contemporary attacks on women's beauty practices: 'pride so transformeth the inward ornaments of the minde'.[41] When the nature of feminine virtue is deconstructed by such rhetoric, it becomes the job of Othello to try and discern Desdemona's 'perfect soul'. Iago's metaphorical blackening of Desdemona is the paint that obscures her perfection and she becomes like one of the many women who, according to Barnabe Rich, 'are so be paynted, so be periwigd, so be poudered, so be perfumed, so bee starched, so be laced, and so bee imbroidered, that I cannot tell what mentall virtues they may have that they do keepe inwardly themselves . . .'[42]

It was long acknowledged that 'the ladies of Italy (not to speake of the Curtezans) to seeme fairer than the rest, take a pride to besmeare and paint themselves'.[43] Furthermore, travellers to Italy, such as William Thomas, were conflicted about the beauty of women in Venice; 'as for theyr beautie of face, though they be fayre in deede, I would not highly commend theim, because there is in a maner none, olde or yonge, unpeinc- ted'.[44] Both courtesans and noble women of Venice were attired bravely, making it difficult to distinguish the courtesan from the lady. Hence, Desdemona's inner virtue literally has nothing to do with the Venetian cultural practice of face painting. Nevertheless, the face paints eventu- ally signify Desdemona's identity as it transforms from noblewoman to whore, and probably confuses the issue further for Othello, who finds her increasingly impenetrable. Iago calls the women of Venice 'pictures out of door' (II, i, 112), an obvious reference to the face paint they wear. Next Desdemona implicates herself when she says to Iago, 'I am not merry, but I do beguile / The thing I am by seeming otherwise' (II, i, 125–6). Although she is referring to her fears for Othello at that moment, Desdemona's statement is a fairly poignant reminder of the linguistic construction of women as duplicitous and sexually incontinent in this play: 'With red & white they painte their face, to tice the[m] to their beddes'.[45]

The handkerchief in *Othello* registers female chastity, sexuality, beauty and history. The red and white hues of the handkerchief argu- ably signify the Anglo-European feminine ideal: it is as red as roses and strawberries, and as white as the lily or as snow; it is as red as blood, and as white as flesh. Paradoxically, however, the exotic nature and secret mystery of the handkerchief are tied to Othello's blackness:

'Tis true. There's magic in the web of it.
A Sibyl that had numbered in the world
The sun to course two hundred compasses
In her prophetic fury sewed the work.
The worms were hallowed that did breed the silk,
And it was dyed in mummy, which the skilful
Conserved of maidens' hearts.

(III, iv, 67–73)

The tincture and dyeing of the handkerchief with ingredients such as mummy (which is a preservative) give it its cosmetic significance, but its presence is also a factor in determining and regulating the sexuality of Desdemona (see Figure 7.3 for a sixteenth-century handkerchief).[46] In Philip Massinger's play *The Picture*, the painted portrait of Sophia's face is the site upon which her sexual loyalty is measured; the artist/ magician Baptista designs the picture so that when Sophia is honest her picture remains as it is; however,

if once it varie
From the true forme, and what's now white, and red
Incline to yellow rest most confident
Shees with all violence courted but unconquered.
But if it turne all blacke 'tis an assurance
The sort by composition, or surprise
Is force'd or with her free consent surrendered.[47]

The handkerchief in *Othello* and Desdemona's face may have the same function. Ania Loomba argues that 'Desdemona's fairness depends upon her fidelity: when suspected of being a whore, she is as "begrimed" as Othello's face'.[48] But even more significantly, her glistening cosmetic whiteness becomes an equal register of her sexual darkness. The handkerchief's movement from Desdemona's possession to Bianca's symbolises the material connection these two women now have for Othello. Prior to Othello's suspicions, Desdemona was just a noblewoman who more than likely used cosmetics, but now the paints on her face become evidence of her guilt. In addition to her face, the handkerchief is more physical evidence of Desdemona's whoredom.

Bianca represents an institution in Venice, that of the Venetian courtesan. It is unlike any other community of prostitutes. They were widely criticised for their openness and cosmetic shame, and this fuelled anxieties about their sexual freedom, as well as the secret accesses they had in society. Yet, they were extolled for their seductive beauty, and the countless artistic depictions of them remind us of their erotic appeal. Bianca's role is a complex one and one that is often marginalised. She is a lover, an artist; she paints her face but she is also skilled in other

Figure 7.3   Embroidered handkerchief (1600–30), V & A Images/Victoria and Albert Museum.

arts, as Cassio reminds us when he asks her to copy the embroidery in the handkerchief: 'Take me this work out' (IV, i, 176). Bianca also has a voice, and she uses it to expose her emotional vulnerability; she is stronger than Desdemona in some ways because she articulates the humiliation to which Cassio subjects her:

> O Cassio, whence came this?
> This is some token from a newer friend.
> To the felt absence now I feel a cause.
> Is't come to this? Well, well.
> (IV, i, 175–8)

Bianca is not afraid to admit her weakness for Cassio, nor is she afraid to display her jealousy. At this moment the handkerchief touches her hands, but because of her status in society she stains it with her own sexual identity, implicating Desdemona as a painted whore as well (at least in Othello's eyes). In fact, for Othello, once the handkerchief reappears in Bianca's hands, 'painted' becomes a word exclusively associated with feminine deception, and when he uses it in a fit of rage, it just so happens that Venice has reappeared on the stage in the form of Lodovico:

> Sir, she can turn and turn, and yet go on
> And turn again, and she can weep, sir, weep,
> And she's obedient, as you say, obedient,
> Very obedient. [TO DESDEMONA] Proceed you in your tears.
> [TO LODOVICO] Concerning this, sir – [TO DESDEMONA] O well
>   painted passion!
> [TO LODOVICO] I am commanded home. [TO DESDEMONA] Get
>   you away.
> I'll send for you anon. [TO LODOVICO] Sir, I obey the mandate,
> And will return to Venice. [TO DESDEMONA] Hence, avaunt!
>
> (IV, i, 250–7)

Othello participates in the play's misogynistic discourse and his tone is ironic, disjointed and furious. Desdemona's face is stinging and probably slightly smudged, but her tears reinforce Othello's convictions of her guilt even as they wash away any perceived cosmetic façades. And this is the point in the play at which Othello finds himself literally caught between his loyalty to Dame Venice and his anguish at being deceived by one of her 'whores'.

Conclusion

In her deathbed Desdemona's body takes on a sexual significance similar to that of the female corpse in *The Second Maiden's Tragedy*. It is still, like a picture, quiet and 'fair'. Convinced that her deeds confine her perpetually to darkness, Othello takes on biblical significance by sacrificing the life of his ewe. Othello enters her chamber with 'a light', figuring Shakespeare's use of material stage properties as cosmetic signifiers: the darkly painted Moor brings in light, which will enhance and illuminate Desdemona's white body. Upon seeing the sleeping form of his wife, Othello temporarily returns to Desdemona her original hue, and he takes up Petrarchan language, eroticising her pale flesh, while at last attempting to elevate her spiritually:

> It is the cause. Yet I'll not shed her blood,
> Nor scar that whiter skin of hers than snow,
> And smooth as monumental alabaster.
> Yet she must die, else she'll betray more men.
>
> (V, ii, 3–6)

After she has passed away and the red is indelibly absent from her cheeks, Othello's love increases, as does his victim's aesthetic value. Desdemona's cosmeticised body, like the Lady in *The Second Maiden's Tragedy* and like Hermione in *The Winter's Tale*, becomes a memorial, an effigy, an artistic construction of her former self. When Othello learns Iago has lied, truth and beauty reunite spontaneously and upon Desdemona's corpse. In his guilt Othello's vulnerability, shame and despair 'bewray' again his 'strange kinde of *Beauty*', a type of beauty acknowledged by Thomas Browne: 'we that are of contrary complexions accuse the blackness of the Moors as ugly; But the spouse in the *Canticles* excuseth this conceit, in that description of hers, I am black, but comely'.[49] The phrase 'I am black, but comely' seems hauntingly to epitomise Othello's final moments. The deathbed scene would have been heightened by the dramatic spectacle of his cosmeticised blackness and the glistening white of the boy playing Desdemona, a photonegative beauty through which Shakespeare meta-theatrically enlivens the metaphorical significance and materiality of cosmetics. Thus far on the Shakespearean stage, boys paint to play ladies and twins; rude mechanicals paint to play walls; cosmetic ingredients appear in the form of caskets, and blackness is given a moral value through the contradictory image of two boy actors, one white, one black, who turn out to be equally tragic figures. How then will Shakespeare choose to represent supernatural realism? The ghost of Hamlet's father will be inevitably realised through a cosmetic construction of whiteness that suggests not only his material attachment to Hamlet's world, but also his symbolic relationship to the political ideology of Shakespeare's world.

Notes

1. Hall, 'Satire I', *Virgidemiarum*.
2. Rich, *My Ladies Looking Glasse*, p. 10.
3. Contareno, *The Commonwealth and Gouernment*, p. 3.
4. Coryat, *Crudities*, pp. 37–8.
5. Grieco, 'The Body, appearance, and sexuality', p. 62.
6. Rich, *My Ladies Looking Glasse*, p. 2.
7. Contareno, *The Commonwealth and Gouernment*, p. 178.
8. Bell, *How To Do It*, p. 25.
9. Contareno, *The Commonwealth and Gouernment*, p. 3.
10. Brotton, *The Renaissance Bazaar*, p. 38.
11. Williams, *Powder and Paint*, p. 15.
12. Corson, *Fashions in Makeup*, p. 95.
13. Bell, *How To Do It*, p. 45.
14. Corson, *Fashions in Makeup*, p. 53.
15. Vaughan, *Othello*, pp. 16–17.

16. Žižek, *The Sublime Object*, p. 31.
17. 'Take white Pigeons, and fat them with Pine Apple kernels the space of fifteene days and then kill them: and having cast away the head, the feet, and the guts with al the garbage, distil them in a Limbeck with halfe a loaf of Sucharine Alome, three hundred leaves of fine *silver foile*, five hundred of *gold foile*, and the crum of foure white loaves, steeped or wet in Almond milke, a pound of the marrow of a Calfe' (Ruscelli, *The Secrets of Alexis*, p. 64) [italics mine].
18. Manningham, *Diary*, p. 10.
19. Gainsford, *The Rich Cabinet*, p. 9.
20. Drew-Bear, *Painted Faces*, p. 95.
21. Singh, 'Gendered "Gifts"', p. 152.
22. Freud, 'The theme of the three caskets', p. 292.
23. Ibid. p. 294.
24. Lupton, *A Thousand Notable Things*, p. 41.
25. Della Porta, *Natural Magick*, p. 253.
26. Ibid. p. 245.
27. Tuke, *A Treatise Against Paint[i]ng*, p. 34.
28. Du Bosc repeats this story in 1639: 'there was none could be known by their countenance, their faces were become quite others then they were, all full of spots and frightfullnesse' (*The Compleat Woman*, p. 41). Annette Drew-Bear comments on the link between this story and *Timon of Athens*: 'Timon strips off the false guilding from the painted faces of his deceitful friends, symbolically washing off their false deceptive veneers and revealing their true ugliness' (*Painted Faces*, p. 96).
29. Freud, 'The theme of the three caskets', p. 294.
30. Ibid. p. 294.
31. Doebler, *Shakespeare's Speaking Pictures*, p. 48.
32. Scot, *The Discoverie of Witchcraft*, p. 33.
33. Neill, *Issues of Death*, p. 147.
34. Buoni, *Problemes of Beavtie*, p. 28.
35. Fernie, *Shame in Shakespeare*, p. 144.
36. Neill, *Issues of Death*, p. 147.
37. Harris, *Foreign Bodies*, p. 13.
38. Anonymous, *England's Vanity*, p. 97.
39. Callaghan, *Shakespeare Without Women*, p. 80.
40. MacDonald, 'Black ram, white ewe', p. 194.
41. Averell, *A Dyall for Dainty Darlings*, p. 1.
42. Rich, *The Honestie of this Age*, p. 15.
43. Bulwer, *Anthropometamorphosis*, p. 260.
44. Thomas, *The Historie of Italie*, p. 85.
45. Grange, 'The Paynting of a Curtizan', in *The Golden Aphroditis*.
46. Recently, Ian Smith has challenged the critical orthodoxy that the handkerchief is white; he argues that this passage suggests it is black (see Smith, 'Othello's black handkerchief', pp. 1–25).
47. Massinger, *The Picture*, Sig. B4v.
48. Loomba, '"Delicious Traffick"', p. 217.
49. Browne, *Pseudodoxia Epidemica*, p. 356.

Chapter 8

'Flattering Unction': Cosmetics in *Hamlet*

In a Tragedie (that was prepar'd for the publicke view of the University,) the Actors were privately to be tried upon the Stage . . . two scholars were in this Spanish Tragedy (which was the story of *Petrus Crudelis*) whose parts were two Ghosts or Apparitions . . . and then these two Scholars were put out of their blacks into white long robes, their Faces meal'd, and Torches in their hands . . . just as they put their heads through the hangings of the Scene, coming out at two severall sides of the Stage, they shook so, and were so horribly affrighted at one another's gashly lookes . . .[1]

Although written in the 1650s about a university performance of a Spanish tragedy, Edmund Gayton's description of two scholars/actors having their faces 'meal'd' to represent ghosts is evidence that actors wore cosmetics during dramatic performances in the late sixteenth and throughout the seventeenth centuries. The word 'meal', used here to describe the faces of the actors, recalls the use of crumbs of barley bread and milk in some facial cosmetics; 'meal' is also a term contemporaries used to satirise the painted or powdered faces of women in anti-cosmetic literature.

The first two words of *Hamlet*, 'Who's there?' (I, i, 1), followed forty-five lines later by the entrance of the apparition, played by an actor whose face, undoubtedly, would be 'mealed', encapsulate the play's engagement with the complex network of meanings attached to painted faces on the early modern English stage. The Ghost's painted face in *Hamlet* points to the old King's liminality, and simultaneously registers the wavering stability of his political identity. In addition to such visual cosmetic signifiers, the language of the play also harbours patterns of cosmetic imagery, which are connected to one of the anxieties at the heart of the play: painted authority. I have mentioned in this book that Tudor monarchy depended upon the performance of its power, its opulent, visual self-presentation, and that this manifesto locates its materiality upon the painted face of Queen Elizabeth I. In a stunning example of meta-drama, the Ghost (played by an actor whose face would have been adorned with cosmetics), represents a monarch who is no longer of this world, but whose transition is yet to be made into the next; it is this figure that triggers the events of a play that meditates upon the various forms of paintedness and its potentially destabilising effect upon bodies – physical and political. When Hamlet asks Horatio what the Ghost's face looked like, he asks if it was 'Pale or red?' Horatio responds, 'Nay, very pale' (I, ii, 232–3). The literal expression of 'pale' on the Renaissance stage was achieved with face paint. It can be argued that the image of the cosmeticised ghost walking the Globe stage in armour, with the beaver up so that the actor's face can be seen, and who emerges out of trapdoors to stalk the imaginary battlements, is a startling allusion to the declining political authority and physicality of Queen Elizabeth I. The figure of old Hamlet's spirit becomes, in this context, a visual metaphor, a meta-theatrical sign and a powerful reminder of the virtually impenetrable masks worn by those who rule.

Significantly, the decaying body of the ageing Queen Elizabeth I haunted many playwrights in this period and certainly did so throughout the Jacobean era. As Steven Mullaney has already suggested, most of London and the Queen herself were aware that her physical deterioration was 'a highly fraught political, physical and symbolic issue'.[2] The Queen's anxiety about ageing is crucial in understanding the various attitudes toward painted faces during the English Renaissance. Her compulsion to control the proliferation of her likeness by legislating that her face be painted in portraits by the standard of a facial pattern made when she was much younger, demonstrates the deliberate attempt on the part of a monarch to hide behind a mask of white lead and vinegar (ingredients used in cosmetic *and* canvas paints). This is the art of deception, which takes place within a political framework. This glossing over of reality is consistent with the way in which Shakespeare portrays political deception throughout his plays.

In this chapter I will argue that the use of cosmetic signifiers in *Hamlet* ironically help to uncover the play's preoccupation with the deceptive visibility of power while it demonstrates their meta-theatrical utility. Cosmetic signifiers (meaning cosmetic language in the text and literal cosmetics on the stage) support the play's concerns with vision (seeing, spying, watching), the uses of representation, the surging tension between appearance and reality, and the various performances of power. Shakespeare's appropriation of cosmetic language and allusions to the contemporary preoccupation with ingredients and recipes for bodily restoratives help to construct these concerns through an intense network of image patterns. In Shakespeare's *Hamlet* cosmetics are deemed valuable because of their poetic and theatrical uses;

cosmetic language is often used ironically, recalling, but not necessarily reinforcing, the contemporary arguments condemning women and their technology of beauty.

Appearances and Realities: Painted Faces in *Hamlet*

The cosmeticised complexion of the Ghost in *Hamlet* serves several functions, the most important being to establish his simultaneous otherworldliness and his material attachment to the earth. In the 2004 Royal Shakespeare Company production, the Ghost was not in armour, instead most of his body was exposed and painted thickly with a pale white, which was extremely effective in constructing a tangible distance between the material world of Hamlet and the pseudo-spiritual existence of the alienated old King. Cosmetic bases in early modern England were thick and shimmering, sometimes laced with silver or pearl, and sometimes a powdered complexion was glazed over with a mixture of egg whites or oil, depending on what was readily available to a theatre company. I have argued elsewhere that I believe cosmetic paints were used on the Renaissance stage for a variety of significations, including representations of apparitions or ghosts.[3] The paint materialises the Ghost's unfamiliarity; like the dying old Queen Elizabeth I, whose actual face seemed not to exist because of the layers of facial cosmetics, the face of the ghost of old Hamlet is only a 'likeness' of its former self: 'Looks a not like the King?'(I, i, 46). The Ghost's interment in Purgatory constructs his position as liminal; he is caught between the material and spiritual realms. It can be argued that the pale face of the Ghost is a sign, reminding us not only of the political obfuscation rotting the realm, but also of the lingering materiality of Hamlet's father.

Although, the Ghost acts as the supernatural authority, naturally, Hamlet is unable to accept wholeheartedly that the spirit is who he claims to be. Fundamental to the anti-cosmetic ideology is the notion that 'painting is an enemy to knowledge',[4] and Hamlet's distrust of painted surfaces extends to the Ghost, whose literally limned face simultaneously evokes the contemporary distrust, yet attraction to painted faces in the same way that Hamlet both distrusts and yet is inevitably drawn to his father's apparition. In the 1570s through to the late 1590s it was widely believed that ghosts were either manifestations of the devil's ability to assume any shape, projections of a disturbed mind, or the result of clever theatrical tricks. In an anti-Jesuit tract, John Gee describes the devices of the Jesuit priests of the Counter-Reformation. He reports alleged instances in which the Jesuits attempted to convert young and unsuspecting Protestants: 'I made bold to acquaint my Reader with *Mary Wiltshire*, sometime ensnared and cooped by a packe of *Iesuites* or *Priests*, with the engine of personated Apparitions'.[5] The questionable nature of the 'apparition' in *Hamlet* is captured brilliantly in Gee's tract as he accuses the Jesuits of creating 'special effects' to trick their victims: 'somewhat I thinke may be done this way by Paper Lanthornes or transparent Glasses to eradiate & redouble light & cast out painted shapes by multiplication of the *species visibles*, & artificiall directing of refractions'.[6] Curiously, among the recipes for cosmetic unguents, Della Porta's *Natural Magick* contains instructions on how to create such artificial projections. Gee's accusation here is that the Jesuit priests use specious means to convert Protestants back to the Church of Rome. Gee's anti-theatrical views are bound up with his anti-Catholic views. He argues that 'the *Iesuites* being or having *Actors* of such dexteritie, I see no reason that they should set up a company for themselves, which surely will put down *The Fortune, Red-Bull, Cock-pit & Globe*'.[7] He continues: 'Representations and Apparitions from the dead might be seene farre cheaper at other Play-houses. As for example, the *Ghost* in *Hamlet* . . .'[8] Gee's tract exposes the conversion tactics of the Jesuits as based on false projections, a manipulation of the perceptions of reality. Hamlet's world is permeated by such manipulable forces and the Ghost's face fundamentally points to Claudius's own re-fashioning of reality. His 'painted word' is the true enemy of knowledge, and cosmetic signifiers such as the Ghost's pale complexion register the underlying importance of Hamlet's ensuing battle with the discrepancies between what he sees and what is real. By using cosmetic signifiers in this way, Shakespeare demonstrates their intrinsic importance to his dramatic art.

It is no secret that there are profound political resonances inherent in the theme of appearance versus reality in *Hamlet*. Although critics have acknowledged that cosmetic imagery is an element of this theme, there is more work to be done here. Maynard Mack recognises that in *Hamlet* a 'pattern of imagery springs from terms of painting: the paints, colorings, the varnishes that may either conceal, or, as in the painter's art, reveal',[9] without investigating the historical uses or the material origins of this pattern of imagery. Supporting the idea that cosmetic images form a subset of a broader fundamental discourse, Marilyn French claims that

> the incertitude that informs the play is attributed to some split – between seeming and being, appearance and reality; between an ideal good and a real evil; between a false ideal that is really an outmoded traditional code, and a perversion of that code; between intellect and action; between inside and outside.[10]

French goes on to discuss the themes of spying, intelligence and trapping without necessarily realising the metaphorical and linguistic uses of cosmetics in dramatising and bringing to light these central concerns of the play. If we read the play with an informed awareness of the variety of meanings that cosmetics had in early modern culture, we realise, for example, that the painting reference in the nunnery scene can no longer be reduced to a mere castigation of Ophelia for being 'one of those creatures who substitute new faces for the ones God gave them'.[11] Wolfgang Clemen's study of 'Appearance and Reality in Shakespeare's Plays' describes Shakespeare's incorporation of this theme as developing the 'recognition of the ambiguity, the diversity and the problematic character of human nature'.[12] But the view that Hamlet is morally intolerant of the discrepancies he witnesses between appearance and reality is too simplistic when one considers the problem of the prince's own contradictory relationship with pretence and theatricality. Clemen draws our attention to Hamlet's 'sinister and almost unfathomable manner' of 'blending mask and reality, disguise and exposure'; however, his study does little to register the play's attention to the play's set of cosmetic images that engage with Hamlet's adoration of performance and with the meta-theatrical uses that cosmetic imagery had to offer an Elizabethan playwright.[13] Criticism has not denied the play its obsessive preoccupation with appearances, but neither has it given enough attention to the cultural reception of cosmetics and its decided links with early modern theatricality. The topical allusions to cosmetics in Shakespeare are fraught with ambiguities, as I have been trying to show, insofar as the moralistic position is countered by the inability to deny the contemporary attraction to painted beauty, its erotic effect and its performative value.

In Act I, scene ii, Hamlet's famous defence of his choice of black apparel is not only a subjective interrogation of the word 'seems', but it also suggests that Hamlet has been frustrated by visible, yet fundamentally unreliable representations of power; it is a rejection of theatrical peformance:

> Seems, madam? Nay it *is*. I know not 'seems'.
> 'Tis not alone my inky cloak, good-mother,
> Nor customary suits of solemn black,
> Nor windy suspiration of forced breath,
> No, nor the fruitful river in the eye,
> Nor the dejected haviour of the visage
> Together with all forms, moods, shows of grief
> That can denote me truly. These indeed 'seem',
> For they are actions that a man might play;
> But I have that within which passeth show –
> These but the trappings and the suits of woe.
>
> (I, ii, 76–86)

Hamlet's offence at his mother's suggestion that his demeanour might be 'shows of grief' establishes his frustration not only at the courtly devices of simultaneous concealment and exposure, that is, hiding political strategies while visually and dynamically staging power to the eyes of the people, but all forms of staging the self. However, this speech takes place prior to the Ghost's confession, after which Hamlet recognises that he must partake in the theatrical machinations adopted by the new court. Beginning with a painted ghost and the construction of imagery associated with appearances, apparitions and seeming, the play will soon voice an anxiety about cosmetics and their relationship to power. But *Hamlet* does not merely participate in a morally didactic rant against painted surfaces and the dangers lurking beneath. It instead resists this single-minded interpretation because, ultimately, the play's attention to the materials and metaphorical resonances of cosmetic practice is crucial to its artistic design and its theatrical life.

Mousetraps

Many critics have commented upon the play as a system of traps, and upon the 'Murder of Gonzago' as the central trapping device, but what is often overlooked is the relationship between traps, theatre and cosmetics. Anti-cosmetic writers argued that painted women sought to entrap the bodies and souls of men. As I noted in Chapter 2, Thomas Gainsford, writing in the early seventeenth century, declares that 'a woman is a stinking rose, a pleasing evill, the mouse-trap of a man's soule . . . a sweete poyson'.[14] John Hynd tells women: 'thy body is elegant and neat, why then thou hast a mask for thy face, a snare for thy feet, and lime for thy feathers, which will so entangle thee, as that thou shalt hardly escape'.[15] Hynd stresses that in decking themselves out, women are not only trapping men, but also entangling themselves. This is what happens to Hamlet; after rigging up the stage with the trappings of his imitative theatrical spectacle, he traps himself into committing revenge. Thomas Tuke argues that it is a 'certaine wily kind of folly by theses lime-twiggs, these *painted lime-twiggs*, to labour to thinke or labour to catch a Wood-cocke, or a wild-goose'.[16] Polonius views Hamlet's poetry and courtship of Ophelia as much the same: 'springes to catch woodcocks' (I, iii, 115). In the same text, in which he criticises Shakespeare's art as 'beautified', Robert Greene warns men to 'turne thy eies from vanitie, for there is a kinde of women bearing the faces of Angels, but the hearts of Devils, able to intrap the elect if it were possible'.[17] Equally, Thomas Hall's tract insists 'that some women are not content with their native Beauty, but they adde painting and colouring of their face, breasts, etc. to inamour and ensnare others'.[18]

William Prynne, acknowledging the power of the theatre to influence its audience, writes that to stage plays 'are added the allurements of Flutes and Pipes, and such like musicke enticing to deceit ... preparing the mindes of those that sit there with delight for the traps of Harlots, and causing them to be more easily ensnared'.[19] Stephen Gosson views boy actors as 'flatterers' to 'sight', and their 'effeminate gesture' is meant 'to ravish the sence'.[20] In another anti-theatrical tract, Gosson claims that 'Theaters are snares unto faire women' and significantly, that the devil has 'sente over many wanton Italian bookes, which being translated into English, have poisoned the olde manners of our Countrey with foreign delights', including Hamlet's rendition of 'The Murder of Gonzago' no doubt. [21] As I have noted elsewhere in this book, the lines between anti-theatrical writings and anti-cosmetic discourse become blurred when we look at the language moralists use to disparage both crafts. Hamlet's 'Mousetrap' speaks to the anti-theatrical and anti-cosmetic discourses that argue against the manipulation of surfaces. Hamlet's attraction to performance is in constant tension with his distrust of outward show, and the play within a play becomes the site of his conflicting struggle. If Hamlet, playing the fool, had painted his face for the event, the moment would be even more resonant. His face would literally become the trapping device moralists claimed painted faces were; theatricality and paint become one and the same in this moment to arrive at the truth, simultaneously mocking and legitimising the anti-theatrical claim that the theatre is a trap and the anti-cosmetic position that painted faces ensnare those who look upon them.

The inevitable use of white face paint upon the players in 'The Mousetrap' would encapsulate the ideological tensions between anti-cosmetic theory and the paradoxical notion that 'players cannot keep counsel: they'll tell all' (III, ii, 137). In the 2000 Globe production the players donned white vizards, creating a similar effect as the cosmetic bases would. It conveyed a featureless detachment necessary for this particular type of theatrical device, while demonstrating the theatre's ability to uncover previously well-hidden truths (Figure 8.1). Hence the theatre, which is inextricable from cosmetics because of the use of makeup on the stage, is a type of cosmetic signifier in itself, but, paradoxically, here it is used to protest against painted tyranny. Like Vindice in *The Revenger's Tragedy* and Govianus in *The Second Maiden's*

Figure 8.1 'The Mousetrap', *Hamlet* (2000), photo by John Tramper, Shakespeare's Globe Theatre.

Tragedy, Hamlet combines theatricality, cosmetics and traps to attempt to draw out and extinguish corruption from the court.

Shakespeare, perhaps unwittingly, evokes the contemporary fascination with ingredients and recipes for bodily restoratives, cosmetic ointments, such as dentrifice and hair-growth creams, through the trapping sequences of the play. Mousetraps have a variety of symbolic registers: theological, political and cosmetic. In early modern England the mouse, or white mouse, was considered to be a particularly insidious creature, and mice and moles in *Hamlet* are associated repeatedly with kingship. Claudius is the mouse that Hamlet wants to trap. Edward Topsell's *The Historie of Four-Footed Beastes* tells us that 'moles' or 'myse' are also ingredients in concoctions used to make the hair grow:

> Take a mole and burne her whole in the skin, and mingle the dust or pouder which commeth from the same with hony unto the thicknesse or fashion of an ointment, and this being rubbed or anointed upon the bare or bald place will . . . procure the hair to grow thick.[22]

Hamlet's reference to his father's spirit as a 'mole' may tempt us to consider that one of the Ghost's roles in the play might be as an ingredient in the concoction that will be used to purge and beautify the political body. Another recipe from Topsell is for dentrifice, which calls for the 'dust of a dryed mouse being also mingled with hony and rubbed upon the teeth . . . Of the heads of mice being burned is made that excellent powder, for the scouring and cleansing of the teeth'.[23] The bizarre materials used in some of these recipes from the period relate to the themes in *Hamlet*. The Ghost's description of his bodily death employs the language of ingredients, poison, cosmetics, and witchcraft. He describes the juice of 'hebenon' as the 'leperous distilment', which 'with a sudden vigour it doth posset / And curd, like eager droppings into milk, / The thin and wholesome blood' (I, v, 62, 64, 68–70). The filthy fusion of blood and milk, a grotesque version of red and white not only reminds us of the anxieties about ingredients and consumption in the period, but also foregrounds the play's preoccupation with the decay of the bodies of women, kings and the state.

A recipe for trapping mice consists of 'the iuyce of the roote of the hearbe Camelion, mixed with water and oyle, draweth mice unto it'.[24] Hamlet's cryptic answer to Claudius's greeting immediately before the mousetrap scene – 'of the Chamelion's dish, I eat the air promise-crammed' (III, ii, 85) – is evocative of his own recipe for catching the mouse. Chris Hassel points out that 'black chameleon thistle' was considered a 'dangerous poison and a remedy' for sores.[25] He also cites a recipe containing various medicinal herbs, which are recommended as an antidote to poison:

> the flowers of wormwood, rosemary, black thorn, of each like quantity; of saffron half that quantity: all which being boiled in Rhenish wine let it be given . . . against the poison of Isia (which as I said before, is the root of the black chemeleon) and with Pliny translated *viscum*, mistletoe or birdlime.[26]

Hassel draws together all of the important ingredients that are referred to in the 'Mousetrap' sequence, including 'wormwood' and 'chemeleon'. However, the metaphorical significance of this recipe may also be affected by the cosmetic reference to 'birdlime', which was a sticky substance painted upon branches, used in churches and perhaps even playhouses to catch birds, but the phrase was used socially and satirically as a metaphor for the face paint used deliberately by women to 'entrap' men and by players in their notorious trapping devices known as 'stage-plaies'.

Another trap in the play is set by Polonius and Claudius for Hamlet. Convinced that Ophelia is the cause of Hamlet's 'transformation', Polonius gives her a book to read and places her in the castle hall to bait Hamlet, while Polonius and Claudius hide behind an arras. Setting his trap for Hamlet, Polonius's instructions to Ophelia are rife with allusions to cosmetics:

> Ophelia, walk you here. – Gracious, so please you,
> We will bestow ourselves. – Read on this book,
> That show of such an exercise may colour
> Your loneliness. We are oft to blame in this:
> 'Tis too much proved that with devotion's visage
> And pious action we do sugar o'er
> The devil himself.
> (III, i, 45–51)

Polonius's submission to the deceptive guises of the court is evident in his use of cosmetic language: 'sugaring' over the devil and 'colouring' Ophelia's 'loneliness' are actions with decisively cosmetic parallels. After all, Polonius is one of the primary trap setters and spies in a fictional court that is strongly redolent of the climate of intelligence and intrigue in the court of Queen Elizabeth I. Hiding behind the arras, Polonius and Claudius expressly articulate the notion of masking deception with aesthetic representation, the arras being a reminder to Elizabethan audiences of the fearful mix of art, luxury and power.

The cosmetic tenor of the nunnery scene is underscored by Claudius's aside, in which he expresses some guilt for his own crimes:

> How smart a lash that speech doth give my conscience.
> The harlot's cheek, beautied with plast'ring art,

Is not more ugly to the thing that helps it
Than is my deed to my most painted word.

(III, i, 53–6)

Claudius links his murderous actions with the face painting of a prostitute and with his own 'painted word', his ability to portray monarchical authority and legitimacy through convoluting verbal patterns. However, here Claudius not only acknowledges his duplicitousness through cosmetic imagery, but, more significantly, he sees his actions as an 'art', and the 'word', the unit of communication and ideological signification, as something that is easily painted. There are two distinct views of Ophelia in this scene: first, that she is the 'harlot' that Claudius refers to and that Hamlet believes all women to be, and secondly, that she is the pure and innocent victim of her father's sycophantic political strategies. Marvin Rosenberg agrees that Ophelia is bait and that as 'Hamlet enters on the way to setting his own trap, [he] scents a snare, scents a snare in life itself, can't escape that, confronts the adversary's bait – Ophelia'.[27] In one production, according to Rosenberg, the staging strategy of the 'nunnery scene' had Gertrude 'make Ophelia more sexually attractive, [and] loosened the girl's shoulder strap, put a pair of high-heeled red shoes on her feet, and used her own lipstick and rouge to color Ophelia's face – and, in the event, provoke Hamlet's ire at female painting'.[28] But, by this point Hamlet does not need Ophelia to wear makeup to provoke any 'ire at female painting'. Furthermore, this staging invites the speculation that Gertrude and Ophelia are conspirators actively using cosmetic beauty to manipulate and entrap men, which would conform to the misogynistic construction of female culpability in the play. This type of staging might force most people to draw the conclusion that Gertrude is indeed the manipulative, oversexualised woman that I do not believe Shakespeare intended her to be.

Some anti-cosmetic authors single out married women with 'honest Husbands' who use cosmetics, accusing them of enticing men to adultery, and ultimately their souls to hell. Thomas Hall writes that 'Painting is so farre from making honest Husbands love their Wives, that it makes them loath them'.[29] In 'A Sermon Against Excess of Apparel', the preacher objects to 'some nice and vain women', who say 'that all which we do in painting our faces, in dyeing our hair, in embalming our bodies, in decking us with gay apparel, is to please our husbands'; he continues, 'as though a wise and Christian husband should delight to see his wife in such painted and flourished visages, which common harlots most do use, to train therewith their lovers to naughtiness'.[30] Hamlet's perception of his mother is not only influenced by the Ghost's narrative, but it also takes part in a discourse surrounding beauty, cosmetics, wives and adultery. However, as some feminist critics of Shakespeare have demonstrated, it is likely that Gertrude's guilt extends only to a hasty remarriage, and nowhere else in the play is she seen to justify any of Hamlet's vituperative attacks on her sexuality.[31]

Returning to the 'nunnery scene', Annette Drew-Bear argues that if Ophelia 'appears on stage painted when she is sent to allure Hamlet, then her appearance enforces the deceit in her words, like the lie that her father is at home'.[32] But Drew-Bear does not take into account the various levels of meaning that cosmetics had in Elizabethan dramatic practice. As I argued earlier, it is certain that boy actors were painted to signal their feminine roles, but there are female characters in Shakespeare who declare that they are not painted, and because of the moral symbolism that painted faces have for many of the men in this play, especially Polonius, it is unlikely that an obedient daughter like Ophelia would be painted with the 'slibber-sauces' and fucuses of common harlots and high-born courtly ladies. Drew-Bear asserts that if Ophelia were to be painted later in her madness scene, it would give 'added point to her lines and fits with the bawdy language she uses in the songs'.[33] She contends that 'there is no explicit indication in the text for Ophelia to wear face paint, but the Renaissance stage practice of representing bawdy women as heavily painted would support this'.[34] I agree that by this stage in Ophelia's devolution, there would be paint on her face, and perhaps she could be seen on stage painting her face with manic imprecision. Prior to this, though, in the nunnery scene, Ophelia would be even more profoundly traumatised by Hamlet's words were she plain faced; she can be taken at face value and Hamlet's accusations – 'I have *heard* of your paintings, too, well enough. God hath given you one face and you make yourselves another' (III, i, 142–3: emphasis mine) – indicate that he no longer sees Ophelia for who she truly is. Her grief stems, in part, from the fact that she has become invisible to him, and if she paints in her scenes of madness it would symbolise her attempt to claw back some semblance of visibility.

Cosmeticised Bodies and the Female Interior

Inside Gertrude's Closet

A lady's closet was commonly a site for the interrogation of female sexuality and the secrets of beautification. Although a bedchamber and closet may be two completely different spaces, one with a private purpose, the other a more public or social space, in *Hamlet*, there does not seem to be any distinction between the two. Polonius says, 'My lord, he's going to his mother's closet' (III, iii, 27); but later in the graveyard scene Hamlet instructs the skull to 'get you to my lady's chamber and tell her, let her paint an inch thick, to this favour she must come' (V, i, 186–7). Hamlet is suggesting the chamber is where his lady's cosmetics would be kept and where she would have them applied. The mirror Hamlet holds for his mother to reflect upon her sins, if a literal prop, would be located in the closet; presumably, Gertrude's closet and chamber are the same space or within very close proximity of each other, since her cosmetics would not have been far from her looking glass.

Jerry Brotton's analysis of the closet scene suggests that the closet would be located within the bedchamber itself, and that it was a private space, yet with a socially ambiguous function: 'the closet emerged within the architectural space of the Elizabethan domestic interior as a space of intense and dynamic social interaction, partitioned off from the rest of the household, a secret place where public affairs were conducted'.[35] This negotiation between private and public is what makes the closet an ambiguous and potentially dangerous space. As Brotton's essay suggests, by looking at the objects that might be located in Gertrude's closet, we can imagine a much more socially and culturally engaged Gertrude, whose 'sin', I would argue, is simply being female and surrounded by the cultural objects associated with femininity, trade and luxury. Alan Stewart has argued that a lady's closet would contain a variety of objects, including: 'a table, a cupboard, several chests, caskets and hampers, a desk, working baskets, boxes, glasses, pots, bottles, jugs, conserve jars, sweetmeat barrels, an hourglass, a grater, knives . . .'[36] Earlier, I cited William Averell's story about a woman's chamber, which was decked with herbs, flowers, perfumes and tapestry, which 'beautified' the room. As I cited, she would have her servants assist her as she delighted in 'artificial pleasures', and 'her bed chamber was garnished' with commodities that are implicitly exotic and cosmetic: 'sweete hearbes, such varietie of fragrant flowers, such chaunge of odiferous smelles, so perfumed with sweete odours, so stored with sweete waters, so beautified with tapestrie, and decked so artificially'.[37] The tapestry is an object worthy of discussion in a book about cosmetics in Shakespearean drama.

The arrases in *Hamlet* serve two functions: they are aesthetic properties demonstrating wealth and luxury; but they are also used to hide political treachery and hypocrisy. This ambiguity of the tapestries in *Hamlet* parallels the ambiguity of cosmetics, their simultaneous allure and danger, beauty and poison. Averell describes the tapestry in his story as 'beautifying' a room. 'Beautify' is a word associated explicitly with cosmetics, since it was widely used in the period to describe the cosmetic process: 'beautification'. Interestingly too, Jack Jorgens, in his analysis of Kozinstev's 1964 film, argues that the use of the tapestries seems deliberate as they 'furnish warmth and provide cosmetics for the brutal fortress and are thus part of the "seeming" which disgusts Hamlet'.[38] Averell in the sixteenth century and Jorgens in the twenty-first century both acknowledge the use of tapestry as ornament, but also as a liminal object lying somewhere between aesthetics and the more derided artifice. The arras, a property with important cultural meanings, is also used in Gertrude's closet, perhaps to gesture toward Queen Elizabeth I. Jerry Brotton observes two incidents involving Elizabeth and tapestries: the first one took place in May of 1555 when Elizabeth visited her sister Mary to 'protest at her virtual house arrest since Mary's recent marriage to Philip. Recounting the meeting in his *Acts and Monuments*, John Foxe claimed that, in a moment reminiscent of Polonius's own covert piece of surveillance, "It is thought that King Philip was behind a cloth, and not seen" (Foxe 621)'. The second incident took place in 1601 and is recounted by John Harington, who noted that 'the Queen in an almost comic parody of *Hamlet*, "walks much in her privy chamber, and stamps with her feet at ill news, and thrusts her rusty sword into the arras in great rage" '.[39] Whether or not these stories are true, the play registers cultural anxieties about political deception and the Tudor staging of painted authority. No doubt, Elizabeth's own chamber or closet is present in the play's subtext.

When Hamlet enters his mother's closet, we might imagine that he would be faced with:

> her perfumed odours, sweet-washing-balls, Pomanders, sundry sorts of smelling waters, fannes, hatts, feathers, glasses, combs, brouches, ruffes, falling bands, red and white face-colours, scarfes, verdingales, artificiall locks of curled haire, with up-standing-frisadoes . . . smoothing-skin-clouts, night-smocks, myffles . . . cases, coffers, boxes, and many things more, that if a man intrude himself in a Ladies bed chamber, & look upon everything about him, he shal think him selfe to be no else where, but in an evil shop of Merchandise.[40]

This description rages against the prosthetic and commercial nature of female beauty and reveals not only a common impression of a woman's chamber, but also the patriarchal anxiety about the mysteries of female interiority. Hamlet's own perception of his mother's chamber are paralleled with his perception of her sexuality. He describes her bed and chamber as 'enseamed', 'Stewed in corruption' and a 'nasty sty' (III, iv, 83, 84, 85), equating her interiority with the filth of beasts, seeing no difference between her cervix and her 'incestuous sheets'. Simion Grahame's account of a woman's chamber cited above eventually dissolves into a diatribe using much of the same language as Hamlet does. Here women are demeaned and their bodies are fused with the cultural objects associated with lady's chambers and described as remnants of cosmetic filth:

> when some women in a sluttish estate, hath their bed-chamber like a swines-stie, ill-favoured (and uncovered) Pispot, their combs and brushes, full of loose haire and filth, their foule smocks ill laid-up, their knotty phlegme and spetting on the walls and floore, the black and slaverie circles on their lips, sweating, smoaking, and brathing in their uncleene sheetes.[41]

Such descriptions are reminiscent of Bosola's portrait of a painted lady's chamber as a 'shop of witchcraft' in *The Duchess of Malfi*. In his visceral diatribe, Grahame locates the darker elements of female sexuality and cosmetic practice in the bedchamber. Giacamo's invasion of the chamber of Innogen in *Cymbeline* allows him to survey its contents, aware that he has intruded upon a female space that is shrouded by mystery; he also finds other decorative items:

> Such and such pictures there the window, such
> Th'adornment of her bed, the arras, figures,
> Why, such and such; and the contents o' th'story.
>   (II, ii, 25–7)

'Such and such' are vague terms to describe the chamber, testifying to Giacomo's underlying ignorance of Innogen. In her analysis of textiles on the Shakespearean stage, Susan Frye observes that Innogen's chamber, 'like those of many privileged women, is constructed through tapestry, visual imagery, and text'.[42] But Giacamo has observed enough of the superficialities in the chamber to make it seem as though he has invaded her body as well. The description of Innogen's chamber is evasive because of the mystery associated with female spaces. But Shakespeare is not disparaging about the female closet here. Instead, he intrigues us with his imprecise language – 'figures', 'such and such' – gesturing toward the rich objects of aesthetic pleasure that do not necessarily imply a tainted sexuality. In fact, in Innogen's case (and, I would argue, in Gertrude's too), an innocent woman occupies the chamber. An example such as this brings to mind the 'painted closet' of Hawstead Hall. The only one of its kind in the whole of England, the Oratory of Lady Anne Drury (the mother of Elizabeth Drury, a subject of Donne in his *Anniversaries*), is a chamber in which emblems are painted on three of the walls creating a gallery of paint and text, proving that art 'is not mere decoration; rather it is an aid to thought'.[43] The nature of some of the pictorial images and the moralistic tenor of the mottoes that accompany them suggest that the room's visual art was a means to devout meditation. It is the very richness of the painted closet that moves the occupant to morality. I am not suggesting that Gertrude is devout, nor that her closet is necessarily a place for moral devotion; but I am arguing that the luxurious array of particularly feminine objects, including cosmetic pots, painted artefacts and miniatures, located within a lady's chamber are not necessarily markers of a fallen woman.

Hamlet's behaviour in his mother's chamber is an expression of rage at female mutability. He cannot accept change and his anger, as we all know, is directed at his mother's marriage and her lack of attention to the 'shows' of grief. He links her to the painted harlots of the streets whose foreheads are branded with the mark of 'whore'. In the closet he tells her he will 'set you up a glass / Where you may see the inmost part of you' (III, iv, 19–20). There is no stage direction indicating that Hamlet is speaking literally here; we could take the mirror to be either a metaphorical or a literal prop. If there were an actual looking glass used in this scene, however, the spiritually corrective function of mirrors would be engaged: the Bible, the steel glass, a place to view the soul. Metaphorically, Hamlet will act as the mirror for his mother, so that she may see herself as Hamlet sees her. His sermon is such a mirror in which are reflected the sexual sins of his mother. Hamlet's use of the mirror here suggests an underlying anxiety, once again, about Elizabeth Tudor's rule. Her own status as a mirror for magistrates, a mirror for virtuous women and her use of mirrors for cosmetic purposes contradict each other, and the political uncertainties evolving from this contradiction intervene into this scene. The mirror in this scene in *Hamlet*, then, is tied to female virtue, sexuality and political leadership. S. P. Cerasano and Marion Wynne-Davies talk about the difficulties of applying cultural notions of feminine virtue to female monarchs, particularly Elizabeth, who was unmarried. Virtue was advocated, they argue, through the 'popular Renaissance trope, the mirror. In the case of virtue the glass was intended to provoke women to concentrate upon their moral advancement, rather than to embellish their physical adornment'.[44] This binary function of the mirror in Renaissance thought is problematic, however, because it interferes with the management of women. Among the anti-cosmetic sentiments in his tract, *The Rich Cabinet*, Thomas Gainsford adds to the mix by arguing 'woman, faire, and proude, and wanting wisdome: is a looking glasse of vanitie and a mirror of inconstancy'.[45] Elizabeth's notorious fondness for crystal glasses, which produced a tinted reflection to flatter her image, contradicts her status as the exempla for feminine virtue; in other words, she was meant to be the steel glass in which all women should find their copy.

Cultural fantasies about the objects of Elizabeth's own closet are in play during the closet scene of *Hamlet*. Elizabeth's closet would contain all of the riches, spices, cosmetic pots, combs and brushes, jewels, tapestries, miniatures, caskets and perfumes that we may find in Gertrude's closet. Among the countless gifts Elizabeth was given every new year, for example, were 'a pott of green gynger', 'a pott of the rynds of lemons', perfumed gloves, 'a faire large looking glasse set in frame, corded with crimson velvett, bound with passamayn lace of Venis gold', 'boxes of preservatiues', 'pott of orenge flowers', and 'bottles of sweet water'.[46] The presence of these objects in the closets of women reaffirm the necessary and important role material objects played in the construction of identity, and specifically, here female identity. Gertrude is, when the play opens, a reinvented woman, newly married and fond of cosmetics; she has already shed her grief and her past and she constructs a new identity, but without Hamlet's knowledge or approval. The properties of self-fashioning within her closet would recall this fact for him.

Hamlet's language evokes the cosmetic as he proceeds to diminish his mother; he claims she as committed

> Such and act
> That blurs the grace and blush of modesty,
> Calls virtue hypocrite, takes off the rose
> From the fair forehead of an innocent love
> And sets a blister there . . .
> (III, iv, 40–4)

All the sins of Eve are projected on to Gertrude at this point and she is forced to see 'black and grained spots / As will not leave their tinct' (80–1). These images also form part of the network of cosmetic signifiers scattered throughout the play. Hamlet is constantly associating painting and tinctures with female, sexual and political corruption, without acknowledging the inherent contradiction in his use of painted faces to reassert his father's authority. He draws her attention to the portraits of the two kings, 'Look here upon this picture, and on this, / The counterfeit presentment of two brothers' (III, iv, 54–5); these would be pictures painted with the same ingredients used to paint the face of the queen and her ladies at court. It seems, particularly from Hamlet's comparative use of *ekphrasis*, that he is distinguishing between types of painted surfaces. Here we have two monarchs with embellished faces; prior to this the audience witnessed the cosmeticised ghost of old Hamlet. Yet, the portrait would be more able to demonstrate 'what a grace was seated on this brow, Hyperion's curls, the front of Jove himself' (III, iv, 56–7). Shakespeare forces us to pause in this moment in which he juxtaposes the painted portrait of a monarch with its cosmeticised ghost inside the bedchamber of a painted queen, whose moralising son may also be painted up like a fool. The moment the Ghost enters the closet, Hamlet will have to make an optical adjustment from the limned face of the painting of old Hamlet to the ghostly pallor of the actor playing the apparition. Shakespeare is forcing us to think about painted representations of power here: the portrait signifying the proliferation of powerful monarchical images, the faded pallor of the Ghost signifying the end of power. Significantly, in this moment the queen is frightened by Hamlet whose rage about female sexuality, assassination, succession and marriage have pointed connections with the political concerns at the end of the Tudor reign.

Ophelia's Beautifying Craft

Throughout the play, Ophelia's status has been pictorial. Martha C. Rook argues that she 'seems to move towards the abstract or emblematic throughout as she is represented as dutiful daughter, beloved beauty, mad woman, drowned innocent'.[47] In the 'nunnery scene' she is, according to Rook, rendered into a 'false picture' by Hamlet when he refers 'to the use of cosmetics as painting'.[48] Later on, in her death, through Gertrude's narrative, Ophelia becomes 'a set piece, an arras, a speaking picture'.[49] In the scenes of her madness, Claudius, Gertrude, and Laertes conspire to maintain her status as a silent emblem. Claudius refers to her as 'pretty Ophelia' (IV, v, 55), and argues that because she is 'divided from herself', she is no better than 'pictures or mere beasts' (81–2). Ophelia becomes an active agent and is released from her subjectivity when she dabbles with herbs in her 'madness' scenes. Laertes's 'O Rose of May' (156) prepares us for the pastoral redefinition of Ophelia. John Russell Brown claims that Ophelia's mad scenes evoke 'rural' England and asks what effect 'these pastoral intrusions into the courtly and political world of Elsinore' have.[50] I would argue that the herbal and floral allusions in these scenes are evocative, in part, of recipes that include organic ingredients, such as flowers and herbs to beautify and restore the body. The songs and the flowers serve to accompany Ophelia's expressions of grief, and she is marginally linked to witchcraft in this scene. She hands out rosemary, pansies, fennel, columbines, rue and daisies, and dreams of giving away violets (which commonly represented 'faithfulness'). Flowers and herbs held particular significance in the Renaissance in their own right, but they were also crucial ingredients in many medicinal, culinary and cosmetic recipes.

In order 'to make the face white and faire', one would have to 'Take Rosemary, and boile it in white Wine, and wash thy face therewith'.[51] If a woman wanted a 'well coloured face', Wirtzung recommends 'Aromatical wines, that have Rose-mary in them. Not onely to be drunken, but to wash the face also'.[52] Rosemary was also 'used as a mourning posy, worn and then given to the dead'.[53] To cure melancholy one could use 'violet leaves . . . chamomile, hopes, dill . . . and fennel, decocted in ale of beere'.[54] A sixteenth-century poem for lovers informs us of the symbolic importance of some of Ophelia's herbs and flowers: 'Rosemarie is for remembrance, / betweene us daie and night'; additionally, 'Fenel is for flatterers / an evil thing it is sure . . . / Violet is for faithfulnesse'.[55] Ophelia's madness and death reveal that she has retreated into organic feminine artifice (which would be even more poignant were she painted here); her artful songs simultaneously conceal and give away her traumatised condition. Eventually, when she drowns, Ophelia combines with the earth, fusing flesh, flowers and water, and in a pretty death she returns to the realm of 'Dame Nature'.

Hamlet, however, is unable to see face painting and beautification as anything but corrupt and filthy, even as he engages in the cosmetic himself. In the graveyard scene the skull reminds Hamlet that death is in his hands, and its contagion might make them smell. Rosenberg's survey of theatrical productions of *Hamlet* reveals that 'Hamlet has often again smelled his finger; the more fastidious has wiped his hands against each other, or on his handkerchief, on grass, dust, or dirt'.[56] Hamlet's view of the cosmetic accords with his view of female sexuality: he equates both with the rot of death. Hamlet was not alone in seeing a painted woman as a type of *memento mori*. Steven Mullaney argues that 'sexual allure and the skull are combined in a conundrum that is the ageing female body, for in a period that linguistically coded sexual climax as "dying", the face introduces a third register to the common Renaissance pun'.[57] It is true that women had a morbid fear of old age in Renaissance England. Old women were 'hags' or 'witches' associated with the devil; these prejudices had severe social implications for ageing women: 'the old woman is the antithesis of the idealized young woman and just as youth implies beauty so a lack of youth implies ugliness'.[58] When *Hamlet* was written, Queen Elizabeth I was ageing. Some have argued that her own anxieties about the loss of her youth led her to refuse to 'examine her reflection in a mirror during the last twenty years of her life'.[59] The Queen's desperation to preserve her youth and beauty, to deny the inevitable, seems to be what Hamlet gestures toward when he reviles his mother for not acting her age. It is certain that in the graveyard scene, Hamlet is ruminating upon his mother's actions again.

Hamlet's expression of disgust for the skull after he cynically proclaims, 'Now get you to my lady's chamber and tell her, let her paint an inch thick, to this favour she must come' (V, i, 178–9),[60] belongs to a tradition of criticism that devalued female cosmetic ritual by associating it with the physical deterioration of the human body. For many, to think on cosmetics was immediately to think on death. Preservation, in the minds of anti-cosmetic polemicists, is an impossibility and therefore, a waste of time. In the graveyard scene, the questions resounds: 'Why do ye embellish and adorn your flesh with such port and grace, which within some few dayes wormes will devoure in the grave?'[61] And 'why pamperest thou that carren fleshe so high, whiche sometyme doeth stinke and rot on the earth as thou goest?'[62] Women who paint will only find that their 'morne-like christall countenances, shall be netted over, and (Masker-like) cawbe-visarded, with crawling venomous wormes'.[63] Most critics assume that Hamlet is referring to Gertrude when he talks of his 'lady's chamber' in this scene. For instance, Drew-Bear uses it to support her conclusion that Gertrude's face *should* be painted: the 'tradition of visualizing corruption in the face would strongly suggest that Gertrude's face revealed her moral taint'.[64] And Clayton Mackenzie suggests that 'however much make-up Queen Gertude applies to her face, she will still be reduced to the same state as the jester Yorick'.[65] I would agree that Gertrude would wear makeup, but I do not think it is indicative of her guilt; this is where cosmetic symbolism becomes ambiguous in dramatic representations of painted ladies on the Renaissance stage. The Lady in *The Second Maiden's Tragedy* was painted, but her spirit was clean; the painted skull of Gloriana in *The Revenger's Tragedy* once belonged to a virtuous woman. These ambiguous representations echo the various meanings attached to the painted face of Queen Elizabeth I. In *Hamlet*, through Gertrude's body, we are given a glimpse of the nearly canonised though painted flesh of the last Tudor monarch. Mullaney argues that 'even aside from the necessity to paint "near half an inch thick" . . . the erotic dynamics of Elizabethan rule had always entailed a certain ambivalence and danger, involving as they did the construction of an ambiguous desire for the queen, not as monarch but as woman.'[66] What intrudes upon Hamlet's meditations on death is the notion of sexual desire. The correlations between sex and death made by Elizabethans is familiar to most critics, but it is important to consider in the graveyard scene the added implications of Hamlet's fear of death and desire, and his recognition of his sometimes incestuous attraction to cosmeticised bodies.

Conclusion

I want to end this chapter by recalling the original performance of the play at the Globe in 1601 and by reinvoking the image of a painted ghost. In this play, Shakespeare meditates upon the meanings of paintedness, representation and theatricality, while he explores political questions and anxieties that may be rooted in cultural imaginings about the ageing body of the Queen of England. When Hamlet advises the players to, 'Suit the action to the word, the word to the action, with this special observance, that you o'erstep not the modesty of nature. For anything so o'erdone is from the purpose of playing whose end, both at the first and now, was and is to hold as 'twere the mirror up to nature' (III, ii, 17–24), he alludes to the inherent theatricality of monarchy. Richard Mulcaster's *The Queene Majesties Passage* recounting the pageants of the coronation of Queen Elizabeth I presents an ideal of queenly magnificence and a ceremonial, perfumed, display of authority, the type of display that would dominate her self-presentation throughout her reign. Hamlet's suggestion that the 'purpose of playing' is to hold a mirror up to nature 'to show virtue her feature', taken in this context, is politically resonant when we consider mirrors as models of behaviour. Cosmetics come into play when considering the Tudor court: Shakespeare, like Middleton, Webster and Jonson, recognised the magnificent effect painted faces had on audiences, and therefore demonstrated through his own art that performance necessitates cosmetic materiality. It would not make sense for Shakespeare to cry out unequivocally against painted faces, since he, according to Nicolas Rowe (1709), took the part of the Ghost in *Hamlet*. For this performance, Shakespeare would have worn cosmetics himself for the 'purpose of playing'. It is an extraordinary image: Shakespeare beautified with a concoction of white lead, vinegar and perhaps dusted pearl, illustrating to his critics his own unique blend of physical and textual beautification, and reflecting to his audience the ideological ambiguities inherent in a painted face.

Notes

1. Gayton, *Pleasant Notes*, pp. 94–5 [I would like to thank Tiffany Stern for drawing my attention to this reference].
2. Mullaney, 'Mourning and misogyny', p. 166.
3. See my article, 'Beautied with plastr'ing art', *Around the Globe*, September (2005).
4. Gainsford, *The Rich Cabinet*, p. 7.
5. Gee, *New Shreds of the Old Snare*, p. 1.
6. Ibid. p. 17.
7. Ibid. p. 17.
8. Ibid. p. 20.
9. Mack, 'The world of Hamlet', p. 95.
10. French, 'Chaste constancy in *Hamlet*', p. 96.

11. Hunt, 'A thing of nothing', p. 38.
12. Clemen, *Shakespeare's Dramatic Art*, p. 187.
13. Ibid. p. 176.
14. Gainsford, *A Rich Cabinet*, p. 162.
15. Hynd, *The Mirrour of Worldly Fame*, p. 37.
16. Tuke, *A Treatise Against Paint[i]ng*, p. 12.
17. Greene, *Greens Groats-Worth of Wit*, p. 140.
18. Hall, *The Loathsomenesse of Long Hair*, pp. 99–100.
19. Prynne, *Histrio-Mastix*, pp. 159–60.
20. Gosson, *The School of Abuse*, p. 32.
21. Gosson, *Playes Confuted in Five Actions*, Sig. G6r and B6r.
22. Topsell, *The Historie of Four-Footed Beastes*, p. 502.
23. Ibid. p. 516.
24. Ibid. p. 512.
25. Hassel, 'Wormwood, wormwood', p. 159.
26. Ibid. p. 159.
27. Rosenberg, *The Masks of Hamlet*, p. 457.
28. Ibid. p. 460.
29. Hall, *The Loathsomenesse of Long Hair*, p. 106.
30. Welsby (ed.), *Sermons and Society*, p. 61.
31. 'The traditional depiction of Gertrude is a false one, because what *her* words and actions actually create is a soft, obedient, dependent, unimaginative woman who is caught miserably at the centre of a desperate struggle between two "mighty opposites", her "heart cleft in twain" (III, iv, 156) by divided loyalties to husband and son' (Smith, 'A heart cleft in twain', p. 80).
32. Drew-Bear, *Painted Faces*, p. 98.
33. Ibid. p. 99.
34. Ibid. p. 99.
35. Brotton, 'Ways of seeing *Hamlet*', p. 165.
36. Stewart, 'The Early modern closet discovered', p. 82.
37. Averell, *A Dyall for Dainty Darlings*, pp. 4–5.
38. Jorgens, *Shakespeare on Film*, p. 226.
39. Brotton, 'Ways of seeing *Hamlet*', p. 170.
40. Grahame, *The Anatomie of Hvmors*, p. 31.
41. Ibid. p. 31.
42. Frye, 'Staging women's relations to textiles', p. 231.
43. Farmer, *Poets and the Visual Arts*, p. 78.
44. Cerasano and Wynne-Davies, *Gloriana's Face*, p. 11.
45. Gainford, *The Rich Cabinet*, p. 164.
46. Anonymous, *Progresses and Public Processions*, pp. 13–14, 456–7.
47. Rook, 'Representations of Ophelia', p. 21.
48. Ibid. p. 21.
49. Ibid. p. 22.
50. Brown, *Shakespeare: The Tragedies*, p. 152.
51. Anonymous, *A Closet for Ladies*, Sig. H11r.
52. Wirtzung, *The General Practise*, p. 79.
53. Cunnington and Lucas, *Costumes for Births*, p. 137.
54. Bright, *A Treatise of Melancholie*, pp. 269–70.

55. Robinson, *A Handful of Pleasant Delights*, Sig. Aii*v*.
56. Rosenberg, *The Masks of Hamlet*, p. 845.
57. Mullaney, 'Mourning and misogyny', p. 168.
58. Fitzpatrick, 'Spenser's nationalistic images of beauty', p. 23.
59. Cerasano and Wynne-Davies, *Gloriana's Face*, p. 19.
60. Mullaney and Harold Jenkins in his introduction to the Arden edition of *Hamlet* both acknowledge that the phrase 'let her paint an inch thick' was not used solely by Shakespeare. The letter of a Jesuit priest, Roberto Perino dated 1601 reads: 'It was commonly observed this Christmas that her Majesty, when she came to be seen, was continually painted, not only all over her face, but her very neck and breast also, and that the same was in some places near half an inch thick' (Foley (ed.), *Records of the English Province*, p. 8).
61. Brathwait, *The English Gentlewoman*, p. 17.
62. Anonymous, 'An Homilie Against Excess of Apparel', p. 224.
63. Nashe, *Christ's Tears*, p. 71.
64. Drew-Bear, *Painted Faces*, p. 99.
65. Mackenzie, *Emblems of Mortality*, p. 105.
66. Mullaney, 'Mourning and misogyny', p. 168.

Epilogue

The aim of this book has been to address the question I cited in the Introduction: 'should or shouldn't seemingly vain objects be deemed worthy of serious attention?' Most critics who have examined the theological and misogynistic oppostion to cosmetics argue that the dramatic representation of cosmetics is grounded in a fundamental devaluation of beautification. This view is relatively shortsighted. Early modern English culture had a complex and ambiguous relationship with the notion of paintedness. As I have argued, the painted iconography of Queen Elizabeth I was simultaneously an emblem of political potency, and a marker of an unmistakable femininity. While anti-cosmetic polemicists cried out against the various methods and materials women were using to beautify their bodies, a proliferation of cosmetic recipes, continental and English, were being printed between the 1590s and 1650s. These competing narratives suggest an inevitable tension between prescription and practice, and they demonstrate the increasing significance of material practices in the formation of individual identities.

Cosmetic ingredients and the metaphorical language offered by cosmetic discourses provided dramatists like Middleton, Jonson, Webster and Shakespeare with crucial and vividly dramatic materials for their art. Boy actors were painted, or painted themselves, to signify femininity; actors who played clowns, ghosts, walls, twins and spirits also painted their faces. Dramatists capitalised upon the ironic dimensions of the face painting debate, the rich contradictions in condemning painted faces and the cultural significance of cosmetic materiality. Propping up the action of plays I dub cosmetic drama, such as *The Revenger's Tragedy* and *The Second Maiden's Tragedy*, cosmetic materials are essential stage properties, the prosthetics of theatre regardless of their traditional associations with harlotry, adultery, poison and witchcraft. It is perhaps because of these cultural associations that cosmetics on the stage proved to be controversial and therefore the very 'stuff' of good drama. Dramatists saw fit to transport the notion of beautification out of the domestic space into the theatrical space, recognising the performative value of cosmetic materiality and the poetic richness of cosmetic metaphors. These dramatic representations of cosmetics chip away at the traditionalist moral denigration of cosmetics and focus our attention on a material practice that dynamically reflects a burgeoning industry and a cultural phenomenon that was crucial to the constructions of gender identity, race and the perception of monarchical stability.

Bibliography

Adams, Thomas (1629), 'The White Devil', in *The Workes of Thomas Adams*, London.

Alberti, Leon Battista [1435] (1966), *On Painting*, trans. John R. Spencer, New Haven and London: Yale University Press.

Alexander, Nigel (1970), 'Intelligence in *The Duchess of Malfi*', in *John Webster*, ed. Brian Morris, Mermaid Critical Commentaries, London: Ernest Benn, pp. 93–112.

Anonymous (1627), *A Closet for Ladies and Gentlewomen, Or, The Art of preseruing, Conseruing, and Candying*, London.

Anonymous (1793), *A Complete Edition of the Poets of Great Britain*, London.

Anonymous (1683), *England's Vanity: or the voice of God against the monstrous sin of pride in dress and apparel*, London.

Anonymous (1620), *Haec-Vir: or, The Womanish-Man. Being an answere to a late Booke intituled Hic-Mulier*, London.

Anonymous (1620), *Hic-Mulier: Or, The Man-Woman*, London.

Anonymous (1574), 'An Homilie Against Excess of Apparel', in *The Second Tome of Homilies*, London.

Anonymous (1574), 'An Homilie against Peril of Idolatrie, and superfluous deckyng of Churches', in *The Second Tome of Homilies*, London.

Anonymous (1639), *The Ladies Cabinet opened: wherein is found hidden severall Experiments in Preserving and Conserving, Physicke, and Surgery, Cookery and Huswifery*, London.

Anonymous (1593), *The Phoenix Nest*, London.

Anonymous (1649), *A Precious Treasury of Twenty Rare Secrets*, London.

Anonymous (1597), *The Problemes of Aristotle, with other Philosophers and Phisitions*, London.

Anonymous (1923), *Progresses and Public Processions of Queen Elizabeth*, New York: Burt Franklin.

Anonymous [1520] (1874), *The Tragi-Comedy of Calisto & Melibaea*, in *A Select Collection of Old English Plays*, ed. W. Carew Hazlitt, London.

Ansari, K. H. (1985), *Imagery of John Webster's Plays*, Delhi: Shree Publishing House.

Aristotle (1964), *Metaphysics*, in *Philosophies in Art and Beauty: Selected Readings in Aesthetics from Plato to Heidegger*, ed. Albert Hofstadler and Richard Kuhns, Chicago and London: University of Chicago Press.

Arnold, Janet (ed.) (1998), *Queen Elizabeth's Wardrobe Unlock'd*, London: W. S. Maney & Sons.

Aston, Margaret (1988), *England's Iconoclasts: Laws Against Images*, Oxford: Clarendon Press.

Aughterson, Kate (ed.) (1995), *Renaissance Woman: Constructions of Femininity in England*, London and New York: Routledge.

Aughterson, Kate (2001), *Webster: The Tragedies*, Analysing Texts, Basingstoke: Palgrave.

Austin, William (1639), *Haec Homo, Wherein the Excellency of the Creation of Woman is described by way of an Essay*, London.

Averell, William (1584), *A Dyall for Dainty Darlings, roct in the cradle of securitie*, London.

Averell, William (1584), *A Myrrour for vertuous Maydes*, London.

Averell, William (1588), *A Meruailous Combat of Contrarieties*, London.

Bacon, Francis [1605] (1996), *The Advancement of Learning*, in *Francis Bacon*, ed. Brian Vickers, The Oxford Authors, Oxford: Oxford University Press.

Balsamo, Anne (1999), *Technologies of the Gendered Body: Reading Cyborg Women*, Durham and London: Duke University Press.

Barish, Jonas (1956), 'Ovid, Juvenal, and the silent woman', *PMLA* 71, 213–24.

Barish, Jonas (1960), *Ben Jonson and the Language of Prose Comedy*, Cambridge, MA: Harvard University Press.

Barnes, Barnabe (1607), *The Devil's Charter*, London.

Bateman, Stephen (1569), *A Christall glasse of Christian reformation*, London.

Beier, A. L. and Roger Finlay (eds) (1986), *London 1500–1700: The Making of the Metropolis*, London: Longman.

Bell, Rudolph M. (1999), *How To Do It: Guides to Good Living for Renaissance Italians*, Chicago and London: Chicago University Press.

Belsey, Catherine (1980), 'Emblem and antithesis in *The Duchess of Malfi*', *Renaissance Drama*, XI, 115–33.

Bergeron, David M. (1984), 'Art within *The Second Maiden's Tragedy*', *Medieval and Renaissance Drama in England*, 1, 331–9.

Berry, Ralph (1972), *The Art of John Webster*, Oxford: Clarendon Press.

Boaystuau, Peter (1574), *Theatrum Mundi, The Theatre or rule of the world, wherein may be sene the running and race and course of everye mans life*, trans. John Alday, London.

Boccacio, Giovanni [1349–51] (1972), *The Decameron*, trans. G. H. McWilliam, Harmondsworth: Penguin Books.

Brathwait, Richard (1621), *Time's Curtaine Drawne, or The Anatomie of vanitie. With other choice poems, entituled; Health from Helicon*, London.

Brathwait, Richard (1631), *The English Gentlewoman, drawne out to the full body*, London.

Brathwait, Richard (1640), *Ar't Asleep Husband? A Boulster Lecture*, London.

Briggs, Robin (1996), *Witches and Neighbours: The Social and Cultural Context of European Witchcraft*, New York: Viking.

Bright, Timothy [1586] (1940), *A Treatise of Melancholie*, London; New York: Facsimile Text Society.

Brome, Richard (1659), *The English Moor, or the Mock-Marriage*, London.

Bronfen, Elizabeth (1992), *Over Her Dead Body: Death, Femininity and the Aesthetic*, Manchester: Manchester University Press.

Brooke, Nicholas (1979), *Horrid Laughter in Jacobean Tragedy*, New York: Barnes & Noble.

Brotton, Jerry (2002), *The Renaissance Bazaar: From the Silk Road to Michaelangelo*, Oxford: Oxford University Press.

Brotton, Jerry (2002), 'Ways of seeing *Hamlet*', in *Hamlet: New Critical Essays*, ed. Arthur F. Kinney, New York: Routledge, pp. 161–76.

Brown, John Russell (2001), *Shakespeare: The Tragedies*, New York: Palgrave.

Browne, Thomas (1669), *Pseudodoxia Epidemica: Or, Enquiries into very Many Received Tenents, and Commonly Presumed Truths*, London.

Bruster, Douglas (2004), 'The dramatic life of objects in the early modern theatre', in *Staged Properties in Early Modern English Drama*, ed. Jonathan Gil Harris and Natasha Korda, Cambridge: Cambridge University Press, pp. 67–96.

Bulwer, John (1653), *Anthropometamorphosis: Man Transform'd; or the Artificial Changeling*, London.

Buoni, Thomas (1606), *Problemes of Beavtie and humane affections*, trans. S. L. Gent, London.

Burton, Robert [1621–51] (1989), *The Anatomy of Melancholy*, ed. Thomas C. Faulkner, Nicolas K. Kiessling and Rhonda L. Blair, 4 vols, Oxford: Clarendon Press.

Bushnell, Rebecca (1990), *Tragedies of Tyrants: Political Thought and Theater in the English Renaissance*, Ithaca and London: Cornell University Press.

Callaghan, Dympna (2000), 'Introduction', in *A Feminist Companion to Shakespeare*, ed. Dympna Callaghan, Oxford: Blackwell, pp. xi–xiv.

Callaghan, Dympna (2000), *Shakespeare Without Women: Representing Gender and Race on the Renaissance Stage*, London and New York: Routledge.

Caroll, William C. (1976), *The Great Feast of Language in Love's Labour's Lost*, Princeton: Princeton University Press.

Carroll, Robert and Stephen Prickett (eds) (1997), *The Bible: Authorized King James Version with Apocrypha*, Oxford: Oxford University Press.

Castiglione, Baldesar [1528] (1967), *The Book of the Courtier*, trans. George Bull, Harmondsworth: Penguin Books.

Cave, Richard, Elizabeth Schafer and Brian Woolland (eds) (1999), *Ben Jonson and Theatre: Performance, Practice and Theory*, London: Routledge.

Cerasano, S. P. and Marion Wynne-Davies (eds) (1992), *Gloriana's Face: Women, Public and Private in the English Renaissance*, London: Harvester Wheatsheaf.

Clark, Sandra (1983), *The Elizabethan Pamphleteers: Popular Moralistic Pamphlets 1580–1640*, London: Athlone Press.

Clemen, Wolfgang (1972), *Shakespeare's Dramatic Art: Collected Essays*, London: Methuen.

Cogan, Thomas (1584), *The Haven of Health*, London.

Cohen, Walter (1997), 'Introduction to *Love's Labour's Lost*', in *The Norton Shakespeare*, ed. S. Greenblatt et al., London and New York: Norton.

Contarini, Cardinall Gaspar (1599), *The Commonwealth and Gouernment of Venice*, trans. Lewes Lewkenor, London.

Corson, Richard (1972), *Fashions in Makeup: From Ancient to Modern Times*, London: Peter Owen.

Corson, Richard (1986), *Stage Makeup*, Englewood Cliffs: Prentice Hall.

Coryat, Thomas (1611), *Crudities*, London.

Culpeper, Nicholas (1660), *Arts Master-piece: or the Beautifying Part of Physick*, London.

Cunningham, Peter (ed.) (1842), *Extracts from the Accounts of the Revels at Court, in the Reigns of Queen Elizabeth I and King James I*, London.

Cunnington, Phillis and Catherine Lucas (1972), *Costumes for Births, Marriages and Deaths*, London: Adam & Charles Black.

Daileader, Celia R. (1998), *Eroticism on the Renaissance Stage: Transcendence, Desire, and the Limits of the Visible*, Cambridge: Cambridge University Press.

Davis, Kathy (1995), *Reshaping the Female Body: The Dilemma of Cosmetic Surgery*, New York and London: Routledge.

Della Porta, Giovanni Battista (1658), *Natural Magick in XX Bookes*, London.

Dent, R. W. (1983), 'Imagination in *A Midsummer Night's Dream*', in *Shakespeare: A Midsummer Night's Dream*, Casebook Series, London: Macmillan, pp. 124–42.

Doebler, John (1974), *Shakespeare's Speaking Pictures: Studies in Iconic Imagery*, Albuquerque: University of New Mexico Press.

Dolan, Frances E. (1993), 'Taking the pencil out of God's hand: art, nature, and the face-painting debate in early modern England', *PMLA*, 108, 224–39.

Donne, John (1971), *Selected Prose*, ed. Neil Rhodes, Harmondsworth: Penguin Books.

Downame, John (1656), *A Discourse of Auxillary Beauty or Artificiall Hansomenesse. In point of conscience between two ladies*, London.

Drew-Bear, Annette (1980), 'Face-painting scenes in Ben Jonson', *Studies in Philology*, 77, 388–401.

Drew-Bear, Annette (1994), *Painted Faces on the Renaissance Stage: The Moral Significance of Face-Painting Conventions*, London and Toronto: Bucknell University Press.

Du Bosc, Jacques (1639), *The Compleat Woman*, trans. N. N., London.

Dubrow, Heather (1995), *Echoes of Desire: English Petrarchism and Its Countered Discourses*, Ithaca and London: Cornell University Press.

Dundas, Judith (1993), *Pencils Rhetorique: Renaissance Poets and the Art of Painting*, Newark: University of Delaware Press.

Eamon, William (1994), *Science and the Secrets of Nature: Books of Secrets in Medieval and Early Modern Culture*, Princeton: Princeton University Press.

Earle, John (1628), *Microcosmographie: or a Piece of the World Discovered in Essays & Characters*, London.

Etcoff, Nancy (1999), *Survival of the Prettiest: The Science of Beauty*, London: Little, Brown and Co.

Egerton, Judy (1999), 'Catalogue', *Van Dyck 1599–1641*, Antwerp and London: Royal Academy Publications.

Evans, Maurice (ed.) (1977), *Elizabethan Sonnets*, London: J. M. Dent & Sons.

Farmer, Norman K. (1984), *Poets and the Visual Arts in Renaissance England*, Austin: University of Texas Press.

Fernie, Ewan (2002), *Shame in Shakespeare*, Accents on Shakespeare, London and New York: Routledge.

Ficino, Marsilio (1964), *Commentary on Plato's Symposium*, in *Philosophies in Art and Beauty: Selected Readings in Aesthetics from Plato to Heidegger*, ed. Albert Hofstadler and Richard Kuhns, Chicago and London: University of Chicago Press.

Firenzuola, Agnolo [1541] (1992), *On the Beauty of Women*, trans. Konrad Eisenbichler and Jacqueline Murray, Philadelphia: University of Pennsylvania Press.

Fitzpatrick, Joan (1998), 'Spenser's nationalistic images of beauty: The ideal and the other in relation to Protestant England and Catholic Ireland in *The Faerie Queene* Book I', *Cahiers Elisabethains*, 53, January, 15–25.

Florio, John (1598) *Queen Anna's new World of Words; or Dictionaries of the Italian and English tongues,* London.

Foakes, R. A. (1973), 'The art of cruelty: Hamlet and Vindice', *Shakespeare Survey*, 26, 21–31.

Foakes, R. A. (ed.) (2002), *Henslowe's Diary*, Cambridge: Cambridge University Press.

Foley, Henry (ed.) (1877), *Records of the English Province of the Society of Jesus*, 7 vols, London.

Foucault, Michael (1992), *The History of Sexuality*, vol. 2, *The Use of Pleasure*, trans. Robert Hurley, Harmondsworth: Penguin Books.

Fraunce, Abraham [1588] (1969), *The Arcadian Rhetorike*, Menston: Scolar Press.

French, Marilyn (1992), 'Chaste constancy in *Hamlet*', in *Hamlet*, ed. Martin Coyle, New Casebooks, London: Macmillan, pp. 96–112.

Freud, Sigmund (1964), 'The theme of the three caskets', in *The Standard Edition of the Complete Psychological Works of Sigmund Freud*, trans. James Strachey, Anna Freud, Alix Strachey and Alan Tyson, 24 vols, London: Hogarth Press, pp. 289–301.

Frye, Susan (2000), 'Staging women's relations to textiles in Shakespeare's *Othello* and *Cymbeline*', in *Early Modern Visual Culture: Representation, Race, and Empire in Renaissance England*, ed. Peter Erickson and Clark Hulse, pp. 218–46.

Gainsford, Thomas (1616), *The Rich Cabinet. Furnished with varietie of excellent discriptions, exquisite characters, witty discourses, and delightful histories, deuine and morall*, London.

Garber, Marjorie (1992), *Vested Interests: Cross-dressing and Cultural Anxiety*, New York and London: Routledge.

Garner, Shirley Nelson (1989), '"Let her paint an inch thick": Painted ladies in Renaissance drama and society', *Renaissance Drama*, 20, 121–38.

Gascoigne, George [1575] (1910), 'The Poesies', in *The Complete Works of Gerge Gascoigne*, ed. John W. Cunliffe, 2 vols, Cambridge: Cambridge University Press.

Gascoigne, George [1576] (1910), *The Steel Glas: a Satyre*, in *The Complete Works of George Gascoigne*, ed. John W. Cunliffe, 2 vols, Cambridge: Cambridge University Press.

Gaule, John (1629), *Distractions or The Holy Madness*, London.

Gayton, Edmund (1654), *Pleasant Notes upon Don Quixot*, London.

Gee, John (1624), *New Shreds of the Old Snare*, London.

Goddard, William (1615), *A Neaste of Waspes Latelie Fovnd*, London.

Goreau, Eloise K. (1974), *Integrity of Life: Allegorical Imagery in the Plays of John Webster*, Salzburg: University of Salzburg Press.

Gosson, Stephen [1579] (1906), *The School of Abuse*, ed. Edward Aber, London: Constable.

Gosson, Stephen (1580), *Playes Confuted in Five Actions*, London.

Grabes, Herbert (1982), *The Mutable Glass: Mirror-imagery in Titles and Texts of the Middle Ages and English Renaissance*, trans. Gordon Collier, Cambridge: Cambridge University Press.

Grahame, Simion (1609), *The Anatomie of Hvmors*, Edinburgh.

Grange, John (1577), *The Golden Aphroditis: A Pleasant discourse*, London.

Greenblatt, Stephen (1980), *Renaissance Self-Fashioning from More to Shakespeare*, Chicago and London: University of Chicago Press.

Greenblatt, Stephen (1988), *Shakespearean Negotiations: The Circulation of Social Energy in Renaissance England*, Oxford: Clarendon Press.

Greenblatt, Stephen (1988), 'Invisible bullets', in S. Greenblatt, *Shakespearean Negotiations: The Circulation of Social Energy in Renaissance England*, Oxford: Clarendon Press.

Greenblatt, Stephen (1997), 'Introduction to *A Midsummer Night's Dream*', in *The Norton Shakespeare*, ed. S. Greenblatt et al., London and New York: Norton.

Greenblatt, Stephen (2005), 'The mark of beauty', paper given at 2005 annual meeting of the Shakespeare Association of America.

Greene, Robert (1596), *Greens Groats-Worth of Wit, bought with a Million of Repentance*, London.

Greer, Germaine (2000), 'Uneasy lies the head that wears the crown', *The Daily Telegraph*, 13 May.

Grieco, Sara F. Matthews (1993), 'The body, appearance, and sexuality', in *A History of Women: Renaissance and Enlightenment Paradoxes*, ed. Natalie Zemon Davis and Arlette Farge, Cambridge, MA: Harvard University Press, pp. 46–84.

Gurr, Andrew and Mariko Ichikawa (2000), *Staging in Shakespeare's Theatres*, Oxford: Oxford University Press.

Hackett, Helen (1995), *Virgin Mother, Maiden Queen: Elizabeth I and the Cult of the Virgin Mary*, Basingstoke: Macmillan.

Hall, Joseph (1597), *Virgidemiarum, Sixe Bookes*, London.

Hall, Kim F. (1995), *Things of Darkness: Economies of Race and Gender in Early Modern England*, Ithaca and London: Cornell University Press.

Hall, Thomas (1653), *The Loathsomenesse of Long Hair*, London.

Hallahan, Huston (1977), 'Silence, eloquence, and chatter in Jonson's *Epicoene*', *Huntington Quarterly*, 40, 117–27.

Harrington, John [1618] (1970), *Epigrams by John Harrington*, Menston: Scolar Press.

Harris, Jonathan Gil (1998), *Foreign Bodies and the Body Politic: Discourses of Social Pathology in Early Modern England*, Cambridge: Cambridge University Press.

Harris, Jonathan Gil (2001), 'Shakespeare's hair: staging the object of material culture', *Shakespeare Quarterly*, 52: 4, 479–91.

Harris, Jonathan Gil and Natasha Korda (eds) (2002), *Staged Properties in Early Modern English Drama*, Cambridge: Cambridge University Press.

Harrison, Willam [1577] (1877), *Description of England in Shakespeare's Youth*, ed. Frederick J. Furnivall, London: N. Trubner.

Hartman, G. (1684), *The True Preserver and Restorer of Health*, London.

Hassel Jr, R. Chris (1993), 'Wormwood, wormwood', *Shakespeare-Jahrbuch*, 150–62.

Heywood, Thomas [1603] (1961), *A Woman Killed with Kindness*, ed. R. W. Van Fossen, The Revels Plays, London: Methuen.

Holland, Henry (1590), *A Treatise Against Witchcraft: or, A dialogue, wherein the greatest doubts concerning that sinne, are briefly answered*, Cambridge.

Hull, Suzanne W. (1982), *Chaste, Silent, & Obedient: English Books for Women 1475–1640*, San Marino: Huntington Library.

Hunt, John (1988), 'A thing of nothing: The catastrophic body in *Hamlet*', *Shakespeare Quarterly*, 39:1, 27–44.

Hunter, Lynette and Sarah Hutton (eds) (1997), *Women, Science and Medicine 1500–1700*, Stroud: Sutton P. Thrupp.

Hynd, John [1603] (1811), *The Mirrour of Worldly Fame*, in *The Harleian Miscellany: A Collection of Scarce, Curious and Entertaining Pamphlets and Tracts*, ed. Thomas Park, 24 vols, London.

Jacobson, Daniel Jonathan (1974), *The Language of The Revenger's Tragedy*, Jacobean Drama Series, Salzburg: University of Salzburg Press.

Jardine, Lisa (1996), *Worldly Goods: A New History of the Renaissance*, London: Macmillan.

J. D. (1660), 'A Paradox of a Painted Face', in *A Collection of Several Ingenious Poems and Songs by the Wits of the Age*, London.

Jeamson, Thomas (1665), *Artificiall Embellishments: or Arts best directions how to preserve beauty or procure it*, Oxford.

Jones, Emrys (ed.) (1991), *The New Oxford Book of Sixteenth Century Verse*, Oxford: Oxford University Press.

Jonson, Ben [1600] (1981), *Cynthia's Revels: Fountain of Selfe-Love*, in *The Complete Plays of Ben Jonson*, ed. G. A. Wilkes, 4 vols, Oxford: Oxford University Press.

Jonson, Ben [1603] (1998), *Sejanus His Fall*, in *Ben Jonson: Volpone and Other Plays*, ed. Lorna Hutson, Renaissance Dramatists, Harmondsworth: Penguin Books.

Jonson, Ben [1607] (1995), *Volpone*, in *The Alchemist and Other Plays*, ed. Gordon Campbell, Oxford: Oxford University Press.

Jonson, Ben [1609] (1995), *Epicoene, or The Silent Woman* in *Ben Jonson: The Alchemist and Other Plays*, ed. Gordon Campbell, World's Classics, Oxford and New York: Oxford University Press.

Jonson, Ben, *Catiline* [1611] (1973), ed. W. F. Bolton and Jane F. Gardner, London: Edward Arnold.

Jonson, Ben [1614] (1996), *The Devil is an Ass*, ed. Peter Happé, The Revels Plays, Manchester and New York: Manchester University Press.

Jonson, Ben [1625] (1975), *The Staple of News*, ed. Devra Rowland Kiefer, Regents Renaissance Drama Series, Lincoln: University of Nebraska Press.

Jonson, Ben [1640] (1947), *Timber or Discoveries*, in *Ben Jonson*, ed. C. H. Herford and Percy and Evelyn Simpson, 11 vols, Oxford: Clarendon Press.

Jorgens, Jack (1997), *Shakespeare on Film*, Bloomington: Indiana University Press.

Juvenal (1972), *The Sixteen Satires*, trans. Peter Green, Harmondsworth: Penguin Books.

Karim-Cooper, Farah (2007), '"This alters not thy beauty": face-paint, gender, and race in *The English Moor*', *Early Theatre*, 10: 2.

Karim-Cooper, Farah (2014), 'To glisten in a playhouse: cosmetic beauty indoors', in Andrew Gurr and Karim-Cooper (eds), *Moving Shakespeare Indoors: Performance and Repertoire in the Jacobean Playhouse*, Cambridge: Cambridge University Press.

Kelley, Philippa (2002), 'Surpassing glass: Shakespeare's mirrors', *Early Modern Literary Studies*, 8: 1, May, 2.1–32, http://purl.oclc.org/ emls/08–2/ kellglas.htm.

Kelso, Ruth (1956), *Doctrine for the Lady of the Renaissance*, Chicago: University of Illinois Press.

Keyes, Jean (1969), *A History of Woman's Hairstyles 1500–1965*, London: Methuen.

La Perriere (1614), *Theatre of Fine Devices*, trans. Thomas Combe, London.

Leggatt, Alexander (1981), *Ben Jonson: His Vision and His Art*, London: Methuen.

Lichtenstein, Jacqueline (1989), 'Making up representation: the risks of femininity', in *Misogyny and Misandry*, ed. R. Howard Bloch and Frances Ferguson, Berkeley: University of California Press.

Linthicum, M. C. (1936), *Costume in the Drama of Shakespeare and His Contemporaries*, Oxford: Clarendon Press.

Llewellyn, Nigel (1991), *The Art of Death: Visual Culture in the English Death Ritual 1500–1800*, London: Reaktion Books.

Lomazzo, Paulo (1598), *A Tracte Containing the Artes of curious Paintinge Carvinge & buildinge*, trans. Richard Haydocke, Oxford.

London, William (1658), *A Catalogue of the most vendible Books in England*, London.

Loomba, Ania (2000), '"Delicious traffick": racial and religious difference on early modern stages', in *Shakespeare and Race*, ed. Catherine M. S. Alexander and Stanley Wells, Cambridge: Cambridge University Press, pp. 203–24.

Lupton, Thomas (1601), *A Thousand Notable Things of Sundrie Sort*, London.

Lyly, John [1578] (1997), *Euphues, or The Anatomy of Wit*, in *John Lyly: Selected Prose and Dramatic Works*, ed. Leah Scragg, Manchester: Fyfield Books.

MacDonald, Joyce Green (2000), 'Black ram, white ewe: Shakespeare, race, and women', in *A Feminist Companion to Shakespeare*, ed. Dympna Callaghan, Oxford: Blackwell, pp. 188–205.

Mack, Maynard (1968), 'The world of Hamlet', in *Shakespeare: Hamlet*, ed. John Jump, New Casebooks, London: Macmillan, pp. 86–107.

Mackenzie, Clayton G. (2000), *Emblems of Mortality: Iconographic Experiments in Shakespeare's Theatre*, Lanham, New York and Oxford: University Press of America.

Manningham, John (1868), *The Diary of John Manningham, of the Middle Temple 1602–1608*, ed. John Bruce, London: Nichols and Sons.

Markham, Gervase (1623), *Countrey Contentments, or the English Huswife*, London.

Marston, John, *Antonio and Mellida* [1600] (1965), ed. G. K. Hunter, Regents Renaissance Drama, London: Edward Arnold.

Marston, John [1600] (1965), *Antonio's Revenge*, ed. G. K. Hunter, London: Edward Arnold.

Massinger, Philip [1621] (1978), *The Duke of Milan*, in *The Selected Plays of Philip Massinger*, ed. Colin Gibson, Cambridge: Cambridge University Press.

Massinger, Philip (1630), *The Picture*, London.

Mazzio, Carla (1997), 'Sins of the tongue', in *The Body in Parts: Fantasies of Corporeality in Early Modern Europe*, ed. David Hillman and Carla Mazzio, New York and London: Routledge, pp. 53–79.

McLuskie, Kathleen (2000), 'Drama and sexual politics: the case of Webster's Duchess', in *The Duchess of Malfi: Contemporary Critical Essays*, ed. Dympna Callaghan, New Casebooks, Basingstoke: Macmillan, pp. 104–21.

McMillin, Scott (1984), 'Acting and violence: *The Revenger's Tragedy* and its departures from *Hamlet*', *Studies in English Literature*, 24, 275–91.

Mebane, John S. (1989), *Renaissance Magic and the Return of the Golden Age: The Occult Tradition and Marlowe, Jonson and Shakespeare*, Lincoln and London: University of Nebraska Press.

Middleton, Thomas [1607] (1996), *The Revenger's Tragedy*, ed. R. A. Foakes, Revels Student Editions, Manchester: Manchester University Press.

Millard, Barbara C. (1984), '"An acceptable violence": sexual contest in Jonson's *Epicoene*', *Medieval and Renaissance Drama in England*, 1, 143–58.

Miso-Spilus (1662), *A Wonder of wonders: Or, a Metamorphosis of Fair Faces voluntarily transformed into foul visages. Or, an Invective against Black-spotted Faces: by a well-willer to modest Matrons and Virgins*, London.

Montaigne, Michel de [1615] (1892), *The Essays of Montaigne: Done into English by John Florio (1615)*, ed. George Saintsbury, 3 vols, London: David Nutt.

Montrose, Louis Adrian (1988), '"Shaping fantasies": figurations of gender and power in Elizabethan culture', in *Representing the English Renaissance*, ed. Stephen Greenblatt, Berkeley: University of California Press, pp. 31–64.

Mullaney, Steven (2001), 'Mourning and misogyny: *Hamlet* and the final progress', in *Shakespeare, Feminism and Gender*, ed. Kate Chedgzoy, New Casebooks, Basingstoke: Macmillan, pp. 161–83.

Mullins, Edwin (1985), *The Painted Witch: Female Body, Male Art*, London: Secker & Warburg.

Nashe, Thomas (1594), *Christ's Tears Ouer Ierusalem*, London.

Neill, Michael (1997), *Issues of Death: Mortality and Identity in English Renaissance Tragedy*, Oxford: Clarendon Press.

Ovid (1979), *Ars Amatoria*, in *Ovid: The Art of Love and other Poems*, trans. J. H. Mozley, Cambridge, MA: Harvard University Press.

Peacham, Henry (1612), *Minerva Britania*, London.

Phillippy, Patricia (2006), *Painting Women: Cosmetics, Canvases, and Early Modern English Culture*, Baltimore: Johns Hopkins University Press.

Plato (1997), *Symposium*, in *Plato: Complete Works*, ed. John M. Cooper and D. S. Hutchinson, Indianapolis and Cambridge: Hackett.

Platt, Hugh (1628), *Delights for Ladies to Adorne their Persons, Tables, Closets, and Distillatories; with Beauties, Banquets, Perfumes, and Waters*, London.

Plotinus (1991), *The Enneads*, ed. John Dillon and Stephen Mackenna, Harmondsworth: Penguin Books.

Poitevin, Kimberley (2011), 'Inventing whiteness: cosmetics, race, and women in early modern England', *Journal for Early Modern Cultural Studies*, Spring/Summer.

Pollard, Tanya (1999), 'Beauty's poisonous properties', *Shakespeare Studies*, 27, 187–202.

Pollard, Tanya (2005), *Drugs and Theater in Early Modern England*, Cambridge: Cambridge University Press.

Price, H. T. (1955), 'The function of imagery in Webster', *PMLA*, 70, 717–39.

Price, Michael (1996), '"Offending without witness": recusancy, equivocation, and face-painting in John Donne's early life and writing', *Explorations in Renaissance Culture*, 22, 51–82.

Prynne, William (1628), *The Unlovelinesse of Love-Lockes*, London.

Prynne, William (1633), *Histrio-Mastix: The Players Scourge or Actors Tragedie*, London.

Puttenham, George (1589), *The Art of English Poesie*, London.

Read, Evelyn Plummer and C. Read (eds) (1951), *Elizabeth of England: Certain Observations Concerning the Life and Reign of Queen Elizabeth by John Clapham*, Philadelphia: University of Pennsylvania Press.

Rhodes, Neil (ed.) (1987), *John Donne: Selected Prose*, Harmondsworth: Penguin Books.

Rich, Barnabe (1613), *The Excellency of good women*, London.

Rich, Barnabe (1615), *The Honestie of this Age: Proouing by good Circumstance, that the World was never honest till now*, London.

Rich, Barnabe (1616), *My Ladies Looking Glasse*, London.

Robinson, Clement [1584] (1973), *A Handful of Pleasant Delights*, London: Scolar Press Facsimile.

Romei, Count Annibale (1598), *The Courtier's Academie*, trans. J. K., London.

Rook, Martha C. (1994), 'Representations of Ophelia', *Criticism*, 36: 1, Winter, 21–38.

Rosenberg, Marvin (1992), *The Masks of Hamlet*, Newark: University of Delaware Press.

Ruscelli, Girolamo (1615), *The Secrets of Alexis of Piemont: Containing Many Excellent Remedies Against Divers Diseases*, trans. William Warde, London.

Sammern, Romana (2015), 'Red, white and black: colors of beauty, tints of health and cosmetic materials in early modern English art writing', *Early Science and Medicine*, 20.

Sawday, Jonathan (1995), *The Body Emblazoned: Dissection and the Human Body in Renaissance Culture*, London: Routledge.

Schmidt, Alexander (1971), *Shakespeare Lexicon and Quotation Dictionary*, 2 vols, New York: Dover Publications.

Schuman, Samuel (1982), *The Theatre of Fine Devices: The Visual Drama of John Webster*, Salzburg: University of Salzburg Press.

Scot, Reginald (1584), *The Discoverie of Witchcraft*, London.

Shakespeare, William [1600] (1982), *Hamlet*, ed. Harold Jenkins, The Arden Shakespeare, London and New York: Routledge.

Shakespeare, William (1997), *The Norton Shakespeare*, ed. Stephen Greenblatt, Walter Cohen, Jean E. Howard and Katherine Eisaman Maus, London and New York: W. W. Norton.

Shapiro, Michael (1973), 'Audience v. dramatist in Jonson's *Epicoene* and other plays of the children's troupes', *English Literary Renaissance*, 3, 400–17.

Shepherd, Simon (1981), *Amazons and Warrior Women: Varieties of Feminism in Seventeenth-Century Drama*, Brighton: Harvester Press.

Sidney, Philip (1595), *An Apologie for Poetrie*, London.

Sidney, Philip [1595] (1989), *The Defence of Poesy*, in *Sir Philip Sidney*, ed. Katherine Duncan-Jones, Oxford Authors, Oxford: Oxford University Press.

Singh, Jyotsna (2000), 'Gendered "gifts" in Shakespeare's Belmont: the economies of exchange in early modern England', in *A Feminist Companion to Shakespeare*, ed. Dympna Callaghan, Oxford: Blackwell, pp. 144–59.

Slights, William E. (1994), *Ben Jonson and the Art of Secrecy*, Toronto: University of Toronto Press.

Smith, Ian (2013), 'Othello's black handkerchief', *Shakespeare Quarterly*, 64: 1, Spring, 1–25.

Smith, Rebecca (1992), 'A heart cleft in twain: the dilemma of Shakespeare's Gertrude', in *Hamlet*, ed. Martin Coyle, New Casebooks, London: Macmillan, pp. 80–95.

Snook, Edith (2011), *Women, Beauty and Power in Early Modern England: A Feminist Literary History*, Basingstoke: Palgrave Macmillan.

Spenser, Edmund [1590–6] (1978), *The Faerie Queene*, ed. Thomas P. Roche and C. Patrick O'Donnell, Harmondsworth: Penguin Books.

Spenser, Edmund [1594] (1989), *Epithalamion*, in *The Yale Edition of the Shorter Poems of Edmund Spenser*, ed. William A. Oram, Einar Bjorband, Ronald Bond, Thomas H. Cain, Alexander Dunlop and Richard Schell, New Haven and London: Yale University Press.

Stallybrass, Peter (1987), 'Patriarchal territories: the body enclosed', in *Rewriting the Renaissance*, ed. Margaret W. Ferguson, Maureen Quilligan and Nancy J. Vickers, Chicago and London: University of Chicago Press, pp. 123–46.

Stallybrass, Peter and Ann Rosalind Jones (2000), *Renaissance Clothing and the Materials of Memory*, Cambridge: Cambridge University Press.

Starkey, David (2001), *Elizabeth: The Struggle for the Throne*, New York: HarperCollins.

Steele, Brian (1997), 'In the flower of their youth: "portraits" of Venetian beauties ca. 1500', *Sixteenth Century Journal*, 28: 2, Summer, 481–502.

Stern, Katherine (1997), 'What is femme? The phenomenology of the powder room', *Women: A Cultural Review*, 8: 2, Autumn, 183–96.

Stevens, Andrea Ria (2013), *Inventions of the Skin: The Painted Body in Early English Drama, 1400–1642*, Edinburgh: Edinburgh University Press.

Stevens, Charles and Jean Liebault (1616), *Maison Rustique, or, The Countrie Farme*, trans. Richard Surflet, London.

Stewart, Alan (1995), 'The early modern closet discovered', *Representations*, 50, 76–100.

Stowe, John (1631), *Annales, or a General Chronicle of England*, London.

Stratton, Jon (1996), *The Desirable Body: Cultural Fetishism and the Erotics of Consumption*, Manchester: Manchester University Press.

Strong, Roy (1977), *The Cult of Elizabeth: Elizabethan Portraiture and Pageantry*, London: Thames and Hudson.

Strong, Roy (1987), *Gloriana: The Portraits of Queen Elizabeth I*, London: Thames and Hudson.

Stubbes, Philip [1583] (1877), *The Anatomie of Abuses*, ed. F. J. Furnivall, London.

Swetnam, Joseph (1667), *The Arraignment of Lewd, Idle, Froward and Unconstant Women: or, The Vanity of them, chuse you whether*, London.

Tassi, Marguerite A. (2000), 'Lover, poisoner, counterfeiter: The painter in Elizabethan drama', *The Ben Jonson Journal*, 7, 129–56.

Taylor, John (1621), *Superbiae Flagellum, or, The Whip of Pride*, London.

Theweleit, Klaus (1987), *Male Fantasies*, 2 vols, Minneapolis: University of Minneapolis Press; Cambridge: Polity Press.

Thomas, Thomas (1587), *Dictionarium Linguæ Latinæ et Anglicanæ*. London: Richard Boyle.

Thomas, William (1549), *The Historie of Italie*, London.

Topsell, Edward [1607] (1973), *The Historie of Four-Footed Beastes*, London; Amsterdam and New York: Da Capo Press.

Tuke, Thomas (1616), *A Treatise Against Paint[i]ng and Tinctvring of Men and Women*, London.

Vaughan, Virginia Mason (1994), *Othello: A Contextual History*, Cambridge: Cambridge University Press.

Vecellio, Cesare (1590), *Degli Habiti Antichi, Et Moderni*, Venice.

Vickers, Brian (ed.) (1999), *A Primer of English Poetry*, in *English Renaissance Literary Criticism*, ed. Brian Vickers, Oxford: Clarendon Press.

Vives, Juan Luis (1592), *A very Fruteful and pleasant booke called the Instruction of a Christian Woman*, trans. Richard Hyrde, London.

Wall, Wendy (2002), *Staging Domesticity: Household Work and English Identity in Early Modern Drama*, Cambridge: Cambridge University Press.

Webbe, William (1586), *A Discourse of English Poetrie*, London.

Webster, John (1927), *The Complete Works of John Webster*, ed. F. L. Lucas, 4 vols, London: Chatto & Windus.

Webster, John (1996), *The Duchess of Malfi and Other Plays*, ed. René Weis, Oxford English Drama, Oxford: Oxford University Press.

Welsby, Paul A. (ed.) (1970), *Sermons and Society: An Anthology*, Harmondsworth: Penguin Books.

Whately, William (1619), *A Bride-Bush, or A Direction for Married Persons*, London.

Whitney, Geoffery [1586] (1969), *A Choice of Emblemes and Other Devices*, Amsterdam and New York: Da Capo Press.

Williams, Clare (ed.) (1937), *Thomas Platters Travels in England 1599*, London: Jonathan Cape.

Williams, Neville (1957), *Powder and Paint: A History of the English Woman's Toilet, Elizabeth I – Elizabeth II*, London: Longman Green.

Wills, David (1995), *Prosthesis*, Stanford: Stanford University Press.

Wilson, Thomas (1570), *The Arte of Rhetorique, for the use of all suche as are studiovs of Eloquence*, London.

Wirtzung, Christopher (1654), *The General Practise of Physick*, London.

Woodbridge, Linda (1987), 'Black and white and red all over: The sonnet mistress amongst the Ndembu', *Renaissance Quarterly*, 40, pp. 247–93.

Woodforde, John (1992), *The History of Vanity*, Stroud: Alan Sutton.

Woolley, Hannah (1675), *The Gentlewoman's Companion: or A Guide to the Female Sex*, London.

Woudhuysen, H. R. and David Norbrook (eds) (1992), *The Penguin Book of Renaissance Verse 1509–1659*, Harmondsworth: Penguin Books.

Žižek, Slavoj (1989), *The Sublime Object of Ideology*, London and New York: Verso.

Index

Note: page numbers in *italics* refer to illustrations